THE
SECRET HISTORY OF
ROCK 'N' ROLL

BOOKS BY CHRISTOPHER KNOWLES

Clash City Showdown:
The Music, the Meaning, and the Legacy of The Clash

Our Gods Wear Spandex:
The Secret History of Comic Book Heroes

The Complete X-Files:
Behind the Series, the Myths, and the Movies

THE
SECRET HISTORY OF
ROCK 'N' ROLL

THE MYSTERIOUS ROOTS
OF MODERN MUSIC

Christopher Knowles

viva
EDITIONS

Published in the United States by Viva Editions, an imprint of Cleis Press Inc., 2246 Sixth Street, Berkeley, California 94710.

Printed in the United States.
Cover design: Scott Idleman
Cover photo: Image Source
Text design: Frank Wiedemann
First Edition.
10 9 8 7 6 5 4 3 2 1

ISBN: 978-1-57344-405-7

Library of Congress Cataloging-in-Publication Data

Knowles, Christopher, 1966-
 The secret history of rock 'n' roll : the mysterious roots of modern music / Christopher Knowles. -- 1st ed.
   p. cm.
 ISBN 978-1-57344-405-7 (trade paper : alk. paper)
 1. Rock music--Religious aspects. I. Title.
 ML3921.8.R63K66 2010
 781.66--dc22
                        2010022117

This book is dedicated to everyone
whose life was saved by rock 'n' roll.

ACKNOWLEDGMENTS

The author would like to thank Brenda Knight for getting the show on the road and keeping the wheels turning. A hearty thanks to Mark Rhynsburger for his surgical eye and to Scott Idleman and Frank Wiedemann for the dazzling visuals. Thanks to Felice Newman, Frédérique Delacoste, and Kara Wuest for setting the stage. Thanks to Scott Rowley for lighting the flame. And as always, eternal love and gratitude to my family for keeping me grounded.

TABLE OF CONTENTS

XI INTRODUCTION

1 PART I: A BRIEF PREHISTORY OF ROCK 'N' ROLL
3 Prelude
4 Initiation
7 Building a Mystery
11 Isis and Osiris
14 The Great Gods
16 The Eleusinian Mysteries
21 The Bacchanalia
27 Hermes, Hecate, and Apollo
30 Mysterious Sacraments
33 The Korybantes
35 Orpheus
39 The Mysteries of Cybele and Attis
44 The Official State Cults of Rome
48 Isis, Queen of Heaven
52 Blood and Fire: The Mithraic Mysteries
57 The Fall of the Mysteries, and Then of Rome Itself
61 The Middle Ages and the Renaissance of the Gods
64 Transmission
65 Merrymount, or the Puritan Woodstock
67 The Masonic Mysteries
68 The Druidic Roots of American Folk Music
71 The Mysteries of the Yoruba
73 East Meets West
75 The Modern Magi—Jung and Crowley
81 Gospel Music and the Holiness Movement
84 A (Very) Short History of 20th-Century Bacchanalia

86 Technicolor Gods

87 Psychedelia

91 PART II: THE MODERN MYSTERIES OF ROCK 'N' ROLL

95 VOX POPULI: THE NEW APOLLOS
Elvis Presley ☆ The Beach Boys ☆ Bob Dylan ☆
The Beatles ☆ Elton John ☆ The Eagles ☆
Bruce Springsteen ☆ Journey ☆ Blondie ☆
The Police ☆ U2 ☆ Green Day

121 PARTY ANIMALS: THE NEW DIONYSIANS
The Rolling Stones ☆ Grateful Dead ☆ The Doors
☆ Led Zeppelin ☆ Van Halen ☆ The Beastie Boys
☆ The Red Hot Chili Peppers ☆ Guns N' Roses

143 EARTH MOTHERS: THE NEW ELEUSINIANS
Tina Turner ☆ Janis Joplin ☆ Linda Ronstadt ☆
Heart ☆ Chrissie Hynde ☆ Pat Benatar ☆ Courtney
Love ☆ Sleater Kinney

153 GENDER BENDERS: THE NEW GALLOI
Little Richard ☆ Glam and Glitter Rock ☆ David
Bowie ☆ The New York Dolls ☆ Queen ☆ Joan
Jett ☆ Prince ☆ Jane's Addiction ☆ The Future of
Femme

171 WITCHY WOMEN: THE MODERN MYSTERIES OF ISIS
Grace Slick ☆ Stevie Nicks ☆ Patti Smith ☆ Kate
Bush ☆ Siouxsie & the Banshees ☆ Cocteau Twins

182 ART DAMAGE: HERMETIC ROCK
Pink Floyd ☆ Jimi Hendrix ☆ King Crimson ☆
Brian Eno ☆ The Talking Heads ☆ Peter Gabriel ☆
Sonic Youth ☆ Radiohead

195 METAL MILITIAS: THE NEW KORYBANTES
The Kinks ☆ The Who ☆ Cream ☆ Heavy Metal
Thunder ☆ AC/DC ☆ Judas Priest ☆ Iron Maiden
☆ Motörhead ☆ Metallica

208 GOING UNDERGROUND: MITHRAIC ROCK
The MC5 ☆ The Stooges ☆ The Ramones ☆
The Sex Pistols ☆ The Clash ☆ Black Flag ☆
The Bad Brains ☆ Minor Threat

220 PRINCES OF DARKNESS: THE NEW PLUTONIANS
The Velvet Underground ☆ Black Sabbath ☆ Alice
Cooper ☆ Kiss ☆ Public Image Ltd. ☆ Killing Joke
☆ Throbbing Gristle ☆ Ministry ☆ Nine Inch Nails
☆ Devil Music—for real this time ☆ Thrash and
Grindcore ☆ Death Metal ☆ Marilyn Manson

245 WOE IS ME: THE MODERN MYSTERIES OF ORPHEUS
Neil Young ☆ James Taylor ☆ Nick Drake ☆ Ian
Curtis ☆ The Cure ☆ The Smiths ☆ Rites of Spring
☆ Grunge ☆ Nirvana

259 CODA

262 A FUTURE HISTORY OF ROCK 'N' ROLL

265 ABOUT THE AUTHOR

INTRODUCTION

Dancing and music are more pleasing to the gods than rites and prayers.

—The Natya Shastra

I grew up surrounded by music—my mother was a professional musician and I spent a good chunk of my early life in nightclubs, rehearsal spaces, theaters, and assorted houses of worship. But that was just background noise—rock 'n' roll was the only music that really mattered to me.

I'd spend hours sitting alone in my grandmother's house, playing my aunts and uncles' old Beatles, Stones, and Elvis Presley 45s on an old portable record changer. I slept with my radio on, imprinting the great old Top 40 hits of the early Seventies onto my unconscious. Later, albums like *Master of Reality*, *Houses of the Holy*, and *Sheer Heart Attack* introduced me to the rich fantasy worlds of hard rock and metal.

Punk rock entered the equation sometime around 1978 when a local FM station briefly reinvented itself as "New Wave Radio." I spent my 13th-birthday money on *Never Mind the Bollocks*, *Give 'Em Enough Rope*, and *Rocket to Russia*. But all of this was my novitiate. After a megawatt baptism courtesy of the Clash in 1980, I was initiated into the mysteries of the nascent hardcore scene, courtesy of the early lineups of Boston punk legends Gang Green and Jerry's Kids, all of whom I hung out with at school.

Hardcore inspired a vast yet invisible network of bands, clubs, fanzines, and record labels. Flyers for hardcore gigs were completely incomprehensible to outsiders, loaded as they were with violent band names (Minor Threat, SS Decontrol, Negative Approach, etc.) and arcane geometric symbols. The usual punk accessories—spikes, leather jackets, mohawks, and the rest—were left for the poseurs. In their place was a strict, mannered uniform of shaved heads, sleeveless tees (with hand-drawn band logos), bleach-spattered jeans, and canvas sneakers or cheap army boots. Some in the hardcore elite embraced a lifestyle of abstinence and celibacy known as the "straight edge." Straight-edge kids recognized each other by the black *X*s drawn on the backs of their hands.

Whatever it later became, the early days of the scene were magic. (A hardcore band's best record was usually its first.) My favorite kind of hardcore gig was literally in someone's basement, attended by the bands who were playing and a small handful of friends. The laws hadn't been written yet and it was still a very small "us" against an ocean of "them." There was, in fact, a true sense of brotherhood.

And yet, I didn't realize how it had all been done before until I began to study the ancient Mystery cults, particularly the Mithraic cults so popular with the Roman Legions. Even that straight-edge X had a Mithraic precedent in the X-shaped "Cross of Light." I had read any number of articles comparing Woodstock and the rest to the ancient Bacchanalia, but I would come to learn that a variety of ancient Mystery cults bore a striking resemblance to modern, secular subcultures. What was so shocking to me is how unconscious this process was, given the eerie parallels between ancient and modern. I wrote this book to explain why.

I'm also writing in hopes that people will rediscover a culture and an art form too often taken for granted. The old stigma against rock 'n' roll never really went away. Middlebrow cultural critics in the Eighties and early Nineties were always looking for something to replace it, which may speak to an unconscious loathing instilled by their parents and teachers. Hip-hoppers, dance divas, and glossy country acts have been the music industry's darlings since grunge died, usually leaving new rock bands struggling for attention. Pirating and iTunes have reduced the album format to loss leader status.

And somehow rock 'n' roll has survived. I hope to convince you that it continues to survive, for very powerful, compelling, and deep-seated reasons. It survives because in one form or another, it's always been with us and always will be.

Christopher Knowles

PART I:
A BRIEF PREHISTORY OF ROCK 'N' ROLL

PRELUDE

Did rock 'n' roll spring up like some postwar mutant and emerge fully formed with the release of "Rocket 88" or "Rock Around the Clock"? Were the parents of the Fifties and Sixties right; was this some degenerate intruder that disrupted the sanctity of America's suburban utopia? Or is rock 'n' roll something much older, much deeper and much more profound than the dozy sounds of the silken-voiced Rat Pack crooners it replaced?

You can draw a line backward in time at the point of your choosing; pick your favorite rock 'n' roll song or album and trace its roots through the various forms of African American dance music or rural folk. You'll find most of the basic building blocks of the rock 'n' roll sound. But you won't find the true precedent for the psychedelic youth explosion of the rock era. You won't find the fantasy, the revolutionary ambitions, or the larger-than-life drama of the Aquarian Age in the juke joints or honky-tonks of the early 20th century. You won't find the distinctly *religious* intensity that gripped tens of thousands of teenage girls whose screams drowned out the Beatles as the band struggled to hear itself over the hysteria at Shea Stadium.

No, in order to understand rock 'n' roll you have to go back—all the way back—to the earliest days of human civilization. The drugs, the drums, the noise, the wild costumes, the pyrotechnics, the controversy, and the outrage of 20th-century rock 'n' roll are waiting for you there, in temples filled with your horny, blissed-out ancestors who believed that if they got out of their heads and away from the ego, they could actually meet the spirits that their neighbors could only talk about. In the pages to come we'll learn their secrets and discover an ancient culture startlingly similar to our own. We'll learn how ancient cults organized themselves around specific archetypes, and how those same archetypal themes would reemerge largely intact in the rock era, among the various subcultures and genres that evolved out of a musical form itself derived from the pounding music of these ancient cults.

Rock 'n' roll isn't just another form of music—it's an indelible part of the human experience. It may well be the oldest form of cultural expression in human history. It didn't spring up like some Atom Age mutant in the 1950s; it simply shook off the dust of centuries of repression, took on a new incarnation, and picked up where it left off.

INITIATION

Nearly everyone who was a teenager sometime between 1964 and 1992 has that one concert that "changed my life." From the time the Beatles touched down at JFK airport to the time

Nirvana topped the charts with *Nevermind*, rock 'n' roll was the center of gravity for youth culture. So much so that serious people once described it as a new religion. Social critics threw around terms like *Dionysian* and *Bacchanalia*, terms that most rock fans probably didn't understand.

I actually had two concerts that changed my life. The first was the Clash on the London Calling tour in 1980. Being a 13-year-old punk rocker, I was extremely confused by the album, which took away my beloved Clash blitzkrieg and replaced it with radio-friendly pop-rock tunes. But none of that was on display at the Boston Orpheum that night—those same songs sounded like the Invasion of Normandy. I couldn't account for the difference. Sometime later, Joe Strummer would explain that something often took hold of him onstage, something that caused him to lose all sense of himself and drive him into a sweaty, howling rage. A *shamanic* state, anthropologists might say.

The other concert that changed my life was kind of a sequel: U2 at the Orpheum in November of 1981. I hadn't taken anything beforehand, but the excitement and noise fired up my adrenals and endorphins and put me straight out of my head. The funny thing is that at both concerts I had only the barest sense that I was in a room with thousands of other people having a similar kind of experience—I was somewhere else, *inside* the music. I'd later come to realize what an appropriate venue the "Orpheum" was for that kind of experience.

But there was something else at work—the Clash and U2 weren't just bands back then, they were heroes—*gods*, even. These concerts were major events—landmark dates in the calendar of my youth. Those bands stood outside the parade of ordinary rock groups and promised to "change the world" with their music.

Something profound also struck me at a later concert—Nirvana in 1994 at the old New York Coliseum on Columbus Circle. I saw throngs of kids—the same age I had been when I saw the Clash and U2—wandering around the lobby or loitering in the bathroom while the hottest band in rock 'n' roll was a hundred feet away blasting through their biggest hits. Why? Nirvana was certainly doing its part, but something was missing. What was missing was *meaning*, a reason to stand around in a hideous concrete barn and endure the painfully loud noise bouncing off the tiles. After a decade-plus of 24-hour-a-day music and video on demand, something got lost.

While trying to understand what happened to me in 1981—and what happened to rock 'n' roll in 1994—I eventually discovered where the terms *Dionysian* and *Bacchanalia* came from—the ancient Mystery religions of the eastern Mediterranean. Over time, I'd come to realize that rock 'n' roll is in fact the direct descendant of the Mysteries, which had evolved and adapted to suit the needs and customs of postwar American secular culture.

What did the Mysteries offer that other cults of the time did not? Almost *exactly* what rock 'n' roll would, thousands of years later. Drink. Drugs. Sex. Loud music. Wild pyrotechnics. A feeling of transcendence—leaving your mind and your body and entering a different world, filled with mystery and danger. A personal connection to something deep, strange, and impossibly timeless. An opportunity to escape the grinding monotony of everyday life and break all the rules of polite society. A place to dress up in wild costumes and dance and drink and trip all night.

Mystery cult centers were the ancient equivalents of today's clubs and concert halls, which may be why so many of the old pagan place-names are still in use—the "Orpheum," the "Apollo," the "Academy," the "Palladium," and on and on. Just as in the Aquarian Age of the Sixties, some Mystery cults were relatively socially acceptable (think the Beatles) and some were seen as a sign that the world was going to hell in a hand-basket (think the Rolling Stones).

As we'll see, traces of the Mysteries survived long after they were put down by the Christian emperors, even within the Church itself. And with the rise of colonialism and empire in the 17th century, a purer extract of the Mysteries would emerge on the plantations of the New World and slowly begin to exercise its dominance over the popular music and culture of the Western world. Nothing in our society—religion, culture, politics—would ever be the same again.

BUILDING A MYSTERY

> I like to think of the history of rock & roll like the origin of Greek drama. That started out on the threshing floors during the crucial seasons, and was originally a band of acolytes dancing and singing. Then, one day, a possessed person jumped out of the crowd and started imitating a god.
>
> —Jim Morrison

Most historians believe that the Mysteries began at the end of the Neolithic Age (also known as the New Stone Age, roughly 9000 to 4500 BCE), making them one of the earliest cultural developments known to humanity. Coinciding with the development of agriculture, the rituals were designed to appeal to the grain gods of the Underworld by acting out their myths, which celebrated the cycles of planting, growth, and harvesting. The earliest distinct Mysteries were practiced in Egypt, which depended on the yearly flooding of the Nile to fertilize its soil. This process was at the center of all the various (and often contradictory) regional cults that made up what we now generically refer to as "Egyptian religion." From Egypt, the Mysteries migrated into western Asia and the Mediterranean basin, and eventually to the farthest frontiers of the known world.

The Mysteries were known by many names in Greece, including *mysteria, teletai, bakchoi,* and *orgia* (where the modern word *orgy* comes from). Adjectives like "unspeakable" or "forbidden" were often used, adding to their mystique. Mysteries are generally distinguished from other cults by a number of features. The initiates worshipped "suffering gods," and experienced their various deaths and dramas through ritual theater and music. Myths were retold and often acted out on those agricultural themes. These cults practiced secret initiations which were not to be shared with outsiders, sometimes on pain of imprisonment, or even death.

The Mysteries were usually centered on a single god, but they were not technically monotheistic. Instead they were *henotheistic*, meaning they recognized the existence of other gods but focused their energy on one. Most importantly, the Mystery religions weren't about dogma—they were about experience. Music and dance were essential to the rituals themselves, which usually took place at night. And sexual symbols—or practices—were often a crucial part of the process.

The gods of the Mysteries were usually believed to have come from distant lands. Foreign gods have always had that exotic appeal, a cosmic variant on the "grass is always greener" adage. This was especially true before the rise of mass communications, but idealizing someone else's gods was popular in the Victorian era and the Sixties. At its core, religion has always been about *escape*.

Most of the Mystery religions were distinctly countercultural, offering a direct, personal relationship to a god without a priest as middleman. Their voluntary nature was radical for their time, reflecting an overall trend toward individualism in Classical Greece. But even with their wild rituals, the Mysteries required a high degree of discipline and loyalty. These weren't hippie stoners as we would understand them—as with the Central American shamans, the actual Mystery ritual would be the climax of a long period of study, sacrifice, and self-purification.

Less is known about the actual rituals themselves. But songs and dances were performed, usually fast and wild, with crashing drums and screaming flutes—rock 'n' roll, in other words. Simple pyrotechnics were often used (torches, sometimes treated with chemicals for different effects) and public sex often broke out among the wilder cults such as the Roman Bacchanalia. As the eminent German historian Walter Burkert wrote, Mystery festivals were designed to be "unforgettable events casting their shadows over the whole of one's future life, *creating experiences that transform existence*" (which brings us back to that one concert that changed your life). The initiates fully expected to meet their gods in the flesh, and by all accounts, they usually weren't disappointed. The Greek philosopher Proclus wrote that the gods didn't always take human shape, but would "manifest themselves in many forms, assuming a great variety of guises; sometimes they appear in a formless light, again in quite different form."

Like Christianity sometime later, Mystery religions centered on concepts of death and resurrection. The Mysteries prepared believers for their death and descent to the Underworld, where one's favorite god would guide the believer on her voyage. That was part of the pitch; an inscription at the Mystery temple Eleusis declared, "Beautiful indeed is the mystery given to us by the blessed Gods: Death is for mortals no longer an evil, but a blessing."

Aside from the usual nocturnal gatherings, Mystery cults also ran more conventional temples for the uninitiated, which were remarkably similar—if not nearly identical—to liturgical Christianity, offering communion and holy water (imported from the Nile), and preaching doctrines such as salvation, resurrection, and judgment of the dead.

This uncomfortable similarity is the reason early Christian fathers went on the warpath against the Mysteries in their writings, calling their gods demons and their goddesses the whores of Hell. (See Revelation 17:5: "Mystery, Babylon the Great.") But even when the Church became the official cult of state and began literally wiping out the competition, it took a very long time to stamp out the Mysteries. In fact, the Church opted instead to simply adopt many of their rituals, beliefs, and practices.

Ancient historians have cited books and scriptures used in the Mysteries, yet very few of them seem to have survived, other than as fragments. But there's an extensive record of secondary material detailing the Mysteries' beliefs, practices, and influence, which gives a clear picture of the history and power of this remarkable movement. And as is so often the case with Western civilization, our story begins in Egypt.

ISIS AND OSIRIS

Named *Esi* or *Aset* in the Kemetic language of ancient Egypt, Isis first appeared in sacred texts in the third millennium BCE. A synthesis of several older goddesses, Isis (whose name means "throne") became one of the *Ennead,* the nine major gods of the Egyptian pantheon. All these gods were masturbated into existence by the supreme being Atum, who later became Atum-Ra, who then morphed (sort of) into Amun-Ra, and finally (roughly) Ra-Horakhty, a synthesis of Ra and Horus, gods of the Sun. However, Egyptian religion was in constant flux, a reflection of shifting political realities and various priesthoods rising and falling in power and influence. All of which makes it challenging even for experienced scholars to wade through.

Isis and her brother/husband Osiris absorbed the identities of other gods over the millennia in which they were worshipped, but were always associated with agriculture and the yearly flooding of the Nile. Osiris was also lord of the Underworld and judge of the dead and Isis was the goddess of motherhood and magic, as well as the cereal grains that formed the basis of the Egyptian diet. Another brother, Set, represented heat, disease, and storms, and his sister/wife Nephthys was associated with the night, rain, and death.

Boasting a soap opera–worthy plot, the drama of Isis and Osiris was reenacted in a mystery play performed at festivals every year. Set was said to be variously sterile, impotent, or gay, so Nephthys disguises herself as Isis, gets Osiris drunk, and seduces him. Nephthys is impregnated and gives birth to Anubis, the jackal-headed god of the dead. Set freaks out when he hears about all this, and plots to kill Osiris. The dark god throws a dinner party for his brother, where he produces a beautiful sarcophagus that he'll give to anyone it fits. When

Osiris gets in, Set nails the lid shut and tosses the coffin into the Nile.

Isis then goes in search of the sarcophagus, which washes ashore in Tyre (modern-day Lebanon). She poses as a nurse-maid for the royal family, who've taken the beautiful casket into their home as a decoration. Isis heals a young prince by burning away his mortality every night. Things go awry when the Queen discovers Isis putting the baby into the fireplace, but the goddess reveals herself and demands the casket be handed over to her. Isis takes the casket back to Egypt, and with help from Anubis, Osiris is magically revived. Set has Osiris killed again and orders his body parts chopped up and scattered. Isis, along with Thoth and Nephthys, finds all the parts except for Osiris's penis, which Isis recreates from wood (or stone, or clay, or gold, depending on the telling). She then takes the form of a bird and impregnates herself, and Osiris descends to his new throne in the Underworld.

With Set on the warpath, Isis flees to a salt marsh and gives birth to Harpocrates ("Horus the Child"), who as god of silence was seen as the personal embodiment of the Mysteries. Harpocrates grows up to become god of the Sun, saves the world by defeating Set in battle, and takes back his father's throne. Drop the curtain and bring up the house lights.

Mystery religions had a special allure for women, and part of the appeal of these Isis plays is that they allowed housewives an opportunity to vent. Respectable housewives could scream and beat their breasts after the death of Osiris, and then sing and dance after his resurrection. Isis festivals also made for a great night out, complete with torchlight processions and enter-tainers, as well as loud music, dancing, and endless barrels of beer. (Isis was the patron goddess of brewers.) The Egyptians also had their very own pop stars in the form of sultry temple singers, who were known as the "harem of the gods."

Scholars still argue about whether temple prostitutes and sacred sex were common in shrines to Isis, but sexually explicit icons have been found in cult centers like Abydos. In *Ancient Egypt* (1886), British historian George Rawlinson sniffed, "The religious sculptures of the Egyptians were grossly indecent; their religious festivals were kept in an indecent way; phallic orgies were a part of them ... orgies of a gross kind." But all this was part of an ancient and highly structured religious culture, of which sexuality was an important part. It certainly wasn't the kind of mindless hedonism you saw in early Imperial Rome.

Even so, the "Festival of Drunkenness" was no slouch in the sex, booze, and rock 'n' roll department. Held in honor of the goddess Sekhmet in the ancient city of Luxor, this blowout had Egyptians getting as drunk as they could and "traveling through the marshes" (read: screwing) while loud, pounding music drove them on. All of this was meant to celebrate the salvation of humankind from the wrath of the lion-headed warrior goddess Sekhmet, who was tricked into drinking red-dyed beer in the belief it was human blood. Upon waking, she was incarnated as Hathor, the goddess of—you guessed it—sex, booze, and music.

Then there was the Festival of Bast, essentially an Egyptian spin on the modern collegiate Spring Break. Greek historian Herodotus reported on the holiday regattas on the Nile, observing, "Men and women sail together, and in each boat there are many persons of both sexes. Some of the women make a noise with rattles, and some of the men play flutes during the whole journey, while the other men and women sing and clap their hands." When stopping at a town along the way, the women would behave in way more fitting to Mardi Gras or a *Girls Gone Wild* video than a modern religious holiday. Herodotus notes that the girls would "mock the women of the place, others stand up and lift their skirts, while others dance and get up to mischief. They do this at every town lying on the Nile; But when they have reached Bubastis, they make a festival with great offerings and sacrifices, and more wine is drunk at this feast than in the whole year besides."

Egypt has always been a source of fascination to the rest of the world—particularly so in ancient times. Isis cults spread like wildfire all throughout the Hellenistic world following Alexander the Great's conquest of Egypt in 332 BCE. Shrines were established in Athens, Delphi, Sicily, and Spain, even as far north as Germany and Gaul. But it was when she arrived in Rome that the goddess would nearly conquer the entire Western world. More on that later.

THE GREAT GODS

The Mysteries of Samothrace were the oldest known Mystery cult in Greece. Said to be established by the Cabeiri (from the Semitic *kabir*, meaning "almighty"), or the "Great Gods," these mysteries trace their origins to seafaring Indo-Europeans, possibly the Trojans or Pelasgians. These shadowy Cabeiri were believed to be sons of Hephaestus (aka Vulcan) and were sometimes described as being half-human, half-crab. Ancient scholars disagreed on their actual names, which were unspeakable in some precincts.

The Cabeiri were believed to be craftsmen like their father, but they were especially popular with sailors and fishermen, who called on the Great Gods during storms and other crises. The historian Diodorus reported that the Cabeiri would "appear to mankind and bring unexpected aid to those initiates of theirs who call upon them in the midst of perils," adding that heroes such as Jason, Castor and Pollux, Hercules, and Orpheus "attained success in all the campaigns they undertook, because these gods appeared to them." The Cabeiri themselves were devoted to the worship of goddesses roughly equivalent to those celebrated at Eleusis: the Great Mother, Persephone, and Hecate. There was also a phallic god (roughly equivalent to Hermes) in the Samothracian pantheon, and a figure similar to the Chthonian Dionysus (or Hades). The exact roles and identities of these gods were revealed only in the Mystery rites themselves.

The Samothracian Mysteries were celebrated in the city's "Sanctuary of the Great Gods." Unlike Eleusis, the Sanctuary was open to everyone, regardless of sex, age, nationality, or legal status. The Mysteries themselves were celebrated once a year in the "House of the Lords," and were preceded by communal prayers, baptism, and sacrifices of blood and wine, as well as meditations and confession of sins. A hierophant would then produce the icons and read the liturgy of the Cabeiri.

There were the customary ritual dances performed to loud, thrashing music. The Great Gods were themselves closely identified with this manic noise, which often used swords and metal shields as musical instruments. The racket and the accompanying pyrotechnics were intended to instill a sense of terror and awe, preparing the initiate for personal contact with the gods. Herodotus, a Samothracian initiate himself, identified the Cabeiri with "the holy fires of the most occult powers of nature." Strabo wrote that the Cabeiri were "subject to Bacchic frenzy" as well as "inspiring terror at the celebration of the sacred rites by means of war-dances, accompanied by uproar and noise and cymbals and drums and arms, and also by flute and outcry."

The sacred wedding of Cadmus (founder of the city-state of Thebes) and the goddess Harmonia was enacted in a mystery play, also packed with music. Diodorus writes that these nuptials were the first "for which the gods provided the marriage-feast ... (Demeter presented) the fruit of the corn, Hermes gave a lyre, (Athena) a robe and a flute, and Elektra the sacred rites of the Great Mother ... Together with cymbals and kettledrums and the instruments of the ritual, (Apollo) played upon the lyre and the Muses upon their flutes."

Strabo, a particularly sober intellectual type, wrote of the raucous Samothracian rituals, observing that "the religious frenzy seems to afford a kind of divine inspiration and to be very like that of the soothsayer," and that "music, which includes dancing as well as rhythm and melody ... brings us in touch with the divine." Strabo concluded that men can be most like the gods when they are happy, adding that true happiness consists of "rejoicing, celebrating festivals, pursuing philosophy, and engaging in music."

THE ELEUSINIAN MYSTERIES

Like Isis, Demeter was the goddess of agriculture; the word *cereal* comes from her Roman name, Ceres. Educated Greeks were well aware of the links between Isis and Demeter; the two were later syncretized as Isis-Sothis-Demeter, "Sothis" referring to the star Sirius. Both goddesses suffered the loss of a loved one (a daughter in the Greek version). Both were seen as "great mothers"—the name Demeter literally means "Earth Mother." The Mysteries of Demeter, centered in the seaside town of Eleusis, were the most prestigious of the time, and resisted the Church's attempts to wipe them out until the bitter end.

In the myths, Demeter's daughter Persephone (aka Kore, aka Proserpine) is out gathering flowers on the fields of Nysa when she is spotted by Hades (aka Pluto, god of the Underworld). After getting the OK from Zeus, Hades storms in his chariot up to the surface, grabs young Persephone, and drags her down to Hell, where she is raped and held prisoner. The witch-goddess Hecate informs Demeter of the crime, and the two are then told by the sun god Helios that the girl has been abducted by Hades. Helios adds that Zeus (whose role in the mythology is essentially that of a cosmic Mafia don) signed off on the deal.

Apparently not realizing that Hades lives in the *under-world*, Demeter searches the earth for Persephone. Frustrated, she stops near a well at Eleusis (Greek for "advent") to mourn. Just as with Isis, Demeter is taken into the palace to nurse a young child, which ends much the same way as before. Except this time around, Demeter demands that the Eleusinians build a temple and perform rituals to her every year.

Demeter neglects the crops during her search, the soil turns to dust, and a terrible famine results. Zeus and the other gods are inconvenienced by all this, since without food no one can make sacrifices to them. Demeter tells the Olympians it's their tough luck, which finally prods Zeus to demand that Hades return Persephone to her mother. But as Apollodorus tells it, Hades had a trick or two up his sleeve: "Hades gave Persephone a pomegranate seed to eat, as assurance that she would not remain long with her mother." Because of this, Persephone was then required to spend a third of each year in Hell. The early Greeks had three seasons in the year, and accepted the mourning of Demeter as the reason why no crops would grow in the wintertime.

The Mysteries of Eleusis celebrated the responsibility and joy of parenthood, which accounts for their esteemed position in society, particularly with women. "Nothing is higher than these Mysteries," the Roman orator Cicero declared. "They have not only shown us the way to live joyfully but they have taught us to die with better hope." Which is not to say they were boring or sedate. Oh, quite the opposite.

There were two Mystery rites at Eleusis—the greater and the lesser. The greater mysteries took place once every five years; the lesser mysteries were annual. The temple was controlled by two families, the Eumolpus and the Kerykes, to whom control of the *Telestrion*, or main ritual hall, was an heirloom. Anyone could take part—man or woman, slave or free—so long as they spoke Greek and hadn't committed murder or treason. Each initiate needed to bring a sacrificial piglet, and pay an assortment of fees roughly equivalent to an average worker's monthly wages. Initiates began preparation several months beforehand, studying the myths and rites and fasting periodically.

The greater mysteries took place over a nine-day period. There were a number of stages in the ritual. These included the assembly, where pilgrims mingled. There was also a journey to the sea for ritual baptisms, and sacrifices made to the goddess. A parade was held to honor Asclepius the healer, and sacrifices were made to Dionysus. The priestesses brought in the *sacra* baskets, containing ritual symbols such as wool, pomegranates, poppies, and sweet cakes. Ovid wrote that women considered "love and the touch of men forbidden things" during the festival. Quite a bit different from the Bacchanalia, as we'll see.

Torches and various uses of fire were an important part of the nocturnal rituals—some dancers wore headdresses with flaming lamps attached. There was also a solemn torchlight procession in which the initiates were taunted by hecklers as they passed beneath the "Bridge of Jests." The piglets and a black bull would be sacrificed to Dionysus during the revels.

The celebrants would sing and dance once they reached the grounds of the initiation hall. Describing what sounds like an ancient rave, R. Gordon Wasson writes in *The Road to Eleusis* that initiates "danced far into the night beside the well where originally the mother had mourned for her lost Persephone." The exact hymns are since lost, but in his play *The Frogs*, Aristophanes had the initiates sing this to Demeter: "O Lady, over our rites presiding / Preserve and succor thy choral throng / And grant us all, in thy help confiding / To dance and revel the whole day long." The next morning, everyone rested and prepared themselves for the big day, and more sacrifices, of grains and the like, took place. The great drama of Demeter and Persephone was enacted in the mystery play.

Then came the main event where the sacred brew, the *kykeon*, was consumed. The initiates sat on stone bleachers inside the Telestrion, while a male hierophant chanted in falsetto as the brew was prepared using fermented barley, sprigs of mint, and a secret ingredient we'll get to later. The initiates' behavior changed dramatically once they entered the great hall: "About its portals also you will see great tumult and taking of boldness, as some boorishly and violently try to jostle their way toward the repute it bestows," Plutarch observed. "But he who has succeeded in getting inside, and has seen a great light, as though a shrine were opened, adopts another bearing of silence and amazement."

Proclus wrote, "Before the scene of the mystic visions, there is terror infused over the minds of the initiated." How exactly this effect was achieved is lost to us now, but in Aristedes' account, "The mystics were made to experience the most bloodcurdling sensations of horror and the most enthusiastic ecstasy of joy." Then, according to most accounts, the goddesses themselves would appear.

In his landmark volume *The Great Initiates,* Theosophist Edouard Schuré (1841–1929) described this epiphany: "The light of a serene wonder fills the temple; we see the pure Elysian fields; we hear the chorus of the blessed ones ... The heirophant becomes the creator and the revelator of all things; the sun is but his torchbearer, the moon, his helper of the altar, and Hermes, his mystical messenger. The ritual has been consummated, and we are seers forever."

The Eleusinian Mysteries were so popular that imitation cults popped up all over the Mediterranean, Beatlemania-style. Christian bishop Epiphanios (367–403 CE) wrote that a large temple in Alexandria known as the *Korion* was still thriving despite the brutal mob violence that pagan cults faced from Christian mobs in the late 4th century. Epiphanios reported that initiates "passed the night in vigilance with songs and flute playing, singing to the idol." At dawn they would descend to an underground chamber and bring up a statute of Persephone, "seated, nude, bearing on its forehead some seal of a cross, covered with gold." They would then circle the temple with "flutes and drums and hymns" before returning the icon to the chamber and declaring that the new Aion, or Age, had begun.

As with most of the pagan world, Eleusis took it on the chin from the Christian emperors. Valentinian ordered the Mysteries closed in 364 CE, but recanted after hearing protests from the Greek authorities. Eleusis finally fell when the warlord Alaric and a gang of monastic storm troopers desecrated the Telestrion in 396. Strangely enough, Alaric would die of fever before his 40th birthday. Perhaps the Great Mother was getting her last licks in before fading into history.

THE BACCHANALIA

I call upon loud-roaring and reveling Dionysos,
primeval, two-natured, thrice-born, Bacchic lord,
Savage, ineffable, secretive, two-horned and two-
 shaped,
Ivy-covered, bull-faced, warlike, howling, pure.
                    —Orphic Hymn to Dionysus

A lot of writers throw the term *Dionysian* around a bit carelessly, confusing the term with "hedonistic." It's true that Dionysus inspired the most scandalous cults of the ancient Mediterranean, but in their purest form there was a method—and a meaning—to all the sex and drugs and rock 'n' roll. Even so, most rock concerts these days look like a church picnic compared to the ancient Bacchanalia.

Imported into Greece from points east and almost immediately identified with Osiris, Dionysus became one of the 12 gods of the Pantheon, acting as god of wine and the harvest.

Dionysus was also a figure of wild contradictions. Originally depicted as a pudgy, bearded *bon vivant*, he evolved into an effeminate, even womanly figure, but was also worshipped as a fierce black bull. He was the son of Zeus/Jupiter, supreme god of the state, but his cults were often violently put down *by* the state. His most devout disciples were called *Maenads*, and these wild women knew Dionysus (aka Bacchus) as the "Savior" and the "God who comes." Dionysus gave his followers hope for eternal life, but could whip up a hysteria that could drive mild-mannered housewives to rip wild animals limb from limb and eat them raw.

The offspring of one of Zeus's many adulterous flings, Dionysus was worshipped as the god of resurrection. Zeus's jealous wife Hera had Dionysus killed by the Titans, who then cooked and ate him. This led to Zeus destroying the Titans with a thunderbolt and creating humanity from their ashes. This was believed to be the source of our dual nature; the evil came from the Titans, and the good from the parts of Dionysus they had digested. The Dionysus cult preached that the human body was a meat prison, composed of the Titans' remains but animated by the spirit of the Liberator. This belief would later be adopted by the Orphic Mysteries and also have an enormous impact on later cults such as the Gnostics.

Accounts of the Bacchanalia could horrify polite company. The Maenads would consume their "wine" and perform sexual, or violent, or sometimes violently sexual rituals to the thrashing of drums and flutes. Rumor had it that the Maenads used such extreme methods as cutting and flagellation in their initiations, and even that wooden or clay phalli (worn on belts) played some unspeakable role. Wasson writes that when Dionysus took hold of the Maenads and Bacchants, "he was synonymous with Hades, the Lord of Death, and bridegroom to the goddess of Persephone."

Periodic crackdowns on Dionysian excess inspired one of ancient Greece's most famous plays, Euripides' *The Bacchae*. It tells the story of the mythical Theban tyrant Pentheus as he tries to put down the Bacchanalia. Pentheus hears from a messenger who was sent to spy on the Bacchants, who reports that "the entire mountain and its wild animals were in one Bacchic ecstasy. As these women moved, they made all things dance." Dionysus leads the "frenzied dancing in the mountains," inspiring the women to "laugh as the flute plays, to bring all sorrows to an end."

Pentheus even tries to imprison the god, but fails. Dionysus taunts the king, bragging that he's "driven those women from their homes in a frenzy," and they now "live in the mountains, out of their minds," wearing costumes appropriate for his mysteries." As the Maenads dance and scream to the music, Dionysus calls out, "On, Bacchants, on! Chant songs to Dionysus, to the loud beat of our drums!"

Dionysus then invites Pentheus to witness the rituals, but on one condition: the king must dress not only as a woman, but as a woman disguised as a wild beast. Driven insane by the pounding drums and shrieking flutes, the Maenads spot Pentheus lurking in the bushes and tear him to shreds.

The late Harvard classicist Charles Segal sees Pentheus's fear of the Bacchanalia as symbolic of a deeper crisis in ancient Greek culture. "Women are not only sexual objects that escape (Pentheus') understanding," Segal argues, they are more intimately connected to "the biological processes of natural life, to birth, growth, and change" than men. The Maenads connect to the wild god because they are "more closely associated with the release of repressed emotionality that he embodies." This was especially true at a time in Greek history when many women were essentially kept as baby machines and locked away in their homes.

"Greeks ascribed to women the realm of spontaneity and madness," Jamake Highwater explains in *Myth & Sexuality*, adding, "The Dionysian cult gave women a power and importance that were otherwise denied them in fifth-century Athens." Highwater notes that the Mysteries *sanctified* that power, creating a ritual of the wilderness, where inhibitions could run amok. There were other, deeper conflicts at work, stemming from the aspirations of a pretechnological culture that reasonably saw the untamed forces of nature as its mortal enemy.

Having dutifully outraged all of Greece, the Bacchanalia migrated to Rome. The seditious rituals of the Roman Bacchants resulted in a moral panic in 186 BCE, inspiring the Senate to unleash a brutal crackdown, which was later documented by the conservative historian Livy (59 BCE–17 CE) in his landmark *History of Rome*.

As Livy tells it, things got so out of hand that instead of being celebrated three times a year as in Greece, the Roman cults were whooping it up five times a *month*. Stoking up the outrage like an ancient Fox News anchorman, Livy darkly reports that "more uncleanness was wrought by men with men than with women," claiming that anyone who refused to take part in the wanton man-sex was sacrificed to Bacchus. "To regard nothing as impious or criminal was the very sum of their religion," Livy fumes.

To the macho Roman male, effeminate behavior was the problem, not necessarily homosexuality itself. Many powerful

Roman men kept male slaves or teenage boys as "catamites," although it was taboo (illegal, actually) for a free-born adult man to act as a passive sex partner. Roman men were *always* on top. It's the loss of that control—that dominance—that Livy rails against when he writes that "the males, *the very counterparts of the women*" had been "submitting to the foulest uncleanness."

Livy is equally outraged that the men's behavior was hysterical and uncontrolled, noting they were "frantic and frenzied, driven out of their senses by sleepless nights, by wine, by nocturnal shouting and uproar." Livy draws parallels to traditionally female oracles when he writes that the men, "seized with madness and with frenzied distortions of their bodies, shrieked out prophecies." Sure enough, the same kinds of allegations would be made against the early rock 'n' rollers.

For a Roman chauvinist like Livy, the ultimate outrage of the Bacchic Mysteries was that "women form(ed) the great majority, and this was the source of all the mischief." Stoked into a lather, Livy declares, "Never has there been such a gigantic evil in the commonwealth, or one which has affected greater numbers or caused more numerous crimes," a particularly ridiculous statement, seeing that this is ancient Rome he was talking about. Livy then has the cavalry swooping in on this evil conspiracy, and here he relies on records of magistrates for the fate of the Bacchants. And it's a pretty grim account: "Many names were handed in, and some of these, both men and women, committed suicide." Some 7,000 were said to have been arrested and "the number of those executed exceeded the number of those sentenced to imprisonment," Livy reports. "There was an enormous number of men as well as women in both classes." Women found guilty "were handed over to their relatives or guardians to be dealt with privately; if there was no one capable of inflicting punishment, they were executed publicly." Which is to say that hundreds—if not thousands—of men were forced by the Senate to execute their own wives and daughters.

Historians today don't put a lot of stock in Livy's overheated accounts of the Bacchanalia, and generally write them off as politically motivated hysteria. His story of a massive cult that sprung up out of nowhere and took the country by storm is a historical fiction, meant to titillate his audience. In fact, the Bacchic cult had been tolerated for some time in Italy. But then again, Romans were known to take their taste for excess to extremes unequaled in the ancient world, so it's certainly not hard to imagine these shindigs getting out of hand.

The most serious charge leveled against the Bacchanalia was "conspiracy against the Republic," so it's possible the moral charges were simply politically motivated slander. The biggest fear among the elite was that "another people were about to arise" and overthrow the existing order. The greatest boogeyman to the Roman aristocracy was the *demagogue*, meaning anyone who could rally women, slaves, and other noncitizens against the old, landowning families who controlled the Senate. Given the staggering socioeconomic inequalities of both the Republic and the Empire, rebellion was always a clear and present danger. Since many of the Bacchants were immigrants from points east, their rituals were regarded in much the same way modern American Catholics might regard Santeria—a foreign corruption of the true faith.

Contrary to Livy, the Bacchanalia *weren't* prohibited and its shrines *weren't* destroyed but rather tightly regulated and controlled by law. And though they never again reached the fever pitch of the Republican era, the Bacchanalia would be revived by Julius Caesar and Mark Antony. Renamed the *Liberalia* (after yet another of Dionysus's titles) the new Bacchic holiday would become a family-oriented kind of street fair, with honey cakes and sweetmeats replacing all the drugs and sex. Sacred rituals, street entertainers, and other entertainments made it a very popular holiday. The booze and sex snuck back in along the way, but in a much less scandalous fashion.

The Liberalia is still very much with us. In fact, we celebrate our modern version of it on the very same day that the Romans did. In our modern version, people still march and drink and stuff themselves and play flutes and drums and all the rest of it. We still pig out on beer, beef, and cabbage (which dates back to the Osirian fests in Egypt, where cabbage was thought to delay overintoxication). And we even still dress in the color of Osiris-Dionysus-Bacchus, whom the Celts knew as the "Green Man."

Yes, the Liberalia lives on to this day. We just changed the festival's name to "St. Patrick's Day."

HERMES, HECATE, AND APOLLO

Though not the figureheads of prominent Mysteries themselves, the gods Hermes, Hecate, and Apollo were deeply embedded in the Mystery tradition. And seeing that they represented money, magic, and music, respectively, they're deeply embedded in rock 'n' roll as well.

These were everyday gods, responsible for the activities of ordinary life. Hermes was messenger of the gods, as well as patron of trade, medicine, and writing. Hermes was also a *psychopomp,* one who escorted the dead to the Underworld.

He was also the god of coincidence, or synchronicity, if you prefer. The Romans called him Mercury, from the same root as "market" and "merchandise," *mercatus*.

Like Hermes, Hecate played an important role in the Mystery dramas. She—like Hermes, Osiris, Dionysus, and Mithras—was identified with cattle, but was more closely associated with magic, ghosts, witchcraft, and the Under-world. Statues of Hecate were placed at city gates for protection against intruders, particularly those of the demonic variety. Dogs were sacrificed to the goddess, herself often depicted in canine form. Isis was sometimes identified with Hecate in her role as goddess of magicians, as well as through their sacred animals; Isis was identified with Sirius, the Dog Star. Most importantly, Hecate was associated with psychoactive drugs such as belladonna, opium, and mandrake.

Apollo was one of the most important gods in the ancient world. Among other roles, he was the god of prophecy, archery, music and the arts, and healing. He was a god of the *polis*, or city-state, and his oracles were consulted before major battles and other important decisions of state. Although Apollo had several Oracles, or prophetic shrines, all over Greece, the most important was at Delphi. There he prophesied to the Pythia, priestess of the Oracle, as she was gripped by violent convulsions, brought on either from a toxic gas or a hallucinogen, take your pick.

Most importantly, Apollo was himself the ultimate rock god. The *Homeric Hymn to Pythian Apollo* depicts him as ancient cross between Hendrix and Bowie, "clad in divine, perfumed garments ... at the touch of the golden key his lyre sings sweet." When Apollo did his act for the Olympians, "the undying gods think only of the lyre and song." He was not only a rock god, but also the god of rock: another Homeric hymn to Apollo reports that "the sweet-tongued minstrel, holding his high-pitched lyre, always sings both first and last" to the god. But Apollo was a god of plagues as well as healing, and the metallic thrashing of his bow and arrows rivaled the Cabeiri's. The *paean*, or "healing song," was believed to calm Apollo when he got his wrath on.

Healing, prophecy, music, and identification with the Sun; these are traits that link Apollo to shamanic figures all throughout history. In his paper *The Shamanic Origins of Religion and Medicine,* Weston LaBarre notes that the powers attributed to Apollo can be "clearly seen as merely the expectable traits of the ancient Eurasiatic shaman. Apollo is the Sun, giver of all animal and plant life; he is the fertility demon of cattle. (He) sends the plague with his archer's arrows and he is likewise the great healer." At his very core, then, Apollo is directly connected to the gods of the Mysteries. But what other connections does shamanism have with these mysterious journeys into the world of the gods?

MYSTERIOUS SACRAMENTS

> *Either through the influence of narcotic drink, of which the hymns of all aboriginal humans and peoples speak, or with the invigorating springtime's awakening that fills all nature with passion, these Dionysian impulses find their source, and as they grow in intensity everything subjective vanishes into complete loss of self-recognition.*
> —Friedrich Nietzsche, *The Birth of Tragedy*

A growing number of modern researchers have argued that the "mystery" behind the Mysteries was the use of powerful hallucinogens like *Amanita muscaria* and psilocybin mushrooms. Some argued that the Eleusinian *kykeon* contained a dose of lysergic acid amide (LSA), a cousin of LSD isolated from ergot fungus. Others have argued that Dionysus cultists actually used an elixir of psychedelic mushrooms and herbs as their "wine," not the usual mix of fermented grapes. Ancient texts call for this wine to be watered down for safe consumption, even though grape wine could have had no more than 14 percent alcohol before the invention of distillation.

The most prominent advocates of the "entheogenic thesis" vis-à-vis the Mysteries were R. Gordon Wasson (1898–1986) and Terence McKenna (1946–2000), both ethnobotanists and amateur mycologists (*Entheogen* is a Greek word meaning "to create the god within"). A banker by trade, Wasson came to experiment with psychedelic mushrooms and realized that the drug cults of Mexico bore an uncanny similarity to the Mysteries. He enlisted the help of Harvard classical scholar Carl Ruck and penned *The Road to Eleusis*,

laying out his controversial mushroom and ergot theories—
and got his coauthor fired from his post in the process. In
breathless prose, Wasson explained that mushrooms "leap
forth seedless and rootless, a mystery from the beginning
... They express religion in its purest essence, without intellectual content. Aristotle said of the Eleusinian Mysteries
precisely the same."

Wasson reinterprets the abduction myth as a descent into
the unconscious, since the *narkissos* flower, which Persephone
had been gathering, had narcotic properties. Wasson also
points out that the Mycenaean Age (1600–1100 BCE) was
the era in which most of the great Greek myths and dramas
are set, and then traces the etymology of "Mycenaean" to the
mykes or mushroom.

McKenna published his own theories in the 1993 book
*Food of the Gods: The Search for the Original Tree of Knowl-
edge*, in which he expanded on Wasson's concepts. McKenna
was a tireless advocate for organic hallucinogens, advocating
what he called the "stoned ape theory," in which hallucinogens
were the primary catalyst in the development of human intelli-
gence and evolution. McKenna saw hallucinogens as the basis
of *all* religion and mystical experience, a position held in part
by controversial Dead Sea Scrolls scholar John Marco Allegro
(1923–1988), who wrote in *The Sacred Mushroom and the
Cross* (1969) that the blood and wine of Christian communion
were actually derived from psychedelic mushrooms.

Given the links between Christianity and the Egyptian
Mysteries, there may also be a connection to the Eye of Horus.
(Remember that "Horus the Child" was the embodiment of
the Mysteries.) Researcher Stephen Berlant claims that the Eye
was itself a hallucinogenic plant, and cites legendary British

Egyptologist E.A. Wallis Budge, who wrote of the Eye in *Gods of the Egyptians* (1904):

> *The gods nourished themselves with celestial food which was supplied to them by the Eye of Horus, that is to say, they supported their existence on the rays of light which fell from the sun which lit up heaven, and they became beings whose bodies were wholly of light. According to one myth the gods themselves lived upon a "wood or plant of life," which seems to have grown near the great lake in Sekhet-hetep, round which they were wont to sit ... In other places we read of "bread of eternity" and "beer of eternity."*

Seeing that mushrooms thrive in moist climates, the fact that the Eye was found near a lake bolsters Berlant's arguments. The other great solar icon of rebirth in Egyptian religion was the scarab, or dung beetle, which at first seems like a strange choice for such an important archetype until you realize that psychedelic mushrooms often grow in cow manure. Remember that the bull was sacred to Osiris and Dionysus as well.

The most public display of Dionysus worship was the parade of the sacred phallus. This could very well have been a representation of a mature *Amanita muscaria* mushroom, which can look exactly like a well-endowed erection. Mithras, whom we'll meet soon, slits the throat of a bull in his most famous icon, the Tauroctony. Most historians interpret the image as a depiction of the end of the astrological Age of Taurus, but this could be another connection to the mushroom growing on cow manure—perhaps from a belief that the cow *creates*

THE SECRET HISTORY OF ROCK 'N' ROLL   33

the mushrooms. Even more compelling is the hat worn by Mithras, called the "Liberty Cap," whose name and form are shared with a psychedelic mushroom.

Although the eminent religious scholar Huston Smith has lent a qualified endorsement, the academy still hasn't signed off on the entheogenic theory. But renegade scholars continue to ransack old texts for evidence, and a corpus of writings on the theory continues to grow. Hallucinogens weren't the alpha and omega of the Mysteries, by any means, but part of a tightly constructed and highly organized system of conscious-ness-raising that could have you on Olympus even before the potions were served.

THE KORYBANTES
Some people think that heavy metal is a relatively recent musical development, created in the late Sixties by hairy, working-class Brits mangling old blues licks with their amps cranked up to 11. Not exactly. The technology may have evolved, but when you peel away the superficial elements you discover that heavy metal is nothing more than an unconscious 20th-century revival of the Korybantes, the noise-crazed madmen of the ancient Mysteries. These warrior priests performed their insane racket in full hoplite armor, clanging their swords and shields in time to the beat of drums and lyres, literally screaming their songs until their throats were raw.

The exact origins of these Hellenistic headbangers was a matter of considerable confusion among ancient historians, but it's generally believed that they emerged from the Mount Ida region in modern Turkey as priests of Cybele, the Phrygian mother of the gods. The Korybantes were also identified with the Great Gods of Samothrace. There were also similar groups with similarly hazy mythic origins, such as the Kouretes and the Dactyls. All of these groups eventually became interchangeable, particularly with the rise of cosmopolitanism and syncretism. But these macho musical madmen—whatever name they go by—seem to have been a popular feature throughout the various Mystery traditions.

All of the various outfits had two incarnations, however: as mythic beings and as human priesthoods. The Korybantes were demigods, charged with protecting Dionysus during his childhood. As Nonnus wrote in *Dionysiaca*, "The tripping [!] Korybantes would surround Dionysus with their child-cherishing dance, and clash their swords and strike their shields with rebounding steel in alternate movements, to conceal the growing boyhood of Dionysus." The wine god grew up listening "to the fostering noise of the shields," which goes a long way in explaining his own appetite for rock 'n' roll. Similarly, the Kouretes were charged with protecting Zeus as an infant from his baby-eating father, Chronos. For their part, the Dactyls were credited with creating the Olympian games, in some accounts.

Strabo claims that the Korybantes "were sons of Zeus and Kalliope and were identical with the Kabeiroi" who traveled to Samothrace and practiced the Mysteries. Strabo then goes on to say that others believed the Kouretes were the same as the Korybantes and were ministers of Hecate. Diodorus Siculus offers that the "Korybantes were wizards, they practiced charms and initiatory rites and mysteries, and in the course of a sojourn in Samothrace they amazed the natives of that island (with) their skill in such matters ... (Orpheus) also became a pupil of theirs, and he was subsequently the first to introduce initiatory rites and Mysteries to the Greeks."

These Korybantes/Kouretes/Dactyls must have really been something to behold. Ancient literature is filled with breathless tributes to them, as if every poet and historian had a major man-crush on these screaming, armored priests. The author of the Orphic hymns wrote of "leaping Kouretes, who with dancing feet and circling measures armed footsteps beat, (who) move in rhythm to the sounding lyre ... arm-bearers, strong defenders, rulers dread ... preserving rites mysterious and divine: come, and benevolent this hymn attend." Almost sounds like an excerpt from an old Iron Maiden fanzine, no?

So compelling was this metallic racket that "packs of bears joined the dance ... Lions with a roar from emulous throats mimicked the triumphant cry of the priests of the Kabeiroi, sane in their madness; the reveling pipes rang out a tune to honor of Hecate."

Whatever name they went by, the Korybantes became an integral part of the Mysteries in Samothrace, as well as the Mysteries of Cybele and Attis. Given their role in the myths as the guardians of Dionysus, it could well be that the real-life Phrygians first introduced the kind of violent musical blowouts you would later see in the Bacchanalia. Historian Franz Cumont also identified the Korybantes with Mithras, which certainly makes sense in the context of the gonzoid Mithraic rites.

ORPHEUS

Not many religious traditions can trace their roots to a rock star, but according to many ancient sources, the Mystery religions of Greece did exactly that. Of course, the exact prehistory of the Mysteries goes back a bit further, but some ancient Greeks believed that the legendary singer/lyrist/lyricist Orpheus first brought the secret rites to their country. Over time, Orpheus would be credited with a whole lot more besides, including the creation of music itself.

He must have been one hell of a singer.

Strabo describes Orpheus as "a wizard who at first collected money from his music, together with his soothsaying and his celebration of the orgies connected with the mystic initiatory rites" and "procured for himself a throng of followers and power." Unfortunately, as Strabo records, just like 20th-century rockers, Orpheus's secret rites also aroused suspicion among the uninitiated, ultimately leading to his murder.

Like an ancient Elvis, Orpheus then entered into the mythic realm. Reborn as the son of the muse Calliope and a river god, Orpheus was credited with establishing civilization in Greece, as did Osiris in Egypt. Besides creating music and the Mysteries, Orpheus was credited with introducing writing, magic, medicine, and agriculture to the Greeks, depending on which story you read. Orpheus was put aboard the Argo at one point, helping Jason and his sailors escape the Sirens in an ancient battle of the bands, where his famous lyre overpowered the Sirens' shrill singing. Adding to an already impressive résumé, Aeschylus credited Orpheus with the creation of sun worship.

According to 18th-century English mythologist Thomas Taylor, Orpheus "was the son of a king, who was the founder of theology, among the Greeks; the institutor of their life and morals; the first of prophets, and the prince of poets." The Greeks believed that their greatest minds were inspired by the Orphic Mysteries, including "the divine muse of Homer, and the philosophy of Pythagoras, and Plato." Orpheus's musical gifts also had magical properties; "by the melody of his lyre, he drew rocks, woods, and wild beasts, stopt rivers in their course, and ever, moved the inexorable king of hell," Taylor writes.

Orpheus had a wife named Eurydice, who was a daughter of Apollo and may be recorded history's first groupie. While trying to escape a sex-mad satyr, Eurydice stumbled on a nest of poisonous snakes and was fatally bitten. Shattered, Orpheus traveled to Hell, where he serenaded Hades and Persephone. In return they agreed to let Eurydice return with him to the upper world. In one of those frustrating tropes that mythology is full of, everything was copacetic so long as Orpheus didn't look back at Eurydice until they left Hell. Of course he *did* look back and she vanished back into the Underworld forever. Tradition had it that Orpheus renounced sex (well, with *women*, at least) out of grief for Eurydice. This apparently left a trail of broken hearts pining for the pop idol. The Roman poet Ovid wrote, "Many felt a desire to be joined with the poet, and many grieved at rejection. Indeed, he was the first of the Thracian people to transfer his love to (male) youths." Wow, another first.

Orpheus's change of heart in turn led to his murder at the death of a band of Maenads coming off a bender. Ovid wrote that "the frenzied Ciconian women, their breasts covered with animal skins, spied Orpheus from a hilltop, as he matched songs to the sounding strings. (One of them) called: 'Behold, behold, this is the one who scorns us!' and hurled her spear at the face of Apollo's poet, as he was singing." The Maenads tore Orpheus limb from limb, either for forsaking Dionysus or for refusing their drunken come-ons, or perhaps both.

Taylor recounts that following his murder "the soul of Orpheus, being destined to descend into another body, is reported to have chosen rather that of a swan than to be born again of a woman; having conceived such hatred against the sex." Ironically, Orpheus's lyre would be hung in the Temple of Apollo on Lesbos, where his dismembered head was used as an oracle and the lyre played itself in accompaniment.

The Orphic Mysteries dealt in magic as well as music. Pausanias wrote that Orpheus created annual Mystery rites for Hecate in Aegina. In Laconia, he established the mysteries of Demeter of the Underworld. Over time, an entire corpus of poems and hymns credited to Orpheus would appear, many of which were dedicated to the gods and practices of the various Mystery religions.

Despite having a polysexual rock star founder, Orphism wasn't wild and free like Dionysianism. The Orphic Mysteries evolved into a strict, ascetic cult, practicing vegetarianism and preaching a puritanical lifestyle and pessimistic theology. In fact, Orphic teachings offered a foreshadowing of the Christian doctrine of original sin. Because humanity contained traces of the Titans as well as the murdered Dionysus, there was a need to atone for the sins of our Titan fathers.

Later, a trade arose in amulets and magical books credited to Orpheus. In the play *The Cyclops*, Euripedes credited Orpheus with empowering magical charms that could defeat the one-eyed monster. This trade would create an entire profession of door-to-door soothsayers, an ancient Greek version of the Jehovah's Witnesses. In *The Republic*, Plato dismissed them as "begging priests and soothsayers" who "produce a bushel of books of Musaeus and Orpheus, the offspring of the Moon and of the Muses, as they affirm, and these books they use in their ritual, and make not only ordinary men but states believe that there really are remissions of sins and purifications for deeds of injustice."

THE MYSTERIES OF CYBELE AND ATTIS

Androgyny has always been an important part of the esoteric spiritual mind-set. Gender-bending was not only *not* seen as an "abomination" by the ancient pagans, it was often seen as a way to really get down with the gods. Many of the most important gods of ancient Egypt skirted traditional gender boundaries: Atum (the "Great He/She" creator god), Huh (god of Infinity), Neith (goddess of war), Hapi (god of the Nile, usually depicted as a large-breasted man), and Ptah (god of builders and craftsmen, able to change gender at will), as well as Horus and Set.

Egyptian warrior-kings such as Seti and Rameses were often seen in ancient art wearing the ritual drag of wigs, makeup, jewelry, and gowns or skirts. In some cases, the pharaohs are only distinguishable from queens or goddesses by the length of their skirts or their glued-on beards. Egyptologists today believe that Akhenaten (history's first monotheist, ironically) was born a hermaphrodite. Aside from his famous queen, Nefertiti, Akhenaten also had a man-squeeze, Smenkhare. Other Mediterranean cultures followed in the Egyptians' footsteps, particularly the Greeks. Major gods such as Zeus, Hermes (whose androgynous child with Aphrodite gave us the term *hermaphrodite*), Apollo, and Hercules shtupped anything with a pulse, reflecting the values of the time.

The virgin moon goddess Artemis was prominent in Sparta, whose population was commonly divided into homosocial groupings. Same sex mentoring-with-benefits was practiced by men *and* women (who had a much higher social status than their sisters in other Greek city-states). The mythical Amazons were traditionally believed to be lesbians, hooking up with men once a year only to keep the birthrates up. The ancient

Gnostic text *The Divine Pymander of Hermes Mercurius Trismegistus* teaches that humanity was originally androgynous, and that the separation of the genders was part of a Fall from the Godhead.

Likewise, one ancient Mystery cult was centered on the concept of androgyny as salvation. The Mysteries of Cybele and Attis were spread throughout the Roman Empire by a fierce army of cross-dressing eunuch priests, whose fast/loud/wild music and bloody rituals eerily prefigure the glam and glitter movements of the late Sixties and early Seventies, as well as later spin-offs like punk, new wave, and hair metal.

The ancient earth goddess Cybele was one of the most revered figures in the ancient world. Tracing her roots to the wildly religious province of Phrygia, Cybele was adopted as the "Mother of the Gods" in the late 3rd century BCE by ancient Romans, who credited her with their victory in the Second Punic War. Debate had been raging over the inclusion of this foreign goddess in the state cult, but a bizarre series of events made up the Romans' minds for them. The dependably excitable Livy wrote that "the temple of Jupiter and the sacred grove of Marica were struck with lightning" and one municipality "reported a second and more appalling portent; a stream of blood had flowed in at their gate."

Following several reports of stones showering from the skies, the pontiffs decided that bands of virgins "should go through the City singing a hymn" to the goddess, but while they were practicing the hymns in the state temple of Jupiter, the temple of Queen Juno was struck by lightning. Cybele's impending arrival got even stranger. "Two suns were said to have been seen; there were intervals of daylight during the night," Livy writes, adding, "A meteor was seen to shoot from east to west; a gate at Tarracina and at Anagnia a gate and several portions of the wall were struck by lightning; in the temple of Juno Sospita at Lanuvium a crash followed by a dreadful roar was heard."

After frantic deliberation, the legendary general Scipio "was ordered to go to Ostia, accompanied by all the matrons, to meet the goddess." Livy wrote that Cybele's "reputation had previously been doubtful" but the entourage sent to greet her "surrounded her with a halo of chastity in the eyes of posterity."

Cybele was a queenly, maternal, and physically commanding presence, and was often pictured driving a chariot pulled by two lions. She became a favorite of powerful emperors such as Augustus, Claudius, and Commodus, and her cult lasted well into the Christian Era. Such was her reputation that her temples were often converted into shrines to the Virgin Mary rather than being destroyed.

What set Cybele apart from other goddesses was the over-the-top extremism of her followers, who put even the wildest snake handlers of our time to shame. In fact, Cybele commanded such respect precisely *because* she instilled such a bloody passion in her followers. The passion and intensity of Cybele's followers would make them a special target when the Church began its rise to dominance, and her priests would become a special target for their wicked, wanton ways.

Cybele's companion Attis was her son and/or her lover, depending on which version of the myth you read. In some accounts, Attis castrates himself when his mad hermaphroditic lover Agdistis crashes his wedding party. In others, Agdistis and Cybele were the same person. (Mythology can get very confusing.) After his castration, Attis dresses as a woman, takes only male lovers, and travels the countryside leading the people in musical tributes to the Mother Goddess that sound every bit like an ancient version of *Hedwig and the Angry Inch*:

> As Attis, the counterfeit woman, sang this to her
>   companions,
> The choir howled suddenly with tumultuous
>   tongues.
> The tambourine bellows, the cymbals clash again;
> The swift troop moves off to Ida with hurrying
>   feet.
> Crazy, panting, drifting, at her last gasp,
> Attis with her tambourine leads them through the
>   opaque groves
> Like an unbroken heifer refusing the yoke:
> A woman now, I have been man, youth, and boy;
> I was athlete, the wrestler.
> There were crowds round my door, my fans slept
>   on the doorstep

In tribute to Attis, the priests of Cybele—known as *Galli* or *Galloi*—would castrate themselves and dress as women. They would travel the countryside and perform passionate musical tributes to the Great Mother, just as Attis did. An outraged Christian apologist named Hippolytus described the strangely postmodern attitude toward gender these priests held: "For man, they say, is bisexual. So in accordance with this thought of theirs the intercourse of woman with man is in their teaching shown to be most wicked and prohibited ... Attis was castrated, that is, cut off from the earthly parts of the creation here below, and has gone over to the eternal substance above where he says there is neither female nor male, but a new creature."

Ancient historians held a variety of opinions on the Galloi, from admiration to bemusement to ridicule. But everyone seemed to agree that the Galloi loved to rock and roll. Their rituals and festivals made Woodstock look like a ladies' club luncheon.

The public performances of the Galloi were so intense that crowds would be driven into a religious panic. At times pious young men would jump out of the crowd and join the priesthood in a particularly interesting fashion. Roman historian Lucian of Samosata described such a scene:

> On certain days a multitude flocks into the temple, and the Galloi in great numbers, sacred as they are, perform the ceremonies of the men and gash their arms and turn their backs to be lashed. Many bystanders play on the pipes the while many beat drums; others sing divine and sacred songs. Any young man who has resolved on this action, strips off his clothes, and with a loud shout bursts into the midst of the crowd, and picks up a sword ... and castrates himself and then runs wild through the city, bearing in his hands what he has cut off. He casts it into any house at will, and from this house he receives women's raiment and ornaments.

That is one fascinating recruitment technique.

The Galloi even made an appearance in Apuleius's *Metamorphoses*, the classic Roman comic novel. The story concerns an amateur sorcerer named Lucius, who mucks up a spell and turns himself into a donkey. In that form, Lucius is sold to a wandering band of Galloi and dragged around while the priests travel the countryside, often performing their act door to door.

Obviously not a fan, Lucius describes the Galloi's rites, which include an eerily exact precursor of heavy metal head-banging: "They arrived at a rich man's villa and screeching their tuneless threnes from the moment they saw the gates, they rushed frantically inside. Bending their heads, they twisted, writhed and rolled their necks to and fro while their long hair swung round in circles."

With the rise of imperial Christianity, authorities took special care to target the Galloi and their cult. But were the Galloi stamped out, or simply absorbed? Early Christian fathers were known to castrate themselves, and monks and priests and nuns live in homosocial monastic environments to this day. And ornate, sexually ambiguous vestments are still used in ceremonies in any number of denominations or sects.

A studiously meticulous androgyny was the height of fashion among lusty European heterosexuals for centuries, exactly as it had been in Egypt. And all kinds of gender-bending—from dandyism to cross-dressing to alternate sexualities—have been an essential part of human culture throughout history, and would stage a major comeback with the rise of rock 'n' roll.

THE OFFICIAL STATE CULTS OF ROME

Over time, the Mysteries were eventually pulled away from Phrygia and Egypt and Greece, and drawn into the orbit of the dominant superpower of the ancient world. There they would evolve in important ways, blending and merging with their rivals and ultimately becoming institutionalized. But in order to understand that process you first have to understand the Roman religious mind.

Sovereignty, military force, and fertility were the founding principles of Roman religion, represented by Jupiter, Mars, and Juno, respectively. The state cult was centered in the Forum (which held the Shrine of Vesta) and Capitoline Hill (which held the Temple of Jupiter). Greek gods eventually replaced some of the Etruscan ones, though many of the old gods like Janus (god of gateways), Vesta (goddess of the hearth), and Fortuna remained central to Roman life.

The old Republic gave way to the Empire, as the old families declined and new power brokers took hold. The cult of the emperor was then raised alongside the cult of the state. Following Julius and Augustus's example, many emperors saw themselves as descendants of the love goddess Venus. Even so, Augustus's "family values" morality was even more stringent than the Moral Majority's, passing laws against divorce and childlessness.

As its empire continued to grow and expand, Rome found itself invaded by alien gods from the colonies. These cults were usually tolerated (begrudgingly), but they often found themselves suddenly *un*-tolerated. Suetonius reported that Tiberius Caesar (42 BCE–37 CE) banned fortune-tellers and astrologers and "abolished foreign cults, especially the Egyptian and the Jewish rites, compelling all who were addicted to such superstitions to burn their religious vestments and all their paraphernalia." Those who refused were exiled or worse.

Despite his public law-and-order rhetoric, Tiberius wasn't bothered by *any* kind of morality. Foreign gods and secret cults tended to inspire rebellion or sectarian violence, so they had to go, simple as that. In fact, Suetonius reports that when the "old goat" Tiberius had retired to his island villa, "he devised a pleasance for his secret orgies: teams of wantons of both sexes, selected as experts in deviant intercourse and dubbed 'analists,' copulated before him in triple unions to excite his flagging passions."

In the wake of Tiberius's reign came a new movement that would eventually rise to become Rome's imperial state cult. Christianity began as a splinter movement in Judaism, based on the teachings of a traveling rabbi who prophesied the coming of the "Kingdom of God," and whose followers claimed that he rose from the dead and ascended into Heaven. No one paid the Christians much mind, apart from Jewish authorities offended that a crucified troublemaker was being hailed as the Messiah. The Romans were busy enough trying to keep the peace in Judea, which was looking down the barrel of an all-out civil war between various orthodox factions, as well as involving Greeks and Romanized Jews. It wasn't until a Roman citizen from the Mithraic stronghold of Tarsus appeared that the new religion really began to take off.

Saul of Tarsus—aka the Apostle Paul—was a Pharisaic Jew with a mysterious past who claimed to have received a vision of Jesus while on his way to Damascus to suppress a Christian cult. Paul seemed almost completely unfamiliar with the details of Jesus's life and ministry, preaching a doctrine of "Christ" as the fulfillment of messianic prophecies. But Paul was an extremely compelling orator and writer and preached his version of Christianity to the Gentiles, causing bitter schisms in the Jerusalem Church and among the original Apostles.

For a poor tentmaker, Paul was remarkably well traveled, preaching all over the Mediterranean. He was also remarkably lucky—Roman soldiers rescued Paul from an angry mob at one point, and, at another, whisked him off to Caesarea with a 470-man armed escort when a death plot emerged against him in Jerusalem. (Contrast that with what happened to Jesus in much the same situation.) The Romans were also kind enough to let Paul stay with a Christian family for a week when he was supposed to be on his way to trial in Rome. Ostensibly under house arrest for his writing and preaching, Paul was allowed to continue to write and preach in a villa supplied by the Praetorian Guard, of all people. (The Praetorians were a rough equivalent of the modern Secret Service.) Legend has it that Paul was sentenced to death by Nero, but no record of his trial or execution exists anywhere.

In any event, Paul and his new vision of Christ arrived at an extraordinarily convenient time for the Roman power structure. Jews were a powerful minority within the Empire, and were deeply involved in important professions such as education and trade. Judaism was also a missionizing faith at that time, and some Roman citizens had converted, raising the possibility that the growing unrest in Jerusalem could spread to other parts of the Empire. A new form of mystical Judaism, unbeholden to the Temple and to the Holy Land itself, would have been a godsend for the Romans. Especially if it could also attract pagans with themes and rites heavily borrowed from the Mysteries. And in a stunning stroke of blind luck for Rome, Paul preached exactly that.

The revolts in Palestine were brutally put down by the generals Vespasian and Titus, both of whom would become emperors. The historian Josephus claimed that a million people were killed in the assault, and the Jews were banished from Jerusalem. Looking to restore order, Titus's successor Domitian (51–96 CE) appointed himself censor, cracked down on adultery and permissiveness, and suppressed both Judaism and Christianity. Refusing to pray for the emperor was the primary reason Christians were singled out for punishment; Christians had their *own* emperor whose second coming they literally believed was due at any moment. This was certainly not a unique belief at the time—there were any number of other cults that believed their own departed leader would rise from the dead and save the world. These were so widespread that in 98 CE the emperor Trajan banned all secret societies, among which he counted the Christian cults.

The Empire continued to expand, and enjoyed relatively calm periods under Hadrian (who was initiated at Eleusis) and the philosopher-king Marcus Aurelius. But the "Antonine Plague" (believed to be a smallpox epidemic) broke out in 165 CE and killed some 5 million people over the next 15 years. Another plague broke out 70 years later, which threatened the political and military instability of the Empire.

Rome would emerge from a prolonged period of crisis through sheer force of will, as bare-knuckled generals like Aurelian and Probus took the throne and enforced military discipline on their subjects. And it was under these men that the Mystery cults of Mithras, Isis, and Cybele rose to an unprecedented degree of power and influence throughout the ancient world.

ISIS, QUEEN OF HEAVEN

In the 1st century BCE, an assembly of Isis adherents known as the *Pastophori* began to appear in Rome and established a network of shrines throughout the city. These priests were not unlike modern Hare Krishnas; they outraged conservative Romans by shaving their heads in the Egyptian style, and abstained from meat, wine, and marriage. Seeing Isis as a degenerate foreign influence, the Senate ordered her temple destroyed in 65 BCE. Augustus and Tiberius had her priests crucified. Perhaps intrigued by rumors of the cult's temple prostitutes, Caligula legalized Isis worship and ordered the construction of the Iseum in her tribute. Seen as a loving alternative to the cold, old gods of the state, Isis quickly became the *Magna Mater* in the hearts of the Romans. Initially depicted nude, Isis was later depicted in a modest cloak and veil. But her public image was a bit more sedate than the more psychedelic one Isis revealed to her initiates.

In *Metamorphoses,* Apuleius describes how Isis revealed herself to Lucius: "A multiform crown, consisting of various flowers ... in the middle of (her forehead) was a smooth orb ... which indicated that she was the moon. (Vipers) environed the crown on the right hand and on the left (were) ears of corn ... Glittering stars were dispersed through the embroidered border of the robe ... (The full moon) breathed forth flaming fires."

Addressing Lucius directly, the goddess says, "I am she that is the natural mother of all things, mistress and governess of all the elements, the initial progeny of worlds, chief of powers divine, queen of heaven, the principal of the gods celestial, the light of the goddesses."

The Roman Isis also carried a sistrum (a kind of rattle) on loan from Hathor. In Apuleius's description, when "she vibrated these triple chords they produced a sharp shrill cry." To her initiates, this sacred racket had not only a ritual purpose, but also a cosmic one. As Roman scholar Plutarch describes it in his tract *Moralia,* "The sistrum also makes it clear that all things in existence need to be shaken, or rattled about, and never to cease from motion but, as it were, to be waked up and agitated when they grow drowsy and torpid. They say that they avert and repel Typhon by means of the sistrums, indicating thereby that when destruction constricts and checks Nature, generation releases and arouses it by means of motion." In other words, Isis and her music literally kept the devil from your door. It's hard not to think about the rejuvenating powers of rock 'n' roll in that context.

Lucius also describes the welcoming of new initiates into the Isis cult, which sounds like any number of "love-bombing" conversion experiences from modern groups: "From everywhere came crowds of the initiates, flocking around me, and each of them, following the ancient rite, presented me with various gifts. Finally, all the uninitiated having withdrawn, they put on me a new linen robe, and the priest, seizing me by the hand, led me to the very inmost recesses of the holy place."

From there, the experience became considerably stranger, with Lucius descending into what sounds every bit like a powerful acid trip: "I drew near to the confines of death, treading the very threshold of Proserpine. I was borne through all the elements and returned to earth again. At the dead of night, I saw the sun shining brightly. I approached the gods above and the gods below, and worshipped them face to face … As soon as it was morning and the solemn rites had been completed, I came forth clothed in the twelve gowns that are worn by the initiate."

In addition to the Mystery cult there was a network of temples meant for the common folk, in which priests would practice the customary Egyptian rites throughout the day. Their liturgy sounds familiar to us today. Budge writes, "Services were held at daybreak and in the early afternoon daily, and everywhere these were attended by crowds of people. The holy water used in the libations and for sprinkling the people was Nile water, specially imported from Egypt, and to the votaries (monks or nuns) of the goddess it symbolized the seed of the god Osiris, which germinated and brought forth fruit through the spells of the goddess Isis. The festivals and processions ... were everywhere most popular, and were enjoyed by learned and unlearned alike."

Romans knew Osiris as Serapis, the synthesis of Osiris and Zeus created by Alexander's governor Ptolemy in order to calm tensions between Greeks and Egyptians in Alexandria. Serapis's popularity was such that according to the emperor Hadrian, the Patriarch (the pope of the early church) was "forced by some to worship Serapis, by others to worship Christ" when he visited Alexandria. In the Byzantine era, icons of Serapis would simply be revised to depict Jesus, as were Isis and Harpocrates to depict the Virgin and the Baby Jesus.

Aside from the drama of her cult, the exoticism of Isis's native Egypt added to her appeal. Sphinxes and obelisks decorated her temples throughout the Roman world. But her popularity would extend well beyond all that. The archetype of the welcoming, suffering, forgiving mother goddess struck a very deep chord in Rome. As Sir James Frazer wrote in *The Golden Bough*, "In a period of decadence, when traditional faiths were shaken ... Isis with her spiritual calm, her gracious promise of immortality, should have appeared to many like a star in a stormy sky," adding that she inspired "a rapture of devotion not unlike that which was paid in the Middle Ages to the Virgin Mary."

BLOOD AND FIRE: THE MITHRAIC MYSTERIES

Conventional wisdom has it that ancient Rome fell because it became a nonstop carnival of vomit and buttsex. Nothing could be farther from the truth. In fact, an exceptionally harsh brand of Christianity had been the official religion of the state for over a century when the last Caesar was deposed in 475 CE.

By the end of the 2nd century, religion was taking root throughout the Empire, and an explosion of imported cults competed for Roman hearts and minds. The government was usually tolerant of this diversity—just so long as one's faith didn't preach disloyalty to the emperor.

Worship of dying/resurrecting savior gods was popular in Rome well before the birth of Christ, but the Roman take on these doctrines was a bit more colorful than what we're used to these days. Before the rise of Christianity in the 4th century, a henotheistic religion known today as "Mithraism" had become the faith of choice of the business and military classes.

The story goes that Mithraism was handed down from Persian Zoroastrians to Roman soldiers by way of a band of cutthroat pirates from Asia Minor. Zoroaster, who lived a thousand years or so before Jesus, preached that the world was in the grip of an eternal struggle between the forces of light (led by Ahura Mazda) and the forces of darkness (led by Ahriman). Mithras was the son of Ahura Mazda, and Mithraism preached much the same dualist cosmology as its parent religion. It was, as Burkert writes, anti-Gnostic and dedicated to "heroically facing and maintaining the cosmos built on violence and sacrifice."

Since no actual scriptures of the cult survive, its exact beliefs have had to be reconstructed, usually from its enemies' writings. The general consensus is that Mithraic cults demanded that each man must commit himself to the eternal struggle against evil. Mithraism also had a ceremonial meal of bread and wine, practiced baptism, used Sunday as its sabbath, and celebrated its god's birthday on December 25th. Early Christian fathers were reportedly so shocked by the similarities between Mithraism and Christianity that they claimed the cult was some devil's trick meant to muddy the theological waters.

But there were significant differences. Mithraism was exclusively male, and offered seven degrees of initiation similar to military rank. Cultists were expected to partake in fasts and ritual purification, and were often subjected to tests of strength, courage, and endurance. In short, Mithraism was a warrior cult. But it was also, well, *weird*.

Mithraic ceremonies—as well as their basic beliefs—were essentially based in ritual magic, and animal masks and costumes were worn according to each member's rank. And that baptism? Well, on the spring equinox and in the main Mithraic temple (located on Vatican Hill, ironically enough), initiates underwent the *Taurobolium*, in which they were showered in the blood of a sacrificial bull whose throat was cut as he stood above the initiate on a platform. Variations have a ram in place of a bull, which may have symbolized the end of the Age of Aries. A form of this practice may have been used by early Christians as well. (See Revelation 7:14 and 12:11.)

The *Taurobolium* corresponds to the central icon of the cult. The *Tauroctony*, as it's called, typically pictures Mithras cutting the throat of a bull. Often he is surrounded by a Zodiac, and accompanied by a sun god and moon goddess. The seven sisters of the Pleiades are often pictured, as are two torchbearers. A snake and a dog lap up the bull's blood, and a scorpion is seen attached to the bull's genitals. The general agreement is that the *Tauroctony* dates to the end of the Age of Taurus, and that Mithras is moving the heavens into the new age, with the various animals representing constellations, most likely Scorpio, Hydra, and Canis Major.

The other major icon of the Mithraic Mysteries is the winged, lion-headed god Aion, aka the *Leontocephalus*. As god of Eternity, Aion stands atop the X-shaped "cross of light," which represents the intersection of the zodiac and the celestial equator. A giant python coils around his body, and a crab and a goat flank his genitals, representing the solstices in Capricorn and Cancer. Godwise, it's not a warm and fuzzy image.

Then there's the Mithraic liturgy, found in a stash of documents dating from 4th-century Egypt. If the *Tauroctony* and Aion strike you as weird, then the liturgy is completely insane, combining semicogent religious language with strings of nonsense syllables inserted for magical effect, such as this:

> *I invoke the immortal names, living and honored, which never pass into mortal nature and are not declared in articulate speech by human tongue or mortal speech or mortal sound: EEO OEEO IOO OE EEO EEO OE EO IOO OEEE OEE OOE IE EO OO OE IEO.*

Or this:

> *Silence! Silence! Silence! Symbol of the living, incorruptible god! Guard me, Silence, NECH-THEIR THANMELOY! Then make a long hissing sound, next make a popping sound, and say: PROPROPHEGGE MORIOS PROPHYR*

PROPHEGGE   NEMETHIRE   ARPSENTEN
PTTETMI   MEOY   ENARTH   PHYRKECHO
PSYRIDARIO TYRE PHILBA.

Imagine reciting all of that while covered in cow's blood and
standing naked in a dark underground cave. As with the
Mysteries in general, there seems to be a botanical compo-
nent to this, with a kykeon-like admixture referred to, but not
described:

> *Furthermore, it is necessary for you, O daughter,*
> *to take the juices of herbs and spices, which will be*
> *given to you at the end of my holy treatise which the*
> *great god Helios Mithras ordered to be revealed to*
> *me by his archangel, so that I alone may ascend into*
> *heaven as an inquirer and behold the universe.*

It goes on like this, describing the consecrations as being
"bitter," a sensation well familiar to anyone who's tasted
psychedelic mushrooms. It gets even stranger, promising the
initiate that "you will see yourself being lifted up and ascending
to the height, so that you seem to be in midair" and that "you
will hear nothing either of man or of any other living thing,
nor in that hour will you see anything of mortal affairs on
earth, but rather you will see all immortal things."

Stranger still, this experience takes the initiate into outer
space ("You will see the divine order of the skies") and promises that "the visible gods will appear through the disk of god"
and see some kind of ray which the initiate will see "hanging
from the sun's disk like a pipe." Though the "disk" and "pipe"
certainly sound like a mushroom, this particular flying disk

has *doors* as well. Mithras himself appears behind those doors, described as "a youthful god, beautiful in appearance, with fiery hair, and in a white tunic and a scarlet cloak, and wearing a fiery crown."

The initiate is told to present Mithras with his horoscope, and is then confronted with seven snake-headed virgins, and seven bull-headed gods, and on and on. Bear in mind, these are soldiers, politicians, and businessmen going through all this, not a bunch of hippie weirdos. No wonder they kept all of it secret.

The Roman Legions took Mithras with them to the farthest corners of the known world. Based on archaeological evidence, Mithraism appears to be have been especially popular in northern Europe, particularly in Britain and Germany. The blood-and-fire Mithraic cults commonly used caves, grottoes, and basements as their places of worship, which are known to us today as *Mithraeums*. Because these were often hidden, many Mithraeums have been excavated largely intact.

The Liverpool area of England was used as a military base by the Roman Legion long before it was even established as a city. And there is one famous cellar of a uniquely Roman style in a building on the corner of Temple Court and Mathew Street. In point of fact, this cellar is *identical* in construction to a typical Roman Mithraeum: a long half-pipe-shaped space complete with arches, columns, and a curved ceiling, made entirely of brick. In the 1950s, the cellar was converted to a nightclub. You might have heard of it—it's called the Cavern Club.

Apparently, some group named the Beatles made their name there.

THE FALL OF THE MYSTERIES, AND THEN OF ROME ITSELF

Mithras was not the only solar deity in the Roman spiritual supermarket. Sun worship became widespread with a wide assortment of solar saviors like Apollo, Hercules, Horus, and Adonis. And sun worship would briefly become the religion of the state when a flamboyant teenage emperor named Helioga-balus (202–222 CE) took the throne.

Heliogabalus was already unpopular among the elite because of his age and Syrian background, and army revolts broke out when he became emperor. Always happy to poke the Establishment's eye with a sharp stick, he took a vestal virgin for a wife (similar to a president marrying a cloistered nun, only more offensive). Heliogabalus then built a temple for his god El-Gabal, whom he declared the new supreme deity, Helios Sol Invictus ("The Unconquered Sun"). Heliogabalus was just getting started.

Insatiably omnisexual, Heliogabalus married and divorced four other women and married both his chariot driver and a famous athlete in public ceremonies. He also liked to dress as a woman (a very beautiful one, by all accounts) and prostitute himself to the local riffraff. But having pressed one too many buttons, Heliogabalus soon found himself on the wrong end of a Praetorian sword. The Guard also killed Heliogabalus's mother and dragged the naked bodies behind their chariots around the streets of Rome.

Sometime later, another Caesar would make Sol worship the official religion of state. Rising to power as a no-nonsense, bone-breaking general, Aurelian (214–275) decisively put down a number foreign threats and rebellions. With Rome finally at peace, Aurelian set about restoring its former glory. Recognizing the popularity of henotheism and believing that religious confusion was weakening the Empire, he combined the worship of Sol and Mithras into a single cult. Aurelian had a Temple of the Sun built on the Campus Agrippae, and declared December 25 the "birthday of the Unconquerable Sun." This new cult would flourish well after Aurelian's assassination in 275 CE.

A few years later, another hard man took the throne. Diocletian (245–312 CE) would rout the Persians in the east and the Germans in the north, and remain emperor for 21 years. Obsessed with social unity and the rule of law, Diocletian pushed back the spread of foreign cults. He banned Christians from serving in the army and ordered church assets seized, inspiring Christian mobs to set two of his palaces ablaze in protest. Not to be outdone, Diocletian declared Christianity a capital crime, punishable by death by torture. It was under Diocletian that the common lore of Christian persecution arose—being fed to the lions and so on.

Predictably, Diocletian's new world order would fall to infighting after his retirement. His protégé Constantine (272–337) was made emperor but soon found himself at war with the rival emperor Maxentius. On the eve of a decisive battle in October 312, Constantine received a vision. He claimed to have seen the *chi-rho* symbol of Christ written in the sky and heard a voice saying, "In this sign, conquer." Constantine had the army emblazon the symbol upon their shields. When they met the much larger army of Maxentius the next day, Constantine won the battle.

To appreciate the impact created by Constantine's conversion, imagine if an American president converted to Islam. Christians were a generally distrusted minority, comprising no more than a tenth of the population at the start of the 4th century. Seen by many Romans as divisive and uneducated fanatics, Christians also refused to pray for the good of the Empire, which obsessively superstitious Romans believed angered the gods.

So it was a shock when Constantine issued the Edict of Milan in 313 CE. The edict ended state persecution of Christianity, which would blossom under Constantine's generous patronage. Faced with an overwhelmingly Mithraic army, he continued to appease the old gods, minting his coins with Sol on the reverse. But to Constantine, patronage only applied to state-approved Christian sects. Over the coming decades, any bishops or clergymen who disagreed with the prevailing orthodoxy were tortured, exiled, or beheaded—sometimes all three. As the 4th-century historian Ammianus observed, "I never yet found wild beasts so savagely hostile to men, as most of the Christians are to one another."

Constantine's conversion didn't necessarily make him a humanitarian. He outlawed crucifixion, but replaced it with hanging. Slaves could no longer be branded on the face, but could have hot lead poured down their throats if they rebelled. And Constantine could be as ruthless and bloodthirsty as Nero or Caligula, murdering several family members including his brother-in-law, his father-in-law, his nephew, son, and wife. Constantine's children shared in his unique interpretation of religion. Upon Constantine's death, his son Constantius II celebrated by having most of his relatives killed. This left only himself, his brothers, and two cousins to split up the Empire. When he wasn't busy killing his family members, Constantius also played an active role in mediating debates among the clergy on the divine nature of Christ.

Theodosius I (347–395 CE) would be the most brutal

enforcer of Christian faith that the Roman Empire would ever see. But this was only because the Empire was plunged into two separate civil wars under his leadership, and was crippled forever. Not long after Theodosius's reign, the West was overrun by barbarians from the north. The infamous Sack of Rome by the Visigoths took place under the reign of his son, Honorius, in 410 CE.

Starting in 389, Theodosius issued what are now known as the "Theodosian Decrees," where he banished all pagan holidays, outlawed blood sacrifice, banned pagan statues, and ordered the seizure of temple lands by the church. Theodosius also authorized the destruction of pagan landmarks like the Serapeum. Christian bishops led mobs on murderous rampages against pagans, Gnostics, and dissenting Christian factions all across the Empire. In 391, Theodosius extinguished the eternal fire in the Temple of Vesta and had the Virgins disbanded. Witchcraft and divination were outlawed. The Olympian games were abolished in 393. Thousands of texts were gathered up and destroyed. Scribes were forbidden to copy pagan texts on pain of amputation or death.

Among the countless victims of this systematic genocide was Hypatia of Alexandria. The legendary philosopher and mathematician was beaten, stripped, and tortured by a gang of monks on orders of the local bishop. She was hacked to death with stone tiles inside a church, and her severed body parts were charred with fire and then put on public display. She was the last headmster of the Platonist School of Alexandria, and her capital crime was being an educated woman in a Christian city.

The Western Empire was whittled away by packs of barbarians in the 5th century. While Rome's best minds were locked away in monasteries, Europe's educational and technical infrastructure fell apart. With political intrigue at a bloody, all-time high, knights fled to the hinterlands and set up their own mini-kingdoms, inaugurating the era of Feudalism. The Byzantine Empire would continue, but only as a relentlessly shrinking island under the rising tide of Islam (whose popularity in North Africa and Asia was fueled in reaction to the brutality and corruption of the Byzantine Emperor Justinian I). Before the end of the Middle Ages, Byzantium too would be gone.

The last "Roman emperor" was somewhat ironically named Romulus Augustus, after both Rome's founder and its first emperor. Unfortunately, a barbarian warlord would order Romulus off the throne. After he was deposed, Romulus would find his true calling—as a sequestered monk. Roman society had become such a basket case that historians are unable to determine in what years Romulus was born and died.

THE MIDDLE AGES AND THE RENAISSANCE OF THE GODS

The depaganization of Europe was slow and painful and, in many important ways, never completed. The farther away you got from Rome, the less likely the people would be converted, even if their rulers were. The ancient power of the old folkways was simply too much for the Church to overcome. Mythology persisted in the countryside among recalcitrant pagans and in polite company as entertainment. Christian emperors still wore the laurel wreath of Apollo.

Whereas the old Empire espoused religious freedom (more or less), the new one circumvented it simply by absorbing pagan icons and rituals. Realizing that folkways such as Yule trees, Easter eggs, and wishing wells were too deeply rooted,

Pope Gregory the Great (540–604) ordered that any surviving pagan shrines and rituals simply be given a Christian make-over, and that popular gods and heroes be recast as saints. The sex-mad Pan was a bit too much for the bishops, and he became the model for the Devil, one still in use to this day.

Which is not to say that anyone who resisted the *political* power of the Church got off with a slap on the wrist. The first Crusade was not against Muslims but against the Saxons, who refused to give up their old gods. Tens of thousands of them were slaughtered by Charlemagne's army. One of the most horrific Crusades was in the Languedoc region of France in the 13th century, where a mystical Christian sect known as the Cathars had taken root. This Crusade introduced into the lexicon the famous phrase *Caedite eos, Novit enim Dominus qui sunt eius* ("Kill 'em all, let God sort 'em out").

After a long sleep, Europe began to wake up from its intellectual and scientific stupor in the 12th century. The old myths enjoyed a new makeover—it was said that if read properly they could bolster Christian education, not undermine it. Trying to account for the numerous parallels in mythology to Christianity, religious scholars such as Bernard de Chartres and John of Salisbury argued that angels had deviously inserted hidden secret messages about the coming Christ in the old myths to trip up the heathens.

But it was during the Renaissance that the gods really made their big comeback. Images of them were everywhere. Freed of the responsibilities of cults, temples, and priesthoods, the old gods gleefully romped across Europe, inspiring artists and thinkers along the way. Countless works of art depicting the old myths were commissioned. Hercules himself became the patron of Florence.

The reintegration of paganism into the Christian Church was not only extensive, it also became a bone of contention for a new group of radical Christians named the Protestants. The movement's name arose from a famous list of complaints that an eminent German monk named Martin Luther nailed to a cathedral door in 1517. Luther's main beef was the sale of "indulgences," which were essentially bribes to ensure a habitual sinner's entry into Heaven. But his protests caught on with other Christians fed up with a corrupt church hierarchy and sparked a theological rebellion—and a political and social cataclysm—all across Europe.

Leaps in the natural sciences—and more importantly, printing press technology—led to a new wave of resistance against the Vatican. That in turn led to the Reformation and then to the Counter-Reformation, followed by a long period of vicious sectarian bloodletting all across Europe. Disgust with these new holy wars motivated the educated classes to rediscover the ancient skeptics and atheists, eventually leading to the Enlightenment, where Reason became the greatest good.

The Enlightenment took hold especially in England, which had suffered a particularly vicious civil war between Catholic Royalists and Protestant Republicans. The Enlightenment also gave rise to Freemasonry, which itself inspired democratic revolutions in America and France. But all that fertile acreage in North America needed cheap labor to work it, and that's where the next part of our story will pick up.

TRANSMISSION

The spread of customs and beliefs across time and space is an endless source of debate for historians, especially when there's no documentation to trace the sources of these transmissions. How does a belief system from one side of the world end up on the other? It's often hard to determine with prehistoric or preliterate societies. It can be even trickier when these beliefs are secret or even unconscious. And that is certainly the case with the transmission of the Mystery traditions from Europe to the New World.

Protestantism arose at the same time European powers were sending ships and arms to the Americas. The endless religious violence sent a lot of Protestants packing their bags to try their luck in the New World. This new movement was convenient for those bankrolling the colonies, since it didn't require the cumbersome infrastructure of the Roman Church, and Protestant leaders like John Calvin helpfully preached self-denial and total submission to authority. Subsequently, banks in London and Amsterdam created new umbrella corporations like the Virginia Company and the Massachusetts Bay Company to run settlements that sheltered these religious outcasts, in exchange for their labor on the plantations.

Not only did Protestant extremists make the trip, but so did a host of mystics, occultists, Rosicrucians, and Freemasons who were equally (if not more) endangered by the mayhem in Europe. Many of these groups were inspired by the ancient Mysteries, even if they didn't always fully understand them. They pored over the old texts in communities all across the new colonies and would use them as inspiration to imagine a utopian new republic, following the example of Plato and of Sir Francis Bacon's seminal novel, *The New Atlantis*.

But even stronger echoes of the Mysteries would travel to the New World with the slaves from Africa and the indentured servants from the Celtic rim of the British Isles. And when the rhythms and melodies of these oppressed people collided with the archetypes and rituals of their ancestral folkways, it would light a spark that would one day change the face of popular music all across the world. As we will see next, Europeans weren't very long in the New World before they began to rock and roll.

MERRYMOUNT, OR THE PURITAN WOODSTOCK

Thomas Morton was an English lawyer who came to Massachusetts and settled just south of Boston in a seaside outpost he called "Mare Mount" (later Merrymount, now part of Quincy). A freethinker, Morton established good relations with the local tribes (particularly their maidenfolk) and sold them English firearms. He also took in escaped indentured servants from Plymouth Plantation, which then was a Jonestown-like cult compound ineptly run by "Separatists," as the Pilgrims called themselves.

Morton thought his new community would be the perfect spot to revive some of the old European folkways, which he saw as being remarkably similar to some of the local customs. And in 1627, Morton decided to throw an old-fashioned May Day revel, complete with wine, women, and song. Morton later bragged that settlers indulged in "revels and merriment after the old English custom, setting up a Maypole and brewing a barrel of excellent beer," and invited all and sundry to celebrate and bring along "drums, guns, pistols and other fitting instruments for the purpose."

The pious governor of Plymouth, William Bradford, was predictably outraged by Morton and his entourage, cataloging their transgressions in his *History of Plymouth Plantation*: "Drinking and dancing about (the Maypole) many days together, inviting the Indian women for their consorts, dancing and frisking together (like so many fairies, or furies rather) and worse practices. As if they had anew revived and celebrated the feasts of the Roman goddess Flora, or the beastly practices of the mad Bacchanalians."

It was here that Thomas Morton composed America's first rock 'n' roll song, a hilariously bawdy celebration of sex, drink, and chasing after strange gods. The first verse invokes Hymen (an undoubtedly intentional double entendre), son of Dionysus and Aphrodite:

> *Drink and be merry, merry, merry boys*
> *Let all your delight be in the Hymen's joys*
> *Hail to Hymen, now the day is come,*
> *About the merry Maypole take a Room.*
> *Make green garlands, bring bottles out*
> *And fill sweet Nectar freely about.*

There's also a direct come-on to the local Indian girls, giving notice that "nymphs" and "lasses in beaver coats" were always welcome to come drink with the men at Merrymount. Morton's prosperous settlement threw two May Day revels, but the Puritans were having none of it. Morton wrote that the Maypole "was a lamentable spectacle" to the Puritans, adding, "they termed it an idol. They called it the Calf of Horeb and stood at defiance with the place, naming it Mount Dagon."

Sure enough, complaints were lodged, Morton was arrested

and sent back to England, and his settlement was disbanded. He fled England when Cromwell's bloodthirsty thugs took power, but when he returned to Massachusetts he found that the Indian population had been decimated and that the Puritans had a cold, wet jail cell waiting for him. On his release he fled the area and died in Maine in 1647. By the end of the century, the witch trials would be under way in Salem, about 30 miles from Merrymount. Ironically, the city of Salem today is a hotbed for the neopaganism Morton once tried to bring to America.

THE MASONIC MYSTERIES

Though the extent of its influence is debatable, there's no doubt that Freemasonry was a major factor in the American Revolution. Many Founding Fathers including George Washington, John Hancock, and Benjamin Franklin were Masons, as were several key officers in the Continental Army. But after a hot-blooded start, the Masons became increasingly stodgy over the years, attracting left-brained types like lawyers and engineers, as well as drawing heavily from the police and military. In other words, Freemasonry isn't very rock 'n' roll. But at least one prominent Founding Father believed it wasn't always that way.

Thomas Paine was a bit of a black sheep, even among his fellow revolutionaries. His anti-Royalist and antireligious rants earned him a lot of enemies, and nearly cost him his life during the French Revolution. But he authored several influential works of political theory that were widely read during the Revolutionary period, chief among them *Common Sense* (1776).

Paine offered his theories on the secret society in "The

Origin of Freemasonry," written in 1818. Though not a Mason himself, Paine challenged the official history of the order, proclaiming that the Masons were merely the old Celtic Druids trading under a new name, and that "in Masonry many of the ceremonies of the Druids are preserved in their original state." Paine then states unequivocally that the Druids were cut from the same cloth as the Egyptian Mysteries—in fact, they were simply a kind of franchise thereof.

In *the Secret Teachings of All Ages,* occult historian Manly Palmer Hall echoes Paine, claiming that druidic rites "closely resembled the Bacchic and Eleusinian Mysteries of Greece or the Egyptian rites of Isis and Osiris." Hall explains that the ancient Britons received the Mysteries "from Tyrian and Phœnician navigators who, thousands of years before the Christian Era, established colonies in Britain and Gaul while searching for tin."

Despite the Revolutionary-era appropriation of the Great Pyramid icon, the actual rites and symbols of Freemasonry seem to be derived more from Judaism and esoteric Christianity than Egypt or Druidry, so a lot of this could simply be legend-making. But the Freemasons' efforts to trace their lineage to these exotic forebears undoubtedly helped circulate some of the symbols and iconography of the ancient Mysteries, certainly in the popular imagination. Look no further than the smash success of *The Da Vinci Code* and *The Lost Symbol.*

THE DRUIDIC ROOTS OF AMERICAN FOLK MUSIC

The first slaves in the Americas were indentured servants from the British Isles, people so mired in poverty that their debts were paid through labor. Many of these came with their debtholders to the plantations in the American colonies. And many of them came from the Celtic precincts of Britain and Ireland.

The English crown (actually held by a German dynasty) controlled the other countries of the British Isles: the Celtic nations of Ireland, Scotland, and Wales. All these countries had a rich tradition of music that can be traced to ancient times, a tradition that continues to influence the music of our times as well.

Britain was an important hub for trade in the Bronze Age, and its rich deposits of tin were needed for the smelting of bronze. Eventually the island was conquered by the Romans, who settled the city of London. Because Phoenician traders were deeply involved in trade with northern Europe, Celtic music has a resemblance to the ancient music of the eastern Mediterranean. The Celtic music brought to America by British, Irish, and French immigrants would have an incalculable influence on the development of rock 'n' roll. Their "jigs and reels" and "airs"—that is, their raucous dance songs and mournful ballads—would form the backbone of American folksong. And that backbone would be built on an ancient Druid tradition that spread across northern Europe, linking the ancient Mysteries of the Celts to their spiritual cousins in Egypt, Greece, and Asia Minor.

Folk would evolve and splinter throughout the 18th and 19th centuries. The cowboy songs of the American frontier, the bluegrass of the Appalachian rim, and the work songs of the industrial heartland eventually coalesced into the popular genre known today as "country and western."

In the early 20th century, wireless radio and phonographs would spread this music in ways the old songsheets never could. No matter where you lived, a radio or a record player could give you access to the finest music played by the finest musicians. This put rural Americans on more equal terms with their urban cousins. It's hard to overstate the effect this would have on American culture.

The unconscious connection between ancient mythology and American folk music traditions directly informs the movie *O Brother, Where Art Thou?* (2000), written and directed by Joel and Ethan Coen, which allegorized *The Odyssey*. Tracing the adventures of a trio of escaped convicts headed by one Ulysses Everett McGill (played by George Clooney), the film replays the Homeric epic in the context of the Depression-era South, complete with stand-ins for the Cyclops, Penelope, Poseidon, and many other mythic characters.

The film's soundtrack inspired a mini-revival of bluegrass and other rural song styles, unconsciously reflecting the links between the music of the British Isles and its antecedents in the Mediterranean, both structurally and thematically. The Ku Klux Klan also plays a prominent role in the film, the Klan's white robes and hoods being a corruption of earlier druidic ceremonial garb.

By recombining Greek mythology with Celtic-derived music, *O Brother* may have tapped into a deep, unconscious stream in the cultural DNA. In his 2005 book *The Baltic Origins of Homer's Epic Tales*, Italian historian Felice Vinci argues that Homer was in fact Dutch (many historians believe the Celts first emerged as a distinct tribe in the region of Holland) and that *The Odyssey* describes landmarks in the Baltic Sea and Scandinavia, not in the Mediterranean. Vinci argues that climate change had forced certain northern tribes southward and they brought their mythologies and heroes with them to balmy climes such as Greece.

THE MYSTERIES OF THE YORUBA

Like these druidic echoes from the Celtic rim, the culture that came over with the slave trade from Africa also reconnects us to the ancient Mysteries. Probably the most direct parallels to the Mysteries, both in practice and cosmology, are the various syncretic traditions of *Vodoun* and *Santeria*, which combine Catholicism and African tribal religion. This is anything but coincidental. Western African traditions would play host to the rituals, music, and deities of the ancient Mediterranean and carry them over the Atlantic Ocean to the New World.

These synthesized traditions use a dizzying host of sacraments, ritual drumming, and blood sacrifices—just like the Mysteries. A henotheistic approach is taken to interacting with the gods; adherents will often choose one entity to channel and devote their lives to—just like the Mysteries. Women play a central and powerful role in the rites and the hierarchies of the cults themselves—just like the Mysteries. And just as the Church took pagan gods and remade them as saints, the slaves who were brought over to Louisiana, Florida, and the Caribbean took the identities of the saints to mask the polytheistic deities they refused to surrender—deities drawn from the Yoruba tradition of West Africa.

Vodoun ("spirit") is the predominant Yoruba practice in the Francophone territories. The supreme being of Vodoun is *Bondye* ("bon dieu"), a distant and unattainable god (shades of Atum); the *Loa*, lesser deities or aspects of the Creator, commune with human beings in his place. In Haitian voodoo, ceremonies are presided over by the *houngan* (priest), *mambo* (priestess) and the *bokor* (sorcerers). Prominent in the community are the "horses," often women, that the Loa "ride" or channel themselves through.

Voodoo (as Vodoun is commonly known in America) was also widely practiced in the Louisiana territories, itself one of the birthplaces of early rock 'n' roll. Voodoo is legendary in pop culture folklore for its curses and charms, as well as the "voodoo doll," and, last but not least, zombies. Harvard University ethnobotanist Wade Davis studied Haitian Vodoun and came to the conclusion that a complex recipe of toxins were used to *induce* zombieism (essentially a drug-induced brain damage and catatonia).

Like Vodoun, Santeria's roots are in the African Yoruba religion, blended with Catholic and indigenous elements. The term *Santería* itself is pejorative, used by Spanish overlords to mock the slaves' suspicious devotion to the saints. Its ceremonies include the burning of incense, blood sacrifice of livestock such as goats or chickens, and presentation of icons and fetishes. Again, just like the Mysteries.

The reason for the similarities between the Yoruba traditions and the ancient Mysteries is simple; many historians believe that the West African traditions were themselves imported from ancient Egypt. In his book *The Religion of the Yorubas,* J. Olumide Lucas states unequivocally that "the Yoruba, during antiquity, lived in ancient Egypt before migrating to the Atlantic coast," and that "most of the principal (Egyptian) gods were well known" to them. Nigerian historian A.B. Aderibigbe wrote in 1976, "The similarities between Yoruba and ancient Egyptian culture—religious observation, works of art, burial and other customs—speak of a possible migration of the ancestors of the Yoruba from the upper Nile (as early as 2000 BCE–1000 BCE) as a result of some upheavals in ancient Egypt."

Aderibigbe may be referring here to the rise of the Hyksos

people, who some historians believe migrated into northern Africa from Syria around that time. It was the Hyksos who brought the stringed instrument known as the lute into Egypt, where it traveled to other parts of Africa and finally to the Americas. In this light, the electric guitar is part of a cultural continuum which traces its origins from the Yoruba back to ancient Egypt and finally to ancient Mesopotamia.

If these theories are correct, we have still another line of transmission in the eventual secular reincarnation of the Mysteries: from Egypt to West Africa to the New World. The pounding music and sweat-soaked dancing of the Yoruba traditions played a critical role in the development of popular music in the Americas, particularly in the 20th century. Voodoo itself would be lurking in the shadows of early rock 'n' roll, particularly in the music of the influential artists of New Orleans. And its queens and witch doctors would be grist for the lyrical mill, even for bands well outside the city itself. Carnival and Mardi Gras would popularize—and institutionalize—a modern form of Bacchanalia that continues to grow in popularity, influence, and scope. And it all ultimately springs from the same source—the ancient Mysteries.

But hold on, we've got other seasonings to add to this cultural casserole.

EAST MEETS WEST

European colonialism was at its height in the mid-19th century, and riding along with the spices and linens from the Asia and Egypt were some exotic and ancient spiritual notions. Sites all across the Mediterranean had been excavated, leading to earthshaking discoveries like the city of Troy, long believed to be mythical. The excavation of Pompeii shocked Europe with its explicitly erotic frescoes and sculptures. The ashes of Mt. Vesuvius had also preserved Pompeii's "Villa of the Mysteries," whose remarkable frescoes depicted the stages of initiation in the Roman Bacchanalia.

Into all this excitement stepped one Helena Von Hahn (1831–1891), better known as "Madame Blavatsky," a Russian émigré who claimed to have met with a group of immortal spiritual guides she called the "secret chiefs" in their Tibetan stronghold. While working the Spiritualist circuit Blavatsky met a wealthy lawyer named Henry Steel Olcott, and in 1875 together they formed the Theosophical Society, which blended Eastern and Western religious and philosophical ideas into a new synthesis. In 1888, Blavatsky published a two-volume work titled *Isis Unveiled*, in which she laid out the doctrines and philosophy of her new movement.

Theosophy—widely acknowledged as the forerunner of the New Age movement—opened the doors of the West to Eastern religious ideas. The movement splintered in the 20th century and never again reached the heights it achieved under Blavatsky, but the mainstreaming of previously unknown Asian practices like feng shui, yoga, meditation, and herbal medicine can be traced directly back to the Theosophists. Their influence would last well into the 20th century, especially in the Sixties, when imported Asian gods and gurus would be all the rage.

But an important part of this success came from the music; the droning, hypnotic sounds of Indian instruments such as sitars and tablas were just the thing for pot smoking and acid trips. This connection would go mainstream when sitar super-star Ravi Shankar appeared at the Monterey Pop Festival, the coming-of-age party for the psychedelic generation. Bands such as the Beatles, the Beach Boys, and the Moody Blues would offer up a neo-Theosophist synthesis of rock and raga in the late Sixties.

THE MODERN MAGI

Even as strange gods arrived from the colonies, the old gods of Europe shook off centuries of dirt and rust and toured the great museums and galleries of their former empire. At the same time, artists and architects unleashed the Neoclassical Movement in the late 18th century, where the gods of the ancient world were *literally* cast in stone in the major cities of the West. The old gods were more ubiquitous than at any time since the Renaissance.

In Germany, Richard Wagner was introducing the Norse sagas to a new audience in his *Ring of the Nibelung* operas, to which numerous metal bands like Judas Priest and Iron Maiden certainly owe a spiritual debt. Wagner inspired the philosopher Friedrich Nietzsche to write a series of texts which themselves would inform heavy metal, with their machismo and emphasis on "the death of God" and "the will to power."

Nietzsche's work—and the sociomythic explosion of the time—would inspire two very different men to reinterpret the ancient Mysteries in ways more suited to the modern world. Artists across the spectrum would be inspired by their writings and introduce their ideas to the culture at large, a process that continues to this very day. Strangely enough, both men were born in 1875, the same year the Theosophical Society was established.

CARL JUNG

In 1987, author-professor Joseph Campbell sat down with PBS host Bill Moyers for a series of interviews aired in the miniseries *The Power of Myth* and later published in a best-selling book. For many, it would be their first exposure to the academic study of mythology. Though most people credit Campbell with reviving interest in ancient myths, he was building on ground broken by the Swiss psychiatrist-philosopher Carl Jung (1875–1961), who took a special interest in the Mysteries. Jung began his career as a clinical psychiatrist in a Swiss hospital, but would later undertake a long and strange spiritual journey that would transform both himself and Western culture.

Jung arrived at exactly the right time in history. *Fin-de-siècle* Europe was a hotbed not only of psychiatry, but also of alternative religions, drugs, and lifestyle experimentation. The German territories were in the midst of a revival of ancient paganism, driven by artists and bohemians. Jung always had a soft spot for the paranormal, and was fascinated by the spread of Spiritualism and its offshoots.

He was also a brilliant clinician, and caught the attention of Sigmund Freud, the most esteemed psychiatrist in Europe. Bonding almost instantly, Freud and Jung developed an intense, emotionally charged relationship. But Jung soon began to drift back toward mysticism and the occult, causing a rift between the two pioneers.

As his conflicts with Freud intensified, Jung experienced what many observers described as a psychotic break in 1916. Jung would emerge from his "night sea journey" a changed man, and would begin laying the groundwork for a new, transpersonal psychology.

Jung became a celebrity intellectual and built a psychiatric movement to rival Freud's. He introduced several concepts that have made it into the popular lexicon, such as the psychological complex, introversion and extroversion, and the classification of four personality traits used in the well-known Myers-Briggs personality inventory. Jung also played a role in the development of Alcoholics Anonymous, for which countless rock 'n' rollers are in his debt.

Jung proposed the existence of a "collective unconscious," a kind of universal psychic database. Needless to say, this idea was not well received by mainstream psychiatry. Working from that theory, Jung developed new concepts such as the *anima* and *animus* (the female aspect of the male psyche, and vice versa), synchronicity (meaningful coincidences), and individuation.

Most important for our purposes here, Jung argued that mythology was so powerful—and remains so—because it symbolically replays the struggles of human life, and that in the most durable myths, the gods suffer like us. Jung also reimagined the ancient gods as *archetypes*, arguing that gods like Mercury, Apollo, and Demeter were memetic constellations of a sort, and each represented certain aspects of the human psyche. Jungian psychologists have since used the archetypes to classify aspects of culture and human experience, a practice that has spread out into the culture at large. It is through a Jungian lens that we will classify and understand the archetypal categories into which the various offshoots of rock 'n' roll fall.

Jung's work had a powerful influence on the counterculture in the Sixties and beyond. The Beatles, Peter Gabriel, King Crimson, and Tool have all paid tribute to the man and his work, and the Police's seminal album *Synchronicity* (1983) was built explicitly on his concepts. More important, the accidental revival of the ancient Mysteries in the late Sixties would confirm Jung's groundbreaking theories on the power of the collective unconscious.

ALEISTER CROWLEY

Though he died broke and alone, legendary British occultist Aleister Crowley left an enormous imprint on pop culture, particularly rock 'n' roll. Born Edward Alexander Crowley in 1875 in Warwickshire, England, young Aleister joined a family who were members of the extremist Christian sect known as the Plymouth Brethren, but they made their fortune with a lucrative brewery, allowing Crowley's father to retire early.

Fascinated from an early age with the Book of Revelation, Crowley earned his favorite nickname in childhood: "Great Beast 666." But the deaths of his father and a baby sister rocked Crowley's faith, and gave him a taste for the occultism that was sweeping the British demimonde. So after dropping out of college, Crowley used his inheritance to indulge his tastes for prostitutes, drugs, and sorcery.

Crowley eventually fell in with the Hermetic Order of the Golden Dawn, a legendary occult circle that was on the verge of imploding. He didn't last long, due to conflicts with luminary A.E. Waite, the creator of the best-known Tarot deck in use today. Waite's success inspired Crowley to create his own deck, which he named *The Book of Thoth*. From London Crowley traveled to Asia, where he gained a reputation as a mountaineer, leading expeditions to K2 and other challenging peaks. In 1903, Crowley married a young widow named Rose Kelly, who would soon change the course of his life and work.

During a visit to Cairo in 1904, Rose fell into an oracular

trance in which she claimed to channel Horus. This eventually resulted in *The Book of the Law*, which announces the dawn of a violent and ruthless new era Crowley named the "Aeon of Horus." Sounding a bit more like Dionysus than Horus, *The Book of the Law's* Horus commands initiates to "stir the hearts of men with drunkenness. To worship me, take wine and strange drugs." Prophetic, old Aleister was.

Reflecting Crowley's own Nietzschean leanings, *The Book of the Law* proclaimed the tenet of *Thelema*, or "true will" in Greek. Thelema became the centerpiece of Crowley's work, through which he laid down an eleventh commandment: "Do what thou wilt shall be the whole of the Law." Soaking up mojo from the ancient Mysteries, Crowley whipped up what he called "the Rites of Eleusis" for his new secret society, the Astrum Argentum ("Silver Star"). Around the same time, Crowley was approached by a German "sex-magick" order called the Ordo Templi Orientalis (OTO), which Crowley soon took over.

Supporting himself writing pornographic poetry and occult novels, Crowley traveled the world setting up OTO lodges. He established a Thelemic commune in Sicily, which scandalized Italy for three years until the group was deported by Mussolini. He became a tabloid whipping boy during a 1934 libel trial in which the judge declared that it was impossible to libel Crowley, since his reputation could not possibly be worse than it already was. Crowley allegedly did some spying during the wars, though it was never certain which side he was actually spying for.

His fortune long since frittered away, the Great Beast fell on hard times, nursing a monstrous heroin addiction and living in a boarding house. One of his few sources of income was the tithes paid to him by a scattered handful of OTO lodges, most notably the Agape Lodge in Pasadena, California. Agape counted Scientology founder L. Ron Hubbard, actress Jane Wolfe, and the legendary rocket scientist Jack Parsons as initiates. It was through Agape that a young filmmaker named Kenneth Anger entered the netherworld of occult secret societies, on his way to creating the basic template for modern music videos.

Following his death, Crowley joined Jung and many other luminaries on the album cover of the Beatles' *Sgt. Pepper.* Led Zeppelin's Jimmy Page is a devotee of Crowley and has compiled rare editions of his work into a massive library. Ozzy Osbourne recorded a tribute, but Iron Maiden singer Bruce Dickinson went one better and produced a feature film in which Crowley is reincarnated. Killing Joke printed Crowley's poetry on its album sleeves. Artists as diverse as industrial thrashers Ministry, avant-jazz artist John Zorn, techno mutants Psychic TV, and art-metal icons Tool are devotees. But one Crowleyite in particular would have an incalculable influence on modern American music.

In the early Fifties, musical archivist Harry Smith compiled the landmark *Anthology of American Folk Music,* whose influence cannot be overstated. The collection introduced an entire generation of musicians to the forgotten roots of American music, particularly the earthy blues and folk that inspired earnest young bohemians throughout the Sixties.

Himself a born bohemian, Smith was raised by Theosophists and was later initiated by a Native American shaman. Fascinated by Crowley, Smith joined the OTO and was ordained as bishop in its "Gnostic Catholic Church." No less an expert than Kenneth Anger later called Smith the greatest occult magician of his time. These two American Crowley-ites would have an unimaginable effect on the development of classic rock and music video, though neither would get rich for their troubles.

Like many occultists of his time, Crowley spent his life rebelling against a repressive religious upbringing. But in many important ways, the Great Beast never truly left the Plymouth Brethren. He simply chose to play the part of the villain in the great fundamentalist mystery play, a role that many former Christians-turned-Satanists continue to play today. In that, Crowley would have an enormous influence on the heavy metal movement some 30 years or so after his death.

Before all that devilry could come to pass, however, the Good Lord's faithful would first set the stage, reintroducing the Western world to the pounding, driving rhythms that their European ancestors left behind centuries before.

GOSPEL MUSIC AND THE HOLINESS MOVEMENT

Although many historians cite blues music and jazz as primary in the development of rock 'n' roll, it is this writer's opinion that by far the greatest—and most direct—influence on what we know as rock is gospel music. Gospel, which began to emerge as a distinct musical form toward the end of the 19th century, traces its roots to traditional African song styles, as well as Diaspora adaptations such as field hollers and voodoo drumming.

The collision of sacred and secular music is an intrinsic part of the American experience. Many of the hymns that early Americans sang were taken from folk melodies (the tune for "Amazing Grace" comes from a Scottish pipe melody), or in some cases, hijacked from English drinking songs. All this would arise in spiritual conditions unique to the New World.

The difficulty in ministering to scattered settlements on the American frontier gave rise to a group of itinerant preachers known as "circuit riders," who traveled the American frontier on horseback and led revival meetings in the rural boondocks of the colonies. The circuit riders' ministry gave rise to an informal, personal religion that would later inspire a series of religious revivals now known as "Great Awakenings."

The Third Great Awakening (roughly 1850–1900) produced what became known as the "holiness movement," which emphasized the "gifts of the Spirit" such as faith healing, speaking in tongues, and miracles, as well as being "slain in the Spirit," a term for the powerful physical reactions such as fainting or convulsion that were common in holiness meetings. At the dawn of the 20th century, this movement would coalesce into a new variety of Christianity: Pentecostalism.

The first great Pentecostal leader was an African American preacher named William J. Seymour, who kicked off the first great Pentecostal explosion in Los Angeles in 1906. Seymour began meetings in an African Methodist Episcopal Church, which was housed in a converted livery. The "Azusa Street Revival," as it came to be known, offered ecstasy and transformation, with its racially mixed congregants often staying up all night being spiritually slain. Crowds ranged from a handful up to 1,500 people over the next 10 years, variously speaking in tongues, crying on their knees, passing out on the floor, or simply singing along to the raw, vigorous music.

A front-page story in the *Los Angeles Times* from the period (titled "Weird Babble of Tongues") reported that congregants were "breathing strange utterances and mouthing a creed which it would seem no sane mortal could understand," adding that "the devotees of the weird doctrine practice the most fanatical rites, preach the wildest theories and work themselves into a state of mad excitement in their peculiar zeal." Which, of course, sounds *exactly* like the ancient Mystery rites.

Another newspaper account observed that the congregants "cry and make howling noises all day and into the night. They run, jump, shake all over, shout to the top of their voice, spin around in circles, fall out on the sawdust-blanketed floor jerking, kicking and rolling all over it." Echoing Livy's opinions of the Bacchanalia, the reporter concludes that "these people appear to be mad, mentally deranged or under a spell."

From these descriptions it's clear that the Azusa Revival was itself a drugless Bacchanalia, providing the same kind of badly needed emotional release for its poor and marginalized audience. But the driving music and emotional intensity of Pentecostalism would soon spread into other denominations and independent churches all across the American South. Most of the great early rock 'n' rollers—both black and white—cut their teeth in these churches, and the frantic beats, passionate howling, and call-and-response choruses of American gospel music would form the building blocks of "race music" and rhythm and blues. When seasoned with the surly guitars of the electric bluesmen, the mix would give birth to rock 'n' roll itself.

It's no accident that many early rock 'n' rollers such as Elvis, Little Richard, and Jerry Lee Lewis (not to mention the legions of R & B and soul artists) would record some of their most passionate performances in the gospel genre. It was in the holiness churches that they were first consumed by spiritual fire.

A (VERY) SHORT HISTORY OF 20TH-CENTURY BACCHANALIA

The Jazz Age brought the Bacchanalia back to America in a big way. Not that America had been lacking for hoedowns and juke joints, or for moonshine and reefer and all varieties of fornication—it's just that those were largely *local* phenomena, and the Jazz Age made it all big business.

America was on the winning side of the Great War and helped itself to the spoils. This brought on the Roaring Twenties, an era of prosperity, urbanization, mass entertainment, and easy credit. Women had earned the right to vote, and GIs returning home brought the loose Continental attitudes toward pleasure with them, inspiring the hit song "How You Gonna Keep 'Em Down on the Farm After They've Seen Paree."

The guardians of morality tried to put a lid on all the carousing with the prohibition of alcohol, but all that did was empower organized crime and inspire contempt for moral guardians. Cocaine was popular as well, as it helped keep the boozers boozing and dancers dancing. Wireless radio brought the latest sounds into American living rooms and the newfangled automobiles provided a venue for sexual trysts. Radio played a sweetened kind of pop-jazz, but the kids who went to Harlem and other hot spots heard music as loud and relentless as rock 'n' roll. The Twenties also saw the rise of the big bands, which would rule unchallenged until the rise of rock.

A harder, faster take on jazz called "swing" began to take hold during the Depression. Frantic "jungle drums" were a big part of the swing sound, making stars of hyperactive pounders like Gene Krupa and Buddy Rich and band leaders like Benny Goodman and Duke Ellington. Of course, there was resistance to the earthier new sounds. From the start, religious groups saw jazz as a threat, part of an overall Bolshevik conspiracy to corrupt American youth. Their counterparts in Germany and Italy would systematically eliminate this corrosive influence of jazz when Hitler and Mussolini rose to power.

During the war, yet another new form of dance music, one that favored smaller combos and a rougher, simpler sound, began to take hold. "Rhythm and blues" or R & B was heavily influenced by the driving sounds of gospel churches, so much so that sometimes only the lyrics set them apart. Many of the original rock 'n' roll stars—Chuck Berry, Little Richard, Fats Domino, Bo Diddley, and all the rest—thought they were playing R & B, but at some point the name changed and rockabilly acts like Jerry Lee Lewis, Carl Perkins, and Bill Haley and the rest started poaching on their turf. R & B would become slicker and more urban, morphing into soul music in the early Sixties, when it would become an important part of the civil rights struggle.

But throughout the 20th century, things stayed much the same; fast, loud music of largely African American origin was the preferred soundtrack for pleasure and leisure. But the potent cultural mix that gave rise to the Classic Era of Rock wasn't just about music—it was about an exploration of the deepest recesses of the human psyche. There was still a ways to go before old-time rock 'n' roll would become classic rock. Our next detour might seem a little strange, but it takes us to an important source of inspiration for the larger-than-life, heroic mystique of the great rock 'n' rollers of the Sixties.

TECHNICOLOR GODS

At the same time kids were filling their ears with pre–British Invasion pop, the old gods were making a major comeback in the culture—this time as movie stars. A series of Italian-produced films based in pagan and Biblical mythology flooded the market in the late Fifties and early Sixties, giving teenagers a Technicolor immersion in classical mythology no textbook could hope to equal.

American bodybuilder Steve Reeves helped start the "sword and sandal" craze, playing Hercules in two productions in 1957 and 1959. Both films were major hits, inspiring a deluge of imitators who plundered Greco-Roman, Egyptian, and Biblical mythologies without worrying too much about accuracy or coherence. (Hercules fought space aliens at one point.) So immensely popular were these films that the Three Stooges (enjoying a big comeback thanks to TV) tangled with the hero in 1962's *The Three Stooges Meet Hercules,* earning the aging comedians their biggest box-office hit.

Hollywood studios took notice and weighed in with upmarket sword and sandal epics of their own. Charlton Heston played the title role in a 1959 remake of *Ben-Hur.* Stanley Kubrick directed Kirk Douglas in *Spartacus,* based on the real-life gladiator turned rebel leader. Hollywood "It couple" Elizabeth Taylor and Richard Burton starred in a four-hour version of *Cleopatra.* Probably the most popular of these films with the younger audience was *Jason and the Argonauts* (1963), which had the Argonauts doing battle with giant statues and reanimated skeletons, as well as enjoying personal contact with the gods themselves.

These mythic themes would repeatedly surface in the classic rock era, directly or otherwise. One of Donovan's biggest hits was a paean to Atlantis, and Cream sang "Tales of Brave Ulysses." Pink Floyd recorded a performance film at Pompeii, the Grateful Dead played a series of concerts at the Great Pyramids, and King Crimson warbled "In the Wake of Poseidon." Boston's biggest psychedelic band was named Orpheus. Unlikely stars like Elton John, Billy Squier, and Boz Scaggs all sang odes to Hercules, and the Cocteau Twins sang hymns to Pandora, Persephone, and the Sirens. The list goes on.

Along with a superhero revival around the same time, the sword and sandal films whetted a new generation's appetite for heroes and gods. Mere musicians would no longer suffice—rock 'n' roll would need to be bigger than life. The excitement and grandeur of these stories would find a musical counterpart in the massive arena and stadium rock shows of the late Sixties and Seventies. Note that both the "arena" and the "stadium" were Roman terms for venues in which very similar spectacles were staged.

With loud dance music and the archetypes of the gods wreaking havoc in young minds all across the Western world, there was just one more piece of the puzzle to put into place.

PSYCHEDELIA

Alcohol, caffeine, cocaine, opium, and marijuana have been a central part of human culture since the dawn of time, and they have always been popular with musicians and their audiences. Hallucinogens like psychedelic mushrooms and peyote were widespread in indigenous American religions long before Europeans arrived. But those were firecrackers—the world was about to meet the psychedelic atom bomb.

The modern psychedelic age began with a peculiar bicycle

ride Albert Hofmann took one spring afternoon in 1943. After accidentally ingesting an experimental migraine cure called *lysergic acid diethylamide*, this mild-mannered Swiss scientist had history's first recorded LSD trip. "I perceived an uninterrupted stream of fantastic pictures, extraordinary shapes with intense, kaleidoscopic play of colors," Hofmann recalled.

LSD would remain in the psychiatric field as a therapeutic tool, but it was also used for more nefarious purposes, as when the CIA began its notorious MK-Ultra mind control experiments, often dosing unsuspecting subjects in an attempt to create remote-controlled spies and assassins. With the rise of the Beat movement, psychedelics like peyote and psilocybin mushrooms came into vogue, and seekers made pilgrimages to the shamans of Mexico and the Southwest. Novelist Aldous Huxley recorded his own peyote trip in the 1954 classic *The Doors of Perception,* from whose title the Doors took their name. A 1957 article by Gordon Wasson in *Life* explored the mushroom cults in Mexico. A rogue CIA man named Andrija Puharich would even entice *One Step Beyond* host John Newland to televise his own mushroom trip in 1961.

All of this inspired a young professor named Timothy Leary to begin his own experiments with students in the Harvard Psilocybin Project. Later, a shady Briton named Michael Hollingshead introduced Leary and his group to LSD, and all bets were off. Leary became the self-appointed evangelist for the drug, preaching his mantra "Turn on, Tune in, Drop out."

Novelist Ken Kesey's experiences as an MK-Ultra guinea pig inspired his classic 1962 novel *One Flew Over the Cuckoo's Nest.* Flush with royalties from the best seller, Kesey roamed America's highways spreading the LSD gospel with his "acid tests." This was just one case of MK-Ultra blowback; another guinea pig was Ted Kaczynski, the anarchist mathematician turned "Unabomber."

With abuse of the potent drug rampant, acid was finally outlawed in 1966. Undaunted, Kesey settled in San Francisco, which had become a virtual psychedelic city-state. Acid fever peaked with the Summer of Love in 1967. But the resulting media hype blew up in the faces of the original hippies, who tended to be highly educated and relatively mild-mannered types. Pilgrims began to arrive by the busload, screwed-up kids who had only the faintest idea what the counterculture was about. And things started to get a little heavy.

In the wake of the army of runaways and transients came a horde of pimps, pushers, and sickos. By the following summer the streets of San Francisco were flooded with hard drugs like heroin and speed, as well as a nasty LSD variant called STP and a dangerous animal tranquilizer nicknamed "angel dust." With drug culture spreading, the city became the unholy land to the Silent Majority. Footage of long-haired freaks dancing naked in the streets defied the repression of human pleasure that had defined American conservatism since Plymouth. It's no accident that Clint Eastwood's reactionary hero "Dirty Harry" Callahan plied his trade by the Golden Gate.

But the Aquarian Age did away with the discipline and focus—as well as the delayed gratification—of the ancient Mysteries. Drugs that were sacraments in the strict sense of the word were reduced to toys for thrill-seeking baby boomers, much to the horror of psychedelic pioneers like Alan Watts, Robert Anton Wilson, and others deeply involved in the serious study of these compounds. The results were disastrous—whereas the Mysteries survived for thousands of years, the Aquarian counterculture barely managed to last for five

The outcome was as inevitable as it was predictable. Sex 'n' drugs 'n' rock 'n' roll are all wonderful forms of entertainment, but they weren't enough to build a culture—never mind a society—upon. With vibes and drugs growing bad, many hippies took off for the hinterlands to build communes and alternative communities, hoping to weather the backlash that Nixon whipped up during the 1968 campaign. But new countercultures would arise, and timeless archetypes would continue to run rampant throughout the culture, radically recreating what had begun as simple dance music.

PART II:
THE MODERN MYSTERIES OF ROCK 'N' ROLL

Throughout the Classical Age of Rock, certain genres and subgenres would evolve into virtual cults, many of which bear a startling resemblance to the cults of the ancient gods. But this wasn't "religion" as the word is commonly understood; this was a return to the raw, experiential roots of human culture. But ironically, many of the cults would come to develop their own doctrine and dogma, even their own languages and dress codes. Many of these continue to survive to this day—punk, skinhead, metalhead, hippie—long after their original inspiration has been forgotten. Their longevity is a testament to the power of archetypes to manifest themselves in ways that are easily grasped by successive generations.

In Part II, we'll look at these new cults and new rock gods, how they are defined and how they came to be. This is not intended to be a complete historical account, but a selective survey of some of the most definitive artists that fit the ancient archetypes. I've named these categories after the major gods of the ancient world—particularly those of the Mystery traditions, of course. Due to space limitations, we will look only at artists working within the commonly accepted definition of rock. As tempting as it is to explore related genres such as funk, reggae, country, and pop, the archetypes are often different, as are the history and the reasons behind them.

Another important aspect of these artists is the role spirituality plays in the lives and work of many of them. Music is itself inherently spiritual in the best way—an expression of unseen forces that the artist receives and transmits, as the mediums and channels of Spiritualism were supposed to. Now that rock 'n' roll has its own Valhalla (the Rock and Roll Hall of Fame in Cleveland, Ohio), the stories of these artists can often pass into the mythic realm and become archetypes unto themselves. But there is another narrative at work: the startling evolution of rock music itself and how it has acted as an outlet for deep memetic currents that were once thought to have been consigned to history. So just as we saw how rock 'n' roll the ancient Mysteries were, now we will examine how like the Mysteries our modern rock 'n' roll is.

VOX POPULI:
THE NEW APOLLOS

Apollo was the original rock god, and the artists of the Apollo archetype serve up heroic, populist music for the masses. These are the superheroes of rock 'n' roll, the gods of the arenas and stadiums. The sunny aspects of Apollo are reflected in the predominant use of major keys and up-tempo rhythms. The Apollonian archetype often trades in political and religious moralism, serving up its sing-along anthems with a social conscience.

One of the defining characteristics of an Apollonian band or artist is the successful transformation of Dionysian song styles into mainstream pop. For instance, the Beatles were influenced by pop stylists like Chuck Berry and the Everly

Brothers, but they also followed the music back to rootsier blues artists. The Fab Four made their bones in the beer halls of Hamburg, where any self-respecting Maenad would have felt at home.

ELVIS PRESLEY

The original Apollo of 20th-century rock was also its first superstar, a man whose ferocious charisma would eclipse the superheroes and method actors he modeled himself after. Elvis is more a figure of rock's Golden Age than its Classic Era, but he has come to embody an archetype all his own, one that is instantly recognized by people all around the world. It's hard to imagine rock 'n' roll becoming the phenomenon it became without him.

Elvis's story is well known: Sun Records honcho Sam Phillips wishes he could find a white man who can sing like a black man, and one appears in the form of a young truck driver from Memphis, Tennessee. Not only can Elvis Aron Presley bring the blues, he has matinee-idol good looks to boot. A ruthless Dutch cutthroat named Colonel Tom Parker signs on as his manager, and Elvis sets the youth of America ablaze with a string of hits that effortlessly fuse rhythm and blues and up-tempo country swing under the new name "rock 'n' roll," an old slang term for coitus or the sound of a railroad train, take your pick.

The Establishment frets that Elvis is too potent a sexual force for Fifties America, and the singer is drafted into the army. The rock 'n' roll movement cools down considerably. Elvis comes home after a stint in Germany, but some of the old fire is gone. Worse still, Parker commits Elvis to a string of corny B movies, featuring schmaltzy, watered-down performances by the singer. Elvis stews as the British Invasion takes over the rock world in the mid-Sixties, even though the Brits all worship the man. Finally returning to his raw rock roots, Elvis stages a comeback with his famed 1968 TV special. He enjoys a string of hit singles well into the Seventies and wins three Grammys—all for his impassioned gospel recordings. But a prescription drug habit and obesity bring the old Apollo to his knees, and he plays out his string, sweating and stumbling in Las Vegas. Worse still, he dies on the toilet in 1977 at the height of punk and disco, movements which see him as an object of ridicule.

None of that matters. The savage young Elvis lives on forever, as does the survivor Elvis, dressed up in the rhinestone 'n' leather finery modeled on Captain Marvel Jr., his childhood hero. Elvis lives forever alongside other icons of the Fifties such as James Dean and Marilyn Monroe—even his bloated Vegas years can fascinate. *That* is charisma—the gift of the gods.

THE BEACH BOYS

By the early Sixties, rock 'n' roll was seen as just another youth fad, replaced by prefab teen idols like Fabian and Frankie Avalon and slick vocal groups like the Four Seasons. Urban dance music from Detroit was making waves on the Motown label, run by a former autoworker named Berry Gordy. The folk revival was all the rage on campus.

Young Jewish songwriters were working up hits for African American vocal groups in New York's Brill Building. Out of that nexus came Phil Spector, a brilliant but troubled young producer who gave his urban girl groups like the Crystals and the Ronettes a lush, thrilling orchestral sound. Spector's "Wall of Sound" was perfectly suited to the runaway optimism of the Kennedy Administration, which the media had dubbed the "American Camelot."

Rock 'n' roll was down, but not out. The cavalry came storming out of the beaches of southern California, ready to reintroduce guitar rock to the masses. The surf culture the Beach Boys drew upon was Apollonian to its core—sun-drenched, athletic, heroic. But at night those same golden gods morphed into true Dionysians with their beer, babes, and bonfire beach parties. This archetypal tension would inform the best music in the Beach Boys' canon.

The band cashed in on the surfing craze of the early Sixties, serving up basic rock 'n' roll strongly influenced by Chuck Berry and doo-wop. With their clean-cut looks and collegiate harmonies, the Beach Boys mirrored the optimism and confidence of Los Angeles in the early Sixties. But as with the rest of the Camelot myth, that facade hid a more problematic reality.

The band was made up of the Wilson brothers—Brian, Dennis, and Carl—with their cousin Mike Love on lead vocals, and managed by the Wilson boys' father, Murry, himself a failed songwriter and a rock 'n' roll Little League dad, who relentlessly bullied his charges. But it was this role as task-master that got the band in shape to compete at a time when guitar-driven rock 'n' roll was out of fashion. The Beach Boys eventually became successful enough to cut Murry loose, but Brian's obsessive perfectionism and drug use began to tear at his sanity. The Boys toured without Brian, leaving him to construct ever more complex productions in the studio, such at the ornate 1966 psych-rock classic "Good Vibrations" and that year's *Pet Sounds* LP.

Brian wasn't the only one with problems, though. Dennis suffered from serious drug and sex addictions. In 1968, his compulsions led him to pick up two hippie scruffbags for some afternoon delight back at his Sunset Boulevard love nest. Sometime later, Dennis returned home to find his house filled with a ragtag band of freaks led by one Charles Milles Manson. Charlie welcomed Dennis as if he owned the place, eventually bringing the Beach Boy under his spell. Dennis booked Manson some studio time and tried talking the band into recording some of his tunes, but Manson's career stalled and he blamed Beach Boys producer Terry Melcher for his woes. Dennis cut Charlie off, which earned him a death threat. In the summer of '69, Charlie would send his minions to a home on LA's Cielo Drive and instruct them to kill everyone inside and paint cryptic slogans on the wall in their blood. The house belonged to Terry Melcher.

The Beach Boys' sunny image began to lose its appeal in the grim late Sixties, and Brian was sidelined in the studio as his cocaine use grew out of control. He would become a virtual recluse and later be diagnosed as schizophrenic. After battling various addictions, Dennis drowned in 1983 when he fell from his boat after a heavy day of drinking. The brand name continued on with a touring band, but no Wilsons remained after Carl's death in 1998. Like most of these Apollonian artists, the Beach Boys were closely identified with spiritual practice, Transcendental Meditation in their case, which the Beach Boys were instrumental in popularizing. Mike Love still remains involved in promoting TM.

BOB DYLAN

Out of the late-Fifties folk revival came another great Apollonian archetype, one whose poetic ambitions would rewrite the rock 'n' roll rule book in the Sixties. Born Robert Zimmerman in Hibbing, Minnesota, the young singer immersed himself in the popular and folk traditions of the Fifties, renaming himself in honor of the Welsh poet Dylan Thomas and relocating to Manhattan. Folk icon Woody Guthrie was Dylan's early touchstone, whom he followed until his electric period. From the mid-Sixties onward, Dylan became an archetype unto himself and "Dylanesque" became an instantly recognizable adjective for serious music fans.

Dylan's notorious electric set at the 1965 Newport Folk Festival divided his audience straight down the middle between the folk purists and the folk rock avant-garde. Older critics were scathing in their reviews (folk icon Pete Seeger was seen running from the stage with his hands over his ears), and many Dylanologists believe the angry rant "Positively 4th Street" was Dylan's response to the attacks. But like Apollo, Dylan clearly saw the future, one where folk would again recede and electric rock would rule. Beginning with 1965's *Bringing It All Back Home*, the "electric" Dylan consistently landed albums in the Top 10. His singles were less successful, but he scored major hits with ballads like "Lay Lady Lay" (1969) and "Knocking on Heaven's Door" (1973).

Dylan's next big reinvention would be less well received. Following a period of career crisis brought on by a critical backlash and commercial doldrums, Dylan claimed he received a vision of Jesus in a motel room, which inspired him to hitch his wagon to the rapidly growing Evangelical movement. Strange company for a rebel type like Dylan, but Christianity was a central facet of the Americana he lived and breathed. He was inspired enough to record a vigorous gospel-rock album, which he titled *Slow Train Coming* (1979).

The publicity from his conversion and support from flush Evangelicals was enough to make *Slow Train* a hit, but his next two gospel offerings flopped. Dylan didn't need a weatherman to see which way the wind was blowing, and he downplayed the born-again stuff on 1983's reggae-tinged *Infidels*, produced with Dire Straits honcho Mark Knopfler, himself nursing a Jesus jones at the time. By 1985's *Empire Burlesque*, it seemed Dylan had been virtually unborn-again. Since then, Dylan's commercial and critical fortunes have waxed and waned, but he has toured incessantly, sometimes bewildering audiences with indifferent or bizarre performances.

As befits a modern Apollo, Dylan was once seen as "the conscience of a generation." Since his conversion and de-conversion, it's difficult to say if anyone outside his aging cult sees much of him at all. But his stamp on the very way rock songs are written is indelible. Certainly, it's impossible to imagine the Sixties without him.

THE BEATLES

Elvis, Dylan, *and* the Beach Boys would all be overshadowed by four young lads from England, who cut their teeth on the American rock 'n' roll and rhythm and blues records being shipped into the port of Liverpool, from where they hailed. Originally a five-piece band decked out in denim and leather, the Beatles found little success in an England, where lush pop was all the rage on the charts. The band shipped over to Hamburg, where they honed their chops in the rough-and-tumble beer halls of that city's red light district. Coming back to Britain, they set up shop in Liverpool's Cavern Club, where their pretty faces and frantic mix of rock and blues excited the passions of the local fraüleins. The band coalesced around singer/guitarists John Lennon and George Harrison, singer/bassist Paul McCartney, and drummer Richard Starkey, aka Ringo Starr.

There the Beatles were discovered by local businessman Brian Epstein, who saw the ragtag rockers as the next big thing. The only problem was, nobody else agreed with him. Guitar groups were dead, he was told. Undaunted, Epstein caught the ear of EMI house producer George Martin, a secret genius bored with his workaday job. Martin took Epstein's pack of Scouse ruffians under his wing and produced demos for "Please Please Me" and "Love Me Do." Soon Martin and the Beatles were cranking out British hits and Epstein cast his eyes on the vast market across the pond.

John Lennon would later dismiss the Beatles' phenomenal success in America as an accident of history. JFK had promised a new Camelot to young Americans, but his assassination in late 1963 put the country into a state of shock. The Beatles were booked for three consecutive appearances on *The Ed Sullivan Show,* then watched by nearly everyone in the country. The Beatles not only brought a radical new look with their long hair and collarless suits, they were also witty, charming, articulate, and extremely hardworking, churning out an endless stream of singles, albums, and even feature films before they stopped to catch their breath in 1966.

Along the way they were introduced to hallucinogens by none other than Bob Dylan, who offered them their first joint. Synapses they never knew they had started firing, a process that only accelerated when they later discovered LSD. Out of this came the record that this writer argues marked the dawning of the Classic Era of Rock—1965's *Rubber Soul*. For it was at this point rock 'n' roll evolved from simple dance music to a form with the potential for creating challenging and mutable expressions of modern art.

Eschewing the usual pop idioms, the Beatles took on an array of new styles, notably Indian ragas on "Norwegian Wood" and Baroque flavoring on "In My Life," both written by Lennon. McCartney's preternatural melodic gifts bore full fruit with "Michelle" and "You Won't See Me." But *Rubber Soul* was just a prelude. Just eight months later, *Revolver* (1966) displayed a compositional virtuosity never before heard in rock, as well as an LSD-inspired surreality on freak-outs like "She Said, She Said" and the album's closer, "Tomorrow Never Knows." Martin was the hidden hand in all this—his genius for arrangement and studio trickery allowed every random whim the Beatles approached him with to be committed to tape.

As a spiritual force, the Beatles peaked in early 1967 with their double A-side single "Strawberry Fields Forever/Penny Lane," two mini-symphonies informed by the band's prodigious acid intake. That summer's *Sgt. Pepper's Lonely Hearts Club Band* was seen as a generational moment in which the Beatles personified the utopian aspirations of the Sixties generation. But as it did for so many, that summer ended badly for the Beatles when Brian Epstein died from an accidental overdose of sleeping pills.

Struggling to rebound, the Beatles tried to wrest more mileage out of psychedelia with the *Magical Mystery Tour* TV special and accompanying soundtrack. Seeking to recover through spiritual exploration, the Beatles then flew to India for a Transcendental Meditation retreat. The Maharishi had big plans for the Fab Four, but the trip ended badly when the holy man put the moves on Mia Farrow. Leaving the TM orbit, Harrison would later switch his allegiance to the Krishna Consciousness movement, as did Lennon for a short time.

Back in England, the band began to splinter. Their self-titled 1968 double LP (better known as *The White Album*) felt to many like a collection of solo tracks. Next, the Beatles attempted a back-to-basics film and recording project, which was scrapped when intraband tension killed the vibe. On the verge of splitting up, the band reconvened for one last triumph, 1969's *Abbey Road,* a 17-track opus that acted as a kind of career retrospective, touching on all the high stylistic points of their career—and featuring two appropriately Apollonian anthems in "Here Comes the Sun" and "Sun King."

In 1970, the band split up to pursue solo careers, but only McCartney seemed able to manage lasting success. Both Harrison and Lennon developed drug problems in the uncertain Seventies, and both retired from the limelight for long spells. Lennon and his wife, Yoko Ono, reemerged in 1980 with the hit-laden *Double Fantasy,* but the former Beatle was gunned down by a crazed fan that December. But the story of the Beatles didn't end—it will never end. Several reissue projects, documentaries, and biographies have reintroduced successive generations to rock's greatest myth. In 2009, the Beatles were reborn in the virtual world, becoming animated characters in their own video game titled *The Beatles: Rock Band.* Now they've finally made it big.

ELTON JOHN

Born Reginald Dwight in 1946, Elton John is not only a musical legend but one of the best-known gay celebrities in the world today. But in the early Seventies, Elton presented a dowdy image, going around unshaven and clad in badly tailored denim and flannel. While beefy ex-mods were dressing like Liza Minnelli and blasting out sexually ambiguous glam, Elton John was belting out bluesy anthems like "Burn Down the Mission" and love ballads like "Tiny Dancer," all with lyrics written by his (hetero) collaborator, Bernie Taupin.

From 1970 onward, the John-Taupin team was a prodigious hit machine, sending singles to the Top 40 in rapid-fire succession and topping the charts with FM staples like "Crocodile Rock," "Bennie and the Jets," and "Island Girl." Elton came late to the glam party, but he made up for lost time with flamboyant outfits and eyewear in 1973 for his smash single and double LP *Goodbye Yellow Brick Road,* whose title came from *The Wizard of Oz,* an iconic touchstone for countless gay men. By 1976, Elton was exhausted. The yearly album-tour grind was hard enough on artists, but the pressures of superstardom were unbearable. While touring for 1976's *Blue Moves,* Elton announced his retirement during a London concert. He also whipped up controversy when he outed himself as gay in *Rolling Stone.* His subsequent singles and albums sold poorly, which some blamed on his coming out.

But Elton returned to the Top 10 in 1980 with "Little Jeannie," sounding like he'd never been gone. And, in 1983, he stormed into the video age with hit videos/singles such as "I'm Still Standing," and "Sad Songs (Say So Much)." Elton was a natural for MTV and he soon became as ubiquitous in the Eighties as he was in the Seventies. Elton also initiated a new songwriting partnership with Tim Rice (*Jesus Christ Superstar, Evita*), which resulted in the soundtrack to Disney's 1994 smash hit film *The Lion King*. A Broadway production of the film is still playing as of this writing. Elton and Rice also produced *Aida* for Disney, another long-running hit, this time steeped in ancient Egyptian mysticism.

These days, Elton John has become one of those celebrities as well known for being a celebrity as for his astonishing catalog of hits. But he's helped make the gay community considerably less threatening to mainstream audiences, an Apollonian feat if ever there was one.

THE EAGLES

Drawing influence from the late-period, countrified material of LA folk rockers the Byrds, armies of West Coast post-hippie longhairs combined rock, folk, and country and birthed the "soft rock" movement of the Seventies. The first major soft rock group was Crosby, Stills and Nash, formed by former Byrd David Crosby along with Steven Stills and Graham Nash, of Buffalo Springfield and the Hollies, respectively. The trio would make a big splash at Woodstock and expand to a quartet with the addition of Stills's old bandmate Neil Young.

But by far the most popular and enduring product of the new mellow movement was the Eagles, whose members had played with various Byrds on various side projects. Spearheaded by drummer/vocalist Don Henley and guitarist Glenn Frey, the Eagles brought a romantic-yet-tough, adventurous-yet-conservative energy to Seventies soft rock. Their earthy pop became the soundtrack of choice for the Me Generation, and inspired a whole new generation of country acts to take on trappings of rock.

The Eagles peaked with *Hotel California*, released at end of 1976. James Gang leader Joe Walsh had joined on lead guitar, bringing a harder edge to the sound, resulting in epics like "Life in the Fast Lane" and "Victim of Love." The title track brought moody reggae into the mix, resulting in a monster hit that is still in heavy rotation on rock radio. Massive ego struggles spilt the Eagles after 1979's ironically titled *The Long Run* but the band reunited in 1994 for the *Hell Freezes Over* tour, and it has toured with some regularity ever since. Sensing the shift in their demographic base, the Eagles sold their 2007 studio album *Long Road Out of Eden* exclusively through Walmart stores for the first year of its American release.

SPIRIT IN THE SKY

Rock 'n' rollers who came out of—or converted to—the Christian tradition.

Jerry Lee Lewis—The Killer is the cousin of disgraced televangelist Jimmy Swaggart.
Pat Boone—A born-and-bred stalwart of the Christian right.
Cliff Richard—The so-called British Elvis, one of England's last remaining Christians.
Alice Cooper—A minister's son who found Jesus at the bottom of a Budweiser can.

Marvin Gaye—The son of a cross-dressing preacher who tragically ended his life.

Osmond Brothers—The bubblegum popsters are squeaky-clean scions of a large Mormon clan.

Michael Jackson—Raised a Jehovah's Witness but converted to Islam, possibly when an Arab sheik started paying his bills.

Bob Dylan—Famously found Jesus in the late Seventies, then lost him.

U2—Protestant Charismatics from Catholic Dublin.

Stryper—These blow-dried metal poseurs tossed Bibles to the headbangers during their live shows.

Prince—His lifelong struggle between faith and the flesh was won with an assist from the Jehovah's Witnesses.

Korn—Two members of this nihilistic nu metal band have turned to Jesus for succor.

Creed—Singer Scott Stapp often struck a Jesus Christ pose onstage—until the temptations of the flesh won out.

Lou Gramm—Leather-lunged rocker quit Foreigner to sing for Jesus.

The Killers—The new wave revivalists are Mormons in mascara.

The Jonas Brothers—Squeaky-clean pop-punk trio made virgin rings a fashion statement.

BRUCE SPRINGSTEEN

The "New Dylan" tag became a cliché in the Seventies, applied to any number of gritty singer-songwriters. One of these was New Jersey's favorite son, Bruce Springsteen. "The Boss" got his start in bands in his teens, playing the working-class bars of the Jersey Shore with a mix of rock and R & B covers and his romantic, wordy originals. He slowly assembled the top local players for his "E Street Band," and was signed to Columbia in 1972 by legendary A&R man John Hammond.

His first album, *Greetings from Asbury Park, NJ*, featured a poetic mix of R & B and folk numbers, but went nowhere. His second album, *The Wild, The Innocent and the E Street Shuffle*, foundered until FM stations started playing the rambunctious LP track "Rosalita." A relentless touring schedule marked by lengthy, spirited live sets made Springsteen an underground smash.

For his third LP he dropped most of the jazz and R & B flourishes for an epic, guitar-driven rock 'n' roll, heavily influenced by Phil Spector's "Wall of Sound" productions of the early Sixties. Bolstered by the breathless title track, 1975's *Born to Run* was a smash success, landing the artist on the cover of both *Time* and *Newsweek*. Springsteen was hailed by critics and fans as a working-class messiah who'd save rock 'n' roll from disintegrating completely in the post-Beatles era.

But a legal struggle with his former manager kept Springsteen out of commission for almost three years. His next album, *Darkness on the Edge of Town* (1978) featured a grim new lyrical vision matched by a stripped-down sound bordering on hard rock. The loss of his earlier joy and optimism reflected the economic troubles that the working-class folks Springsteen grew up with were facing during the late Seventies.

Springsteen continued to whittle away at his once-complex sound on the nostalgic 1980 double LP *The River*. Both musically and lyrically, the album is an elegy to the vanishing glory days of the American working class, drawing heavily on pre-Beatlemania party-rock styles. Reaganism and the deep recession of 1981 inspired *Nebraska*, a haunting collection of folk and country ballads that Springsteen originally recorded as demos. *Nebraska* had Springsteen drawing on the primitive spirituality of the old Heartland, a quality embedded in the DNA of the traditional music he was immersed in. Biblical themes and motifs were always part of his lyrical vision.

Delving further and further into a nostalgic brand of Americana, Springsteen and his band recorded their most rudimentary rockers yet for the phenomenally successful *Born in the USA* (1984). A last-minute pop number, "Dancing in the Dark," was quickly added when management felt the album offered no obvious hits. How wrong they were—nearly every song on the album became a hit single, including the unlikely title track, a one-chord stomper whose lyrics recounted the troubles of an unemployed Vietnam vet.

At the same time America's farms and factories were being decimated, Ronald Reagan was serving up a reelection campaign heavy with Heartland nostalgia. Republican advisers heard "Born in the USA" 's rousing beat and chorus, but somehow missed the bitter lyrics in the verses. Soon, conservative candidates were bizarrely citing the song as a tribute to a born-again American patriotism. In 1988, Springsteen returned with *Tunnel of Love*, a stripped-down, synth-heavy album filled with countrified pop that Springsteen sang in a distinctly un-Jersey cornpone accent.

Then, the Boss began to stumble. He ditched the E Street

Band and released *Human Touch* and *Lucky Town* simultaneously in 1992. Both albums were filled with hook-free, histrionic rock songs that verged on self-parody. Neither was the type of best seller the singer was accustomed to, and many diehard fans have refused to accept the albums as canonical. Perhaps as an act of penance, Springsteen went back to his roots, recording *The Ghost of Tom Joad* (1995), an album filled with bitter, politically charged folk ballads, and touring as a solo act.

He returned to the spotlight with his post-9/11 album, *The Rising* (2002), whose title song was later adopted by Barack Obama's 2008 Presidential campaign. *The Rising* was Springsteen's first US multi-platinum album in 14 years. Seemingly ageless, Springsteen soldiers on and still attracts enormous audiences to his concert tours.

JOURNEY

After wavering throughout the late Sixties and early Seventies, the record industry finally began to wrest control of the direction of mainstream rock from all the freaks and geeks in the mid-Seventies. Industry moguls began to groom a parade of slick, Midwestern hard rock bands such as REO Speedwagon, Styx, and Kansas for stardom, to offer more palatable versions of edgier sounds drifting over from the UK.

Results were mixed until 1976, when a tech head from Massachusetts named Tom Scholz unleashed a studio concoction featuring himself, singer Brad Delp, and a hired rhythm section burning through a drop-dead repertoire of 200-proof Apollonian rock. The band and its eponymous album would be named Boston, and would terrify every hard rock band on the planet with bulletproof harmonies, airtight compositions, and an immaculate production job that still sounds futuristic. Soon after, Dionysian hard rock would begin to split into Plutonian heavy metal and Apollonian arena rock. Perhaps the most archetypal band of the arena rock movement was Journey, which emerged from the unlikely environs of San Francisco.

Journey was an assembly of musicians consisting of former Santana guitarist Neil Schon and a revolving cast of Bay Area hotshots. The band's early output failed to impress, and their label insisted the band add a slick singer to the lineup. Journey struck gold in late '77 when they found Steve Perry, a singer-songwriter with a searing tenor. In 1978, Perry put Journey on the charts his first time at bat with two singles, the smoochy "Lights" and the portentous "Wheel in the Sky."

Perry methodically took control of the group, and its 1980 album *Departure* stormed the Top 10. Curiously enough, the album featured Egyptian Mystery symbolism on its record sleeve, in this case the winged scarab that would become the band's unlikely trademark. Journey went to the next level in 1981 with *Escape*, which featured three monster hits, "Who's Crying Now," "Open Arms," and the evergreen "Don't Stop Believing." The LP went on to sell 9 million copies. Their next LP, 1983's *Frontiers*, sent four singles to the Top 40.

But Perry upset the band the following year by releasing a hit solo album that sounded suspiciously like a Journey LP, and when he returned to the band in 1986 he had its rhythm section replaced with session players, including future *American Idol* judge Randy Jackson. The new lineup was successful, but Perry developed health problems and left in 1987. After a successful reunion in 1996, Perry begged off again and the band soldiered on with varying degrees of success. Showing that Journey is well implanted in the 21st century, they discovered the Philippines-based Arnel Pineda after hearing him perform karaoke versions of Journey hits on YouTube.

BLONDIE
Cartoonish punk-poppers Blondie were one of the first bands to put New York punk on the map. Their pop hooks—and their singer Debbie Harry's impossible beauty—got them a deal and overseas stardom while their fellow NYC punk bands struggled. Blondie topped the charts in 1978 with an atypical disco number, "Heart of Glass," and scored hits with the punkier "One Way or Another" and "Hanging on the Telephone." Transfiguring the Dionysian/Plutonian energy of punk into easily digestible pop, Blondie became the first genuine hitmakers to emerge from the Bowery punk rock scene.

Rather than chase after easy disco dollars, the band punked it up again for 1979's *Eat to the Beat,* and then split the difference on 1980's "Call Me," taken from the *American Gigolo* soundtrack. However, the pressures of stardom took their toll and creative exhaustion set in on *Autoamerican,* also from 1980. The band had two great moments left in its original incarnation: a reggae cover, "The Tide is High," and "Rapture," an early appropriation of hip-hop. Debbie Harry's solo career never got much traction and she spent a good chunk of the late Eighties caring for Blondie's leader Chris Stein when he contracted a rare and debilitating illness. But Blondie enjoyed a successful reunion in 1999 and the band continues to work the new wave nostalgia market.

THE POLICE

Back in the late Seventies all the energy and excitement was in the clubs, particularly in the punk clubs. Subsequently, intrepid labels like Sire and Virgin went on a signing binge and scooped up all of the top punk acts and rushed them into the studio. The problem was that the lucrative US market *hated* punk and most of the records bombed. Facing a major financial crisis, desperate record execs came up with the "new wave" marketing strategy, which enabled the industry to channel the anarchic energy of punk into a sellable package.

Acts like Squeeze, XTC, and the Joe Jackson Band had nothing to do with anarchy or revolution, but were able to adopt the surface trappings of punk and apply their old-school chops to the new style and score hits when punk fizzled on the charts in mid-1978. Established punk acts began toning down the mayhem to earn airplay, and the fruits of this effort were heard on the Clash's *London Calling* and the Ramones' *End of the Century* (produced by none other than Phil Spector).

Far and away the greatest beneficiaries of the new wave strategy were the Police, whose very name reeks of Apollonian order. The band was formed by Stewart Copeland, son of an exiled CIA bigwig and drummer with veteran progressive rock outfit Curved Air. Copeland scored a major coup when he found Gordon Sumner, an aspiring jazz musician who was nicknamed "Sting" for his black-and-yellow-striped pullovers. Both were talented, ambitious, and desperate to become stars. With the semi-amateur Henry Padovani on guitar, the Police began gigging but were seen as interlopers by the punk elite.

After putting out a couple of 45s, they ditched Padovani for Andy Summers, a journeyman guitar whiz who collaborated with Copeland and Sting in a short-lived studio band named

Strontium 90. With their punk sound going nowhere, the Police lifted the punk-reggae fusion concept from the Clash, and added touches of jazz and Latin to the mix. The new style clicked, and soon the band scored UK hits like "Roxanne" and "Can't Stand Losing You." The Police undertook a Spartan touring schedule, traveling through America in a beat-up old station wagon in 1978. Their second album, 1979's *Regatta De Blanc*, topped the UK charts and featured two big US hits in "Message in a Bottle" and "Walking on the Moon."

With their trademark bleached-blond hair and tropical-tinged rock, the Police oozed Apollo from every pore. Each Police album outsold the one before, and the band's 1983 LP *Synchronicity* was a blockbuster smash, knocking Michael Jackson's *Thriller* from the top of the charts. *Synchronicity* also earned the band three Top 10 singles and set them on a lengthy stadium tour.

After *Synchronicity*, Sting felt there was nowhere for the Police to go but down. He set off on a solo career that saw him venture into the mellow, jazzy pop sound popularized by Steely Dan and the Doobie Brothers in the Seventies. As they say, it was like punk never happened. But after an almost 25-year lull, the Police reunited in 2007 and embarked on a long and lucrative world tour, showcasing jazzy revamps of the old new wave hits.

U2

The cartoonish, synth-heavy new wave sound inspired a back-lash of sorts, and a new generation of guitar-based bands appeared in the early Eighties, inspired by the psychedelic sounds of bands like Pink Floyd and the Doors. Bands like

Echo and the Bunnymen, Simple Minds, and the Psychedelic Furs would themselves be drawn into the new wave whirlpool in the mid-Eighties, but their early output gave British rock a kick in the pants during the uncertain post-punk era. Many of the new guitar bands would find success, but only U2 would become superstars.

U2 grew out a clique of misfits at the Mount Temple School in Dublin who lived and breathed the latest underground sounds coming across the Irish Sea. The seminal moment for the Mount Temple gang was the Clash's Dublin debut in 1977, whose mind-bending ferocity inspired the boys to form their own band. When not bashing out their homemade punk rock tunes, three of the future members of U2—David Evans, Paul Hewson, and Larry Mullen—were involved with a Protestant sect known as Shalom, a bold move considering Ireland was essentially a Catholic theocracy at the time. (What's more, Evans and future U2 bassist Adam Clayton were both born in Britain.)

Practicing and gigging incessantly, U2 forged a new kind of hard rock, drawing on the dark, thorny energy of Joy Division and Public Image Ltd., as well as the Mithraic outrage of the Clash. But they also brought in tinges of traditional Irish and Celtic music, and an optimism and openness inspired by their idiosyncratic Irish brand of Christian Mysticism. It would be a fortuitous mix.

U2's 1980 debut, *Boy*, was polished to a tough, tight sheen by superstar producer Steve Lillywhite. Their single "I Will Follow" became a smash at the clubs and U2 instantly broke into the first rank of the alternative rock scene. Some felt that the band stumbled with the *Boy* soundalike *October*, but a brasher, more political approach emerged on *War*, breaking U2 into the US mainstream in 1983. *War* featured two classic rock radio mainstays, "New Year's Day" and "Sunday Bloody Sunday." Seeking to expand on their arena rock sound, U2 defied their record company's wishes and hired on Brian Eno, the avant-garde producer/musician best known for his work with David Bowie and the Talking Heads. Along with his right-hand man, Daniel Lanois, Eno holed U2 up in an Irish castle and forced them outside their comfort zone. At first blush, the resulting album, *The Unforgettable Fire* (1984), probably didn't seem like a worldwide best seller, but that's exactly what it became, setting U2 on the mainstream rock throne the Police had recently abdicated.

Their next album, *The Joshua Tree* (1987), had U2 serving up its interpretations of traditional roots-rock idioms, which were all the rage during the height of Reaganism. The album sold over 10 million copies, and landed two singles atop the *Billboard* Hot 100. U2 then took a film crew on tour for a concert film to be titled *Rattle and Hum*, and recorded new studio tracks, all of which had U2 veering further and further into John Cougar Mellencamp turf. The album sold 5 million copies but the film was a critical and commercial flop. Bono's strident preachiness along with the film's *Spinal Tap*-type clichés (such as visiting Graceland and jamming with BB King) made U2 the object of widespread ridicule.

Chastened, the band rehired Eno and Lanois for the landmark *Achtung Baby* (1991), which saw U2 shaking off the borrowed old clichés and returning to the rock vanguard. The album was a worldwide blockbuster and put four tracks in the Top 40. In 1993, the band followed *Achtung* with the even more experimental *Zooropa*, which saw Eno acting as a de facto fifth band member. Pushing its luck, the band worked without Eno and Lanois on 1997's *Pop*, a poorly received stab at techno. Chastened once more, the band reunited with Eno and Lanois for *All That You Can't Leave Behind* (2000).

U2 continues to be phenomenally successful, but its distinctly Apollonian relationship to power—both governmental and corporate—overshadows its rebellious, mystical self-image. Even the band's well-publicized philanthropy often seems like an excuse to justify Bono's never-ending media ubiquity. U2 is undoubtedly the biggest rock 'n' roll band in the world, but they are selling a myth that no one much believes anymore—that mainstream corporate rock can "change the world."

GREEN DAY

Green Day came out of the Gilman Street Project in Berkeley. Set up as a private club to circumvent zoning restrictions and filter out neo-Nazis and other troublemakers, Gilman became the flashpoint for a return to the song-oriented punk of the late Seventies. Singer Billie Joe Armstrong and bassist Mike Dirnt had been playing together in various punk bands since their early teens and formed Green Day as a power trio, enlisting drummer Tre Cool when their original skinsman couldn't commit to the band's rigorous touring schedule.

As grunge began to peter out in 1994, bands like Green Day and the Offspring filled the void, serving up a taut mix of good-natured punk rock and pop hooks. Green Day's '94 breakthrough *Dookie* soared to the top of the charts, powered by three instant punk classics: "Longview," "Basket Case," and the surprisingly sentimental "When I Come Around." *Dookie* went on to sell a staggering 15 million copies and establish pop-punk as *the* sound of adolescent America.

While 1995's *Insomniac* and 1997's *Nimrod* offered up increasingly generic punk, the band's knack for instant classics better served them on "Good Riddance (Time of Your Life)," a tender acoustic ballad. With the rise of boy bands and slut pop dominating the airwaves, Green Day struggled for relevance. But a major comeback was just around the corner.

The 2004 elections found the United States more polarized than at any time since the Vietnam War. Easy credit and a real estate bubble were fueling a profligate new American lifestyle. Exurban corporate jobs, prefabricated McMansions (bought on adjustable-rate mortgages), aggressively Evangelical megachurches, and gas-guzzling sport utility vehicles were creating an illusion of prosperity. George Bush rode to reelection with the support of an emboldened religious right, which was scapegoating gays and lesbians and branding anyone opposed to the wars in Afghanistan and Iraq as a traitor.

Green Day's 2004 blockbuster *American Idiot* had an incendiary effect on this new American dream. The album's title track took radio by storm, summing up the frustrations of millions of citizens fed up with a "subliminal mindfuck America" beholden to a "redneck agenda" and living in an "age of paranoia." The follow-up single, "Holiday," offered a sarcastic dissent to the warfare state, with Armstrong lapsing into a parody of a right-wing congressman threatening to bomb the Eiffel Tower during a floor speech.

What makes these songs different from thousands of similar punk rants is their seductive melodies and Green Day's airtight ensemble playing. *American Idiot* recalls not only punk, but the classic rock of the Who and the Kinks as well. At the same time, Green Day adopted a new, more militant look and pose, borrowed heavily from the Clash. Green Day's caustic, satirical punk struck a deep chord in a country tired of being controlled by a belligerent minority consumed by apocalyptic fantasy. In many ways, *American Idiot* became a rallying cry, bolstering a resistance that resulted in massive Republican losses in the 2006 elections.

PARTY ANIMALS:
THE NEW DIONYSIANS

The Dionysian archetype trades in sex 'n' drugs 'n' drink 'n' mayhem—straight up, no chaser. These are the sex-crazed madmen of rock 'n' roll, the bands that caused thousands of parents to lock up their daughters (and sometimes their sons) when they rolled into town. The parallels to the ancient Dionysian cults are many, and the effect was usually the same. The touchstone for the Dionysian rockers was the blues, but many of them have wandered far afield into more exotic musical genres. In their prime, these bands drove teenage girls out of their minds, creating newly converted bands of Maenads wherever they traveled.

THE ROLLING STONES

Storming out of London's rock underground, the Rolling Stones played the bad-boys role in the British Invasion. The young blues fanatics were able to channel the spirit of heroes like Muddy Waters and Howlin' Wolf largely because lead guitarist Brian Jones knew all those old licks by heart. Drummer Charlie Watts and bassist Bill Wyman were also well seasoned in the genres for which band leaders Mick Jagger (vocals) and Keith Richards (guitar) had more enthusiasm than proficiency.

The Stones were swept over to America in the Beatles' wake, but they didn't hit the jackpot until 1965, when "(I Can't Get No) Satisfaction" rocketed to No. 1. From then on, the Stones cranked out one dark, sarcastic hit after another. The band's sexy, druggy aura also earned them scrutiny and scorn from the Establishment; one famous tabloid headline screamed "Would you let your daughter marry a Rolling Stone?" They became a *cause célèbre* after a notorious 1967 drug bust that threatened the band with serious jail time.

Things were going worse for Brian Jones. Marginalized by Jagger and Richards (later dubbed "the Glimmer Twins"), Jones became increasingly obsessed not only with drugs but with exotic foreign music, particularly the Pan Pipers of Morocco. He finally left the Stones in 1969, only to be murdered by a disgruntled handyman in July of that year.

Around the same time, the Stones fell under the spell of Kenneth Anger, who introduced them to the works of Aleister Crowley and Church of Satan founder Anton LaVey. Jagger reportedly wrote "Sympathy for the Devil" under Anger's influence and recorded a startlingly avant-garde soundtrack for his 1969 film *Invocation of My Demon Brother*, using cutting-edge synthesizer equipment. But the Devil would catch up with the Stones by year's end.

Having missed out on Woodstock, the band held its own free festival at the dusty Altamont Raceway on the edge of California's Central Valley. The Stones hired the Hell's Angels to provide security, and the Angels proceeded to pummel with pool cues anyone who got too close to the low-rise stage. The entire concert was a disaster, and the bikers killed a disgruntled fan who rushed the stage with a gun. The Stones survived the ensuing uproar, but they seemed to lose something vital after Altamont.

Still, their 1970 opus *Exile on Main Street* is considered a milestone, and they enjoyed a string of hit singles like "Angie" and "Heartbreaker" throughout the Seventies. *Some Girls* (1978) was a smash hit, giving the band a second wind. Their most satanic innovation came long after "Sympathy for the Devil," when the Stones pioneered the concept of corporate sponsorship of rock 'n' roll for their 1981 world tour. The band continued to score hits throughout the Eighties, but for many diehards the glory days were long over. Many saw their Eighties and Nineties albums as perfunctory, simply excuses to wrest funds from their record company for their mammoth stadium tours. But whatever one thinks of their later records, the Stones' stamina certainly can't be faulted. And their influence is incalculable, even on younger bands who've never heard much of their music. The Stones' lascivious DNA is firmly implanted in rock's genome.

THE GRATEFUL DEAD

To many people, the Grateful Dead embody the Hippie Explosion of the late Sixties. The Dead began as a raw, punchy bar band named the Warlocks, belting out blues and rock standards, with raw-throated organist Ron "Pigpen" McKernan often taking the lead on vocals. Guitarist Jerry Garcia, bassist Phil Lesh, drummer Bill Kreutzmann, and rhythm guitarist Bob Weir rounded out the band, joined later by second drummer Mickey Hart. Auspiciously, the band first performed as the Grateful Dead for one of author Ken Kesey's famous "acid tests" in 1965. It went over so well that Kesey and his "Merry Pranksters" adopted the Grateful Dead as their de facto house band.

The Dead would play anywhere that a crowd gathered, indoors or out, sometimes even on the back of a flatbed truck parked in the middle of the street. Like their neighbors the Jefferson Airplane, the Dead took to expanding their simple tunes into long, rambling improvisations that were essentially impossible to reproduce in the studio. But the hippies ate it up, and the band and the audience fed off of each other, with various chemicals providing a rich medium. An acid-drenched mythology grew up around the Dead, bolstered by their rich and enigmatic iconography of skulls, roses, and winged sun disks.

As the Sixties counterculture faded, the Grateful Dead soldiered on, slowly but surely nurturing a fan base which would evolve into a distinct subculture of its own. No longer a band per se, the Dead were more an itinerant Dionysian priesthood and a traveling hippie museum, trailing a nomadic tribe of drug dealers, idealists, and merchants in their wake. Each concert featured at least one lengthy, abstract improvisation, or "space jam," making every show a unique event. Hard-core fans eventually came to ignore the Dead's studio albums, preferring bootlegs of their epic gigs. The Dead openly encouraged the recording of their shows, eventually setting aside space at each gig for tapers and their equipment. This would spawn a sophisticated network of tape trading that later drew in affiliated bands like Phish.

The Dead built up a major following in the Eighties, offering a counterculture alternative to Reaganism. But an accidental hit ("Touch of Grey") landed them on MTV in 1987, and soon the Dead found itself overwhelmed by new fans, uninitiated into the arcane rules of community that the band had inspired. The Dead stopped having fun but kept making money, supporting a virtual corporation that helped keep the show on the road. But Garcia succumbed to diabetes and a powerful heroin addiction in 1995, stopping the band in its tracks. After regrouping as "the Other Ones," the various members pursued solo projects until regrouping in 2003 as simply "the Dead" and picking up where they left off.

THE DOORS

Most bands of the classic rock era would toy with the arche-types and the trappings of the ancient Mysteries completely unconsciously. Not so the Doors, who burst from LA's Sunset Strip in 1967 armed with a singer/poet who knew the old gods well and was determined to unleash them on an unsuspecting world.

The Doors came out of the unlikely environs of the UCLA film department, where classically trained organist Ray Manzarek met a strange aspiring filmmaker who told none of his classmates that his father was a prominent admiral in the US Navy. Jim Morrison had come to LA after getting into trouble at a Florida college and was eyeing the rock scene as a venue for his idiosyncratic poetry. Possessing a genius-level IQ, Morrison also had the face and voice to make him a star.

The duo enlisted blues-happy guitarist Robbie Krieger and drummer John Densmore and began to jam, intent on bringing their unique musical/poetic synthesis to the hyperactive LA rock scene. It was on the Strip that the Doors' formerly rudimentary rock songs took on a new dimension. It took a while for Morrison to feel comfortable in front of a crowd, but eventually he would be inspired to unleash a host of long, poetic improvisations onstage while the band jammed behind him. The Doors signed with Elektra and essentially put their Whiskey a Go Go set straight to vinyl. They became a media sensation, with journalists grokking Morrison's obscure literary influences and the girls swooning to his manly good looks.

But the Doors found the world outside the Strip disorienting, and were rushed into a series of exhausting tours. After using up the balance of their backlog of club material on *Strange Days* (released nine months after their debut), the band felt pressure to produce follow-up albums they didn't have time to properly prepare for. Morrison's drinking was becoming a major problem, as was his penchant for theatrical provocation, which got the band in serious trouble in Florida when Morrison pretended to expose himself to the crowd. But the booze was the band's real headache, and Morrison was often too wasted to perform. Does it get any more Dionysian than that?

But when the gods of rock willed it, Morrison could take himself, his band, and their fans out of their heads. He could raise pure shamanic energy over from that "other side" he sang about and bring it back to this one. Even though some fans and critics felt the band's later records failed to live up to their early promise, the Doors remained a top live attraction. Anything could happen at a Doors concert, and usually did. The Doors' mystical aura wasn't just hype; in 1970 Morrison was wed to a pagan high priestess named Patricia Kennealy, who went on to refer to herself as "Mrs. Morrison," though the ceremony was not legally binding.

Although their first hit, "Light My Fire," remains their best-known number, the 12-minute opus "The End" truly seals the band's legend. Developed from onstage improvisations in their club days, "The End" evolved into a true Western raga. The song lopes along on Krieger's sitar-like runs, climaxing in a spoken-word passage in which Morrison tells of a modern Oedipus who takes "a face from the ancient gallery" and murders his family before raping his mother. Such was the song's power that Francis Ford Coppola used it at the climax of his own harrowing depiction of human sacrifice in the 1979 Vietnam War epic *Apocalypse Now.*

But the Doors' story didn't end with Morrison's death by OD in 1971. Like any good Dionysus, Jim Morrison rose from the dead and became a superstar all over again. The first stirrings from the grave came in 1978, when the Doors reunited to play tinkly jazz/rock fusion behind tapes of Morrison reciting poetry on the *An American Prayer* LP. But the real revival came in 1980 when former Doors fan club schlepper Danny Sugerman wrote his memoir/bio *No One Here Gets Out Alive* with journalist Jerry Hopkins. The book became a best seller and reignited Doors fandom in high school smoking areas all across America.

Another revival came in 1991 when Doors fan and film director Oliver Stone (*JFK, Wall Street*) cast Val Kilmer as Jim Morrison for the biopic *The Doors*. The film was self-consciously mythological and presented Morrison as an idealized Dionysian martyr and shaman, not as the abusive alcoholic those around the singer knew. The band hated the final product, but it did little to hurt their legacy. Several years later Krieger and Manzarek would form a group called the Doors of the 21st Century with Cult vocalist Ian Astbury on lead vocals. Following a lawsuit by Densmore and the Morrison estate, they changed the band's name to Riders on the Storm.

LED ZEPPELIN

More than any other band, the Mighty Zep has come to define the Dionysian impulse in rock 'n' roll. Emerging in the wake of Woodstock, Manson, and Apollo 11, Led Zeppelin's dark, mystic sound heralded the end of the utopian, Apollonian era of the rock counterculture and its eventual splintering into the mutant subcultures that defined the Seventies and beyond.

Strangely enough, the band itself was formed to fulfill a contractual obligation. Guitarist Jimmy Page was the last man standing in the Yardbirds, the British Invasion blues-rock band that also launched the careers of both Eric Clapton and Jeff Beck. When the rest of the band flaked out and drifted off, Page was left to deal with European tour dates the Yardbirds had committed to—but had no band to play them.

Page spent the glory days of the British Invasion as an in-demand session musician, playing lead guitar on hit records by then-raw acts like the Rolling Stones and the Kinks. It was in the studio that Page met John Paul Jones (né Baldwin), a classically trained multi-instrumentalist who'd also worked on a host of hits in the swinging Sixties. Burned out from relentless sessions and looking to settle into something more rewarding, Jones took his chances with Page.

In forming the so-called New Yardbirds, Page went through the phonebook of available talent on the London circuit, but ultimately settled on two teenage unknowns from the Home Counties, John Bonham on drums and Robert Plant on lead vocals. The four got on like a house on fire the first time they rehearsed. Page kept on the Yardbirds' manager, a fearsome ex-professional wrestler named Peter Grant, to handle the group's business affairs. Grant and the gang of bonebreakers he enlisted from the London underworld kept the sharks and rip-off artists of the music industry at bay for the duration of Led Zeppelin's career.

As seasoned studio pros, Page and Jones understood the value of economy. They knew that the notes you left out were as important as the ones you played. They also understood the effect that endless repetition of a powerful riff had on a listener's subconscious, as it did with voodoo, Sufism, and the ancient Mysteries. Sticking close to this surefire formula, Led Zeppelin released a remarkable string of smash-hit albums. The critics hated it like poison (one condemned their rewrite of Willie Dixon's "Whole Lotta Love," as a "thermonuclear gang rape") but the kids gobbled it up like candy.

The band reached a peak in 1971 with the untitled album commonly known as *Led Zeppelin IV*. Kicking off with two relentless chargers ("Black Dog" and "Rock and Roll"), the album strays into Anglo-Celtic folklore with the Tolkien-inspired "Battle of Evermore" and the epic "Stairway to Heaven." The album's bluesy closing track, "When the Levee

Breaks," opens with the single most iconic drumbeat in rock history (recorded in a three-story stairway to give it its trademark hugeness), which has been sampled by countless artists.

Zep extended this peak for its next two albums, *Houses of the Holy* and the double LP *Physical Graffiti*. The former was pure Dionysian party rock, the latter a masterwork of eclecticism, ballads, and blues jams interwoven with brutal hard rock stompers. *Graffiti* climaxes with "Kashmir," a mystically enigmatic epic spiced with a thunderous orchestral arrangement and Bonham's electronically treated drums.

The band toured relentlessly, logging thousands of miles in America on their private jet. Led Zeppelin concerts were pure Dionysian revival, where stoned, sex-mad kids were bombarded with a tsunami of electric noise and endlessly repeating riffs. But the partying in the audience was nothing compared to the backstage Bacchanals. Led Zeppelin and their entourage were devout party animals, and the booze and the drugs were augmented by an endless parade of nubile, often too-young fans acting as the band's Maenads.

The endless substance abuse and the pressures of touring and recording began to catch up with the band in the mid-Seventies. A serious car accident involving Plant and his family left the singer in traction and at half strength during the sessions for their next album, *Presence*, a back-to-basics attempt further hampered by Page's and Bonham's addiction issues. The years 1976 and 1977 saw Led Zeppelin's enormous good fortune running out. Plant's arduous recovery prevented a world tour. Their concert film *The Song Remains the Same* (taken from a 1973 gig in New York) presented a band out of touch with contemporary reality, and was poorly received. Their 1977 tour also saw several violent incidents involving Led Zeppelin's increasingly dangerous entourage, which jeopardized the band's standing with powerful concert promoters like the late Bill Graham. And after a show at the New Orleans Superdome, the band was shaken to its foundations by the news that Plant's son Karac had died from a viral infection. The remainder of their tour was immediately canceled.

Zep reconvened in 1978 for recording sessions in Sweden, but the involvement of Page and Bonham was limited. Most of the new songs were based on keyboard arrangements, and only two old-time rock stompers made the final cut. The resulting album was dubbed *In Through the Out Door* (a reference to band's endless miseries), but a tour in support of the LP was cut short in 1980 by Bonham's death by overdose. Well aware of the foursome's inherently magical chemistry, Led Zeppelin announced its breakup two months later.

Throughout its career Led Zeppelin cultivated a powerful mystique unparalleled in rock history. The band refused to do interviews or TV appearances. They didn't release singles, or use their portraits on their album covers, replacing them with enigmatic surrealist imagery. This lent them an air not simply of mystery, but of sheer unknowableness. This mystique was compounded by the ubiquitous rumors of the band's involvement in the occult.

These rumors were not unfounded—Jimmy Page was a serious devotee of Aleister Crowley. In 1975, he struck up a friendship with Kenneth Anger, and the two began working on Anger's planned magnum opus, *Lucifer Rising*, which had also involved Mick Jagger and Manson associate Bobby Beausoleil in earlier stages of its production.

Page provided Anger with lodging, money, and equipment,

and recorded a soundtrack for the film. But Page's full attention was focused on his band's remorseless schedule, leaving the notoriously tetchy Anger feeling slighted. The filmmaker took his grievances to the press, bashing Page for his drug use and subsequent loss of musical and magical powers. Page immediately cut Anger loose and the filmmaker returned to the States, eventually reenlisting Beausoleil to score the film—from behind bars, no less.

As their fortunes dimmed, rumors had it the band blamed Page's occult dabbling for all the bad vibes. Page went so far as to address the rumors in the press, admitting his involvement in ritual magic but dismissing rumors of Satanism out of hand. Needless to say, all their setbacks and controversies merely cemented Led Zeppelin's occult mystique in the minds of millions of teenagers around the world. But when Anger's film was released there was little of Lucifer (and certainly no Satan) in sight—the film was in fact a quiet, surreal meditation on the Egyptian Mysteries, ending with Isis and Osiris summoning flying saucers to the Giza Necropolis.

ROCK 'N' ROLL'S SPIRITUAL SUPERMARKET

The rock community has always opened its arms to all kinds of gurus and sects. George Harrison was a generous sponsor of the Hare Krishna movement, and Fairport Convention guitarist

Richard Thompson and Bauhaus singer Peter
Murphy are both followers of Sufism, a form of
Islamic mysticism. The Who's leader Pete Town-
shend and jazz singer Bobby McFerrin have
followed the teachings of Indian mystic Meher
Baba, summed up by McFerrin in his hit "Don't
Worry, Be Happy."

Guitar legends Carlos Santana and John
McLaughlin followed the teachings of Sri
Chinmoy. King Crimson guitarist Robert Fripp
studied the works of math mystic J.G. Bennett.
Kinks guitarist Dave Davies had a Theosophical
spiritual awakening after a close encounter with
disembodied alien spirits in 1981. And Canadian power trio Rush were once followers of the
secular cult of Ayn Rand, who preached liberty
and practiced tyranny. Here are some other
diverse expressions of spirituality and their
famous followers:

Transcendental Meditation is a technique developed by Indian guru Maharishi Mahesh Yogi.
It promises everything from improved well-
being to superhuman powers like levitation.
The Beatles were the Maharishi's first celebrity
followers, but they quit the guru after an ill-
starred pilgrimage to India. Sixties rockers such
as Mike Love of the Beach Boys and Donovan
took up the cause, and outré director David
Lynch and shock jock Howard Stern are also
practitioners.

Buddhism is one of civilization's oldest religious traditions, teaching peace and non-attachment. The Beastie Boys and Bow Wow Wow's Annabella Lwin are two of its most unlikely converts. Leonard Cohen and soft rocker Duncan Sheik try to follow in the Enlightened One's footsteps.

Scientology is a controversial self-help religion created by science fiction author L. Ron Hubbard. Its holy text is Hubbard's *Dianetics*, which made a big splash in the self-improvement craze following World War II. Scientology is especially influential in Hollywood. Alt rock superstar Beck, actress-turned-rocker Juliette Lewis, bass virtuoso Billy Sheehan, R & B legend Isaac Hayes, and albino rocker Edgar Winter are all working to rid themselves of those pesky body Thetans.

Rastafarianism is a Jamaican religion that preaches that Ethiopian dictator Haile Selassie was the messiah and black nationalist Marcus Garvey was a prophet. Similar to certain Christian sects in its cosmology, it trades sacramental bread and wine for copious amounts of ganja. Some of its notable adherents include reggae legends Bob Marley and Peter Tosh, hardcore pioneers Bad Brains, and homophobic dancehall rapper Buju Banton.

Kabbalah is a Medieval form of Jewish esotericism that was traditionally reserved for serious scholars. Hollywood types like Rosanne Barr and Madonna Ciccone famously follow a highly lucrative sect claiming to teach the mystic art.

VAN HALEN

Led Zeppelin inspired—and continue to inspire—legions of imitators. One of the most successful bands cut from Led Zeppelin's cloth was a bar band from Pasadena that boasted one of the most revolutionary musicians in rock history.

Although their popularity didn't quite translate overseas, from 1978 to 1984 Van Halen was *the* party band of adolescent America. Van Halen personified the distinctly Dionysian Southern California of the Seventies, with their odes to easy sex and fast cars and their bad-boys-with-hearts-of-gold image. Unlike the macho, angry British metal bands of the time, Van Halen appealed to girls too, serving up romantic pop-rockers like "Jamie's Crying" and "Dance the Night Away."

The band was named for brothers Eddie and Alex—the former the once-in-a-generation guitar genius and the latter the lucky older brother behind the drum kit. Michael Anthony was a college buddy of Alex's who joined in on bass. Rounding out the band was singer "Diamond" David Lee Roth, whose onstage act was part black belt, part Borscht Belt. Springing from a rich family, Roth landed the gig with Van Halen because he came with his own PA and could provide rehearsal space in his huge family home.

Van Halen made its bones as a local cover band, playing everything from hard rock to disco. Confident in its chops, VH moved from Pasadena to Hollywood and quickly blew every other band on the scene off the stage. Eddie Van Halen's playing—heavily influenced by players like Hendrix and Clapton—terrified a generation of guitarists with its post-psychedelic, high-tech sound. Eddie had plenty of competition in Roth, who outright stole his act from Southern studmuffin Jim "Dandy" Mangrum of boogie band Black Oak Arkansas, right down to the spandex, fringe, and enviable sideburns. Even if purists grumbled over his vocal talents, Roth's energy, charisma, and humor made up the deficit.

Kiss's Gene Simmons caught the live act and tried taking them under his batwing, but Warners honcho Mo Ostin scooped them up and handed them to his star producer Ted Templeman, who'd buffed the Doobie Brothers to a multi-platinum shine. After their first album's release, Van Halen toured with Black Sabbath, blowing the struggling legends off the stage every night. Full of piss and vinegar, VH burned up their advance money trashing hotels while on tour. They also knocked out one instant-party-classic album after another, and Roth bought paternity insurance in case he knocked up one of his fans. Though the song-strapped band had to resort to some old covers on 1982's *Diver Down*, their versions of "Pretty Woman" and "Dancin' in the Streets" were as fresh as anything the new synth pop bands had to offer and put the LP in the Top 3.

Despite Roth's objections, Eddie brought his own keyboards to the sessions for *1984*, which resulted in the band's first No. 1

single, "Jump." Other tracks also scored hits, and the band put three sexy, comedic videos into very heavy rotation on MTV. While the others recuperated, Roth finished off 1984 (the year, not the album) with an iconic (and distinctly Dionysian) video for his version of the Beach Boys' "California Girls." The single was taken from an EP of covers titled *Crazy from the Heat,* which also boasted a smash-hit medley of the old standards "Just a Gigolo" and "I Ain't Got Nobody." However, Roth's solo success would irrevocably rankle his bandmates.

The always touchy relationship between the hard-driving Roth and the emotionally volatile Eddie had broken down following the 1984 tour, and Roth either quit or was fired, depending on whose side of the story you believe. Ted Nugent recommended veteran screecher Sammy Hagar for the position and the new "Van Hagar" lineup got to work. Roth assembled an all-star band, including former Zappa sideman Steve Vai, bassist Billy Sheehan, and drummer Greg Bissonette. Both camps took their cases to the public when VH's *5150* and Roth's *Eat 'Em and Smile* were released in 1986.

Roth started off well, and the goofy videos for singles "Yankee Rose" and "Crazy from the Heat" seemed to pick up where the good times of 1984 left off. But Van Halen did permanent damage to its good-natured reputation when Alex and Eddie relentlessly attacked their former singer in the press. Roth was content to shrug it all off with a few well-rehearsed digs at his former bandmates. Van Halen's brand name and the radio-ready hard rock sound were enough to keep the band raking in the platinum, but not quite on the level of the debut or *1984.* Van Halen no longer made party music for the masses—its new sound was better suited to biker rallies and Las Vegas brothels.

Worse, Roth and VH deeply embarrassed themselves when the original lineup appeared together at the 1996 MTV Music Awards, leading most observers to assume that the classic VH was back. It wasn't, and the Van Halen brothers took to the press to badmouth Roth yet again. Former Extreme vocalist Gary Cherone had already been chosen to replace Hagar, whom Eddie had fired for reasons still unclear. But the Cherone VH album bombed big and Warners dropped the band, an unimaginable fate for a band that had earned the label hundreds of millions of dollars.

But all's well that end's well: Roth rejoined Van Halen in 2006 and enjoyed a hugely successful tour, with Eddie's teenage son Wolfgang on bass. But the image of the lucky, laughing Dionysians from a promised land of endless hedonism was long gone. In its place stood three somewhat haggard, fifty-something men and a teenager, providing a much-needed dose of nostalgia for a Generation X staving off middle age.

THE BEASTIE BOYS

The old hard rock and metal bands found themselves with a new rival at the end of the Eighties—a hybrid brand of party rock pioneered by a gaggle of punks from New York's rough-and-tumble hardcore punk scene. The Beastie Boys cranked out the usual blur of hardcore noise until a parody hip-hop single based on a crank phone call (1983's "Cookie Puss") put the idea in their heads to take the new street style more seriously.

Working with producer Rick Rubin, the Beasties developed a distinctly Dionysian synthesis of punk, hard rock, and hip-hop, all wrapped up in a snotty, rich-kid package that snotty kids of all income brackets found irresistible. Their 1987 debut, *License to Ill*, rode to the top of the charts on the strength of its flagship single, "Fight for Your Right to Party," a Dionysian anthem if there ever was one. The Beasties' success also opened the MTV floodgates for rap, which the network had been hesitant to air.

The 1989 follow-up, *Paul's Boutique,* was a comparative flop (reaching only Gold status in its initial release), but found the Beasties digging deeper for musical inspiration, setting the stage for their next incarnation. Dispensing with sampling, the boys took the time to master their instruments and in 1992 released *Check Your Head,* a bong-hit classic that reinterpreted their favorite old-school grooves in a new signature blend. The Beasties repeated the formula two years later with *Ill Communication*, another huge hit. Along the way the Beasties matured and championed political causes such as the liberation of Tibet. More recently, the Boys have explored more retro styles, as on 1998's electro-flavored *Hello Nasty* and 2002's old-school *To the 5 Boroughs.*

THE RED HOT CHILI PEPPERS

Working in a vein similar to the Beasties was LA's Red Hot Chili Peppers, who turned the violent SoCal punk scene back toward a more Dionysian mind-set. Formed by singer Anthony Kiedis, bass virtuoso Flea (born Michael Balzary), guitarist Hillel Slovak, and drummer Jack Irons, the Peppers drew heavily on Jimi Hendrix and George Clinton as their touchstones, and their raging libidos as their primary inspiration. If their early material was short on tunes and memorable riffs, the Peppers made up for the deficit with their audacious energy and boundless enthusiasm. The alt rock scene was more oriented toward experience than songcraft anyhow, and the Peppers worked hard to make every gig an unforgettable experience. (They would often play nude, or as they put it, "rock out with your cock out.")

The Peppers struggled to score hits, though. And tragedy would tear the band apart when Slovak died of a heroin overdose in 1987. Irons, who'd struggled with depression, quit following Slovak's death. The band rebounded when a young guitarist named John Frusciante showed up with the entire Peppers catalog committed to memory. Drummer Chad Smith signed on and the band hit the road before recording its 1990 breakthrough, *Mother's Milk*.

Milk gave the band much-needed hits with "Knock Me Down" and a cover of Stevie Wonder's "Higher Ground," both of which worked the funk-metal vein. Following that, the Peppers teamed up with Beasties producer Rick Rubin for their 1991 blockbuster, *Blood Sugar Sex Magick*, the first in a long string of hit albums trading in funk, rock, and R & B–influenced balladry. The breakout hit on *Blood* was "Give It Away," a pulsating bit of funk whose award-winning video had the Peppers cavorting in the desert done up as gold-painted satyrs. Frusciante himself fell into heroin abuse, but was pulled out of it by the other Peppers and rejoined for the 1999 comeback, *Californication*, only to quit again in 2010. But the Peppers carry on as one of the most unlikely bands to reach the upper echelon of rock stardom.

GUNS N' ROSES

In the mid-Eighties, the LA metal scene was dominated by "hair bands," glam rockers light on talent and heavy on mascara. It was quite a party; record companies were throwing truckloads of money at every hair band they could find, confident that MTV would put them into heavy rotation if the looks and hooks were right. Throw in the strippers, and the booze and the drugs, and soon LA found itself hosting a true Dionysian madhouse.

But storm clouds were gathering. Hard-core metal fans *hated* the hair bands, whose primary audience was teenage girls. MTV was putting rap into constant rotation, siphoning away a lot of male fans. The glam bands could score quick hits, but most were forgotten when the next hair-whores popped up. Then, out of nowhere, a ragtag band of angry, pugnacious roughnecks hit the scene, dropping a dose of ugly authenticity into a scene that was superficial by definition.

Guns N' Roses was formed by William "Axl" Rose and Jeffrey "Izzy Stradlin" Isbell in 1985. After the usual jostling, the band settled on a five-piece lineup that brought aboard Saul "Slash" Hudson, a biracial English guitarist raised in LA. The band scorned the glitzy metal that ruled the Strip, instead burying themselves in the classics like Led Zeppelin, Thin Lizzy, and Aerosmith.

GnR signed to Geffen Records in 1986 and released a four-song live EP while recording its landmark 1987 LP *Appetite for Destruction*. Guns N' Roses' bluesy, boozy bar-band hard rock was an instant smash, but the band soon found themselves overwhelmed by their new success. Things got rougher when a follow-up mini-LP in 1988 got the band in hot water for racist and homophobic lyrics. Heroin took hold backstage as well, leading Rose to threaten to break up the band if the offenders didn't clean up their acts.

A planned 1991 release turned into two separate albums, *Use Your Illusion I* and *II*. The expensive-sounding albums showed GnR expanding its musical palette, and the band scored a number of hits, all accompanied by costly videos. Then they embarked on a grueling two-and-a-half-year tour that was marked by controversy and infighting. The last original GnR release was *The Spaghetti Incident,* a 1993 covers album. By that point grunge had taken over, and GnR was in danger of becoming forgotten.

That was the least of the band's problems; they spend the next five years falling apart and Rose spent the next 10 years working on the notorious *Chinese Democracy* project, in which he burned through millions of dollars and a small army of musicians before the album was finally released in 2008. While Rose worked on the album, the core of GnR joined up with Stone Temple Pilots singer Scott Weiland to form the short-lived supergroup Velvet Revolver, which managed to produce two LPs in half the time it took Rose to release one. GnR still continues on, ever dependent on the changing moods of Mr. Rose. But no matter what happens, *Appetite for Destruction* will always remain a party rock landmark for that particular breed of fan.

EARTH MOTHERS:
THE NEW ELEUSINIANS

The Eleusinian Mysteries centered on Demeter's role as Earth Mother as well as her role as *Mater Dolorosa*, or "mother of sorrows." And so it is with the Demeter archetype in rock 'n' roll. Many of these artists work in earthy rock idioms, and often present a strong maternal identity. But they all rock as credibly as any men. There is an undercurrent of suffering or tragedy with some of these artists as well, whether in their music, their personal lives, or both. None more so than the next artist.

TINA TURNER

Some believe the first true rock 'n' roll 45 was "Rocket 88," recorded incognito in 1951 by Ike Turner and his Kings of Rhythm. Sometime later, while working the chitlin' circuit in Tennessee, Turner heard the young Anna Mae Bullock belting out the blues and was instantly smitten. Ike invited Anna to join his band as backup singer, but the irrepressible singer quickly took center stage and a new name—Tina. "The Ike and Tina Revue" scored its first R & B hit in 1960, and Ike and Tina wed in 1962. Along the way they raised four children.

Ike kept the rock 'n' roll faith in the Sixties when his rivals switched over to soul, perhaps because Tina was too boisterous and passionate to compete with regal soul queens like Aretha Franklin and Gladys Knight. She was backed by three bomb-shell backup singers known as the Ikettes, whose powerful eroticism and physically overwhelming performances would have given the Maenads a run for their money. Ike and Tina performed barnstorming covers of the big rock hits of the era, including "Proud Mary," "Come Together" and "Honky Tonk Women," and the act was a favorite of bands like the Rolling Stones, who invited the Revue to perform as an opening act on several tours.

But Ike was quietly nursing a drug problem and not so quietly would take his anger out on Tina for years. Worse, their career stalled when a more sedate sound took hold on the radio in the early Seventies, which only escalated the domestic situation. A nasty preshow fight in 1976 was the last straw, and Tina fled, hiding out from Ike's wrath with friends. The two divorced in 1978. Their last hit together was Tina's glam rock stomper "Nutbush City Limits" (1973), featuring T. Rex's Marc Bolan on guitar.

After a showstopping turn as the Acid Queen in the 1975 film adaptation of the Who's rock opera *Tommy*, Turner released her first major solo LP (also titled *Acid Queen*), which included her interpretations of hits by the Who and the Stones, as well as a slow, funky take on "Whole Lotta Love." But after an ill-advised disco album in 1979, Turner's chart prospects faded and she stuck to touring (particularly in Europe, where she commands a huge audience to this day).

But Tina's fortunes rose again in 1982 when she met synth poppers BEF (aka Heaven 17), with whom she recorded hit versions of The Temptations' "Ball of Confusion" and Al Green's "Let's Stay Together," setting the stage for her 1984 comeback. Selling over 20 million copies worldwide, *Private Dancer* featured state-of-the-art production and a sultry mix of rock and R & B. An all-star cast of players gave the album a sleek, contemporary feel and sent five singles to the Top 40. Turner was now more popular than she'd ever been before.

Turner capitalized on her comeback by appearing in the 1985 film *Mad Max Beyond Thunderdome*, whose soundtrack garnered her two more Top 20 hits. The following year, she released another hit album and a best-selling autobiography, *I, Tina*, in which she revealed the physical and emotional abuse she had long suffered with Ike. The book was adapted into a 1993 hit film, *What's Love Got to Do with It?*. Tina still holds the throne as Queen of Rock. A practicing Buddhist, she credits her practice as a central source of strength throughout her career ups and downs.

JANIS JOPLIN

Janis Joplin came out of Texas like a prairie fire, belting out the blues like no good suburban girl should. But she was also a lonely, sensitive girl who latched on to music as her lifeline. She sang with the usual folk groups in high school but was traumatized by a serious case of acne that left deep scars on her face. After a stint at UT–Austin, in 1963 she did what all artsy kids at the time aspired to do: move to San Francisco.

Joplin threw it down with the local blues rockers in SF but developed a particularly extreme drinking/drug problem. An intervention sent her back home, where she cleaned up her act and enrolled in college again, singing in Austin clubs in her spare time. But some demos she had cut in San Francisco caught the ear of heavy-blues band Big Brother and the Holding Company, who invited her back to join them in 1966. The band got gigs and a contract, and Janis also started back with the drugs and drink.

Big Brother was a major draw during the Summer of Love, knocking 'em dead at Monterey in June and releasing its first LP on Columbia that August. They went nationwide and got a couple of TV gigs as well, but the rest of the band resented the attention increasingly paid to Janis. Big Brother's next LP, *Cheap Thrills* (1968), earned them a major hit with "Piece of My Heart" which sent them across the country on a headlining tour. Joplin quit the band while onstage that December.

Joplin enlisted a slick new band and in 1969 recorded her first solo LP, *I Got Dem Ol' Kozmic Blues Again, Mama!* But her heroin bills were skyrocketing and critics and fans resented her diva move. The drink and drugs were beginning to affect her performances, including a spotlight set at Woodstock which was dropped from the final edit of the concert film of the festival.

In 1970, Joplin formed a new band and toured throughout the year before entering the studio with Doors producer Paul Rothschild for what would be her final LP, *Pearl*. During this time, she attended her tenth-anniversary high school reunion, where all the pain and humiliation she had experienced came flooding back, opening up the old wounds. Janis brought that pain to the studio with her, and as a result the music on *Pearl* was more mournful and reflective than her previous rave-ups. But she would never finish the record entirely; on October 4, 1970, she failed to show up for a recording session and was found dead of a heroin overdose in her hotel room. The salvaged *Pearl* was a posthumous hit, powered by her cover of Kris Kristofferson's "Me and Bobby McGee." Joplin's story would be allegorized in the hit 1979 film *The Rose*, which starred Bette Midler.

LINDA RONSTADT

With edgier stars like Joplin out of commission or out of fashion, Linda Ronstadt reigned as the Queen of Rock in the Seventies. She got her start in the Sixties with the Stone Poneys, an LA folk rock band best known for their hit "Different Drum." When the Poneys split up in 1969, Ronstadt launched a solo career, dabbling in country-flavored folk rock. (Her backup band went on to become the Eagles.) It wasn't until Ronstadt teamed with British producer Peter Asher in 1973 than she found solo success. Ronstadt broke through to stardom in 1974 with the *Heart Like a Wheel* LP, which featured two big soft rock hits, "You're No Good" and a cover of the Everly Brothers' "When Will I Be Loved."

Racking up a string of hits, Ronstadt made the cover of *Time* and even hooked up with California Governor Jerry Brown. She later branched out into edgier material, covering songs by Warren Zevon and Elvis Costello, including several of them on her 1980 "new wave" album *Mad Love*. Soon afterward, she moved into a host of other styles outside of rock. Ronstadt's Seventies rock days have fallen down the memory hole for the most part, but she inspired several other singers throughout the decade.

HEART

Ann and Nancy Wilson were gorgeous, fiercely talented military brats who fell in with a local Washington hard rock band and decamped to Vancouver when bandleader Roger Fisher got his draft card. Calling themselves Heart, the band cut their debut album *Dreamboat Annie* for Canadian label Mushroom in 1976. Heart's breakthrough hit was "Magic Man," which urban legend later claimed was about Charles Manson. (It wasn't.)

In 1977, Heart unleashed their masterpiece *Little Queen*, whose cover had the Wilsons dolled up in gypsy finery. Inside the grooves was a Zepesque blend of hard rock stompers and folk rock ballads made magic by the Wilsons' perfect harmonies. The centerpiece of the album was "Barracuda," written in disgust in response to a suggestion by Mushroom—in a print ad, no less—that the sisters practiced incest.

Heart kept themselves on the charts until the MTV explosion of the early Eighties, when their hard rock seemed dated in the age of metal and new wave. They changed labels and reinvented themselves in the slick, Eighties-rock template. The

Wilsons got a big-haired makeover, and Nancy's long legs and ample cleavage became the focal point of their flashy videos. The new-model Heart sent four singles to the Top 10 and topped the US album charts in 1985.

But the record company began to panic when Ann began putting on weight, and their Eighties-vintage sound wasn't so fresh in the Nineties. Sick of the commercial pressures, the Wilsons formed an acoustic side project in 1991 and scaled down the Heart project considerably in the post-Nirvana era, dispensing with the sex-kitten image entirely. A *VH1 Rock Honors* special in 2007 and inclusion of their songs in the popular *Guitar Hero* video game has kept interest in the band alive, and they continue to tour and record.

CHRISSIE HYNDE

Chrissie Hynde was borne and raised in Akron, Ohio, and attended Kent State University. She was on campus at the time of bloody shootings of Vietnam War protesters by the National Guard in 1970. Seeking escape, Hynde moved to London during the height of the glam craze. There she met journalist Nick Kent, who encouraged her to pursue writing. But Hynde's passion was for performing and she soon fell in with the punk crowd, working for Sex Pistols manager Malcolm McLaren and jamming with future members of the Clash and the Damned.

Hynde formed the Pretenders with virtuoso guitarist James Honeyman-Scott, bassist Pete Farndon, and drummer Martin Chambers. The band's first single, a cover of the Kinks' "Stop Your Sobbing," was a UK hit in 1979. Then the Pretenders entered the studio with superstar producer Chris Thomas

(Roxy Music, Sex Pistols), a well-regarded "singer's producer." Hynde had an incredible vocal range for Thomas to exploit—she could purr, whine, and croon, all within the space of a single verse. Blending punk, hard rock, new wave, and reggae into a seamless whole, the Pretenders' debut was a smash hit in the US and UK. Along the way Hynde struck up a relationship with Ray Davies, with whom she would bear a child. *Pretenders II* (1981) was a bit less successful, but the band appeared to have the momentum to become one of the top rock outfits of the Eighties.

Or did they? Farndon was sacked for heroin use in mid-1982, and shortly afterward Honeyman-Scott OD'd. Hynde and Chambers enlisted session players for the mournful 1982 hit single "Back on the Chain Gang," which Hynde dedicated to her fallen former bandmates. Hynde enlisted two new players for 1984's *Learning to Crawl*, an album that equaled the debut's success.

It didn't last long. Personnel changes reduced the Pretenders to a brand name. Hynde had also split with Davies and had taken up with Simple Minds leader Jim Kerr, with whom she had another child, a daughter. In 1994, she created a new Pretenders lineup that brought Chambers back into the fold. That year's *Last of the Independents* album produced the hit power ballad "I'll Stand By You." The album also featured the howling "I'm a Mother," an elemental exclamation in which Hynde, Demeter-like, declares herself "the source" and "the vessel of life." Hynde always made it clear that motherhood was a fierce source of pride to her, as essential to her identity as her lusty ball-buster image. Hynde's nurturing instincts extend to her activism on behalf of animal rights, and she continues to rip it up with the new Pretenders.

PAT BENATAR

Chrissie Hynde had a hard rock counterpart of sorts in Pat Benatar, who scored several hits in the early Eighties. Armed with a glass-breaking soprano, Benatar and husband/guitarist Neil Giraldo fashioned a hook-laden new wave/metal fusion that presented the diminutive singer as a no-nonsense post-feminist with songs like "You Better Run" and "Hit Me with Your Best Shot." As with Hynde, Benatar's tough image was tempered by a strong maternal streak, expressed in the anti-child-abuse rocker "Hell Is for Children."

But the space for women in hard rock shrank with the rise of heavy metal in the Eighties, and Benatar's music veered more toward synth pop as the decade progressed. Metal offered few—if any—opportunities for credible female vocalists.

COURTNEY LOVE

The punk underground would give women a place to raise hell in the Eighties and Nineties, and the Riot Grrl movement took advantage of that. Bands like Babes in Toyland and Bikini Kill offered up shrill, atonal punk that was drenched in postmodernist collegiate feminism for a new generation of fans.

Courtney Love's band Hole took the Riot Grrl aesthetic to the mainstream. The band's first LP, *Pretty on the Inside*, was a nails-on-the-blackboard endurance test, but Love's relationship with Nirvana leader Kurt Cobain seemed to radically improve her songwriting skills. (Love would later give birth to Cobain's daughter, Frances Bean.) Hole's 1994 album *Live Through This* took on a hideously ironic meaning with Cobain's suicide four days before the album's release. Two months later, Hole bassist Kristen Pfaff died from an OD.

The publicity and sympathy bestowed on these tragedies would help make the Hole album a hit and Courtney Love a household name. But the Riot Grrl movement had already peaked, and by the time of Hole's next album, 1998's *Celebrity Skin*, it was long forgotten. The new-model Hole was a slicker Nineties rock outfit, and Love's lyrics reflected her experience as a Hollywood fixture. Love teamed with Smashing Pumpkin Billy Corgan and superstar writer/producer Linda Perry for the 2010 Hole album *Nobody's Daughter*, but a resulting tour was greeted with scathing reviews. Courtney Love is now seen as a gossip page oddity, but her daughter with Kurt Cobain, Frances, is experiencing success as a fashion model.

SLEATER KINNEY

Another Northwest-based band would present a more serious face of the Riot Grrl aesthetic. Portland-based punk trio Sleater Kinney emerged from the same milieu as Hole, but offered a more serious-minded feminist political awareness. The band worked hard and stayed independent, releasing a string of critically praised albums. Although they developed a dedicated following, the band went on hiatus in 2006 so singer Corin Tucker could concentrate on raising her children. Tucker is now working as a solo artist.

GENDER BENDERS:
THE NEW GALLOI

Androgyny has always been a powerful impulse in rock 'n' roll. Even Elvis Presley projected a kind of ambiguous sexuality in his younger days, which he modeled on the rebel archetypes popularized by (bisexual) screen idols like James Dean and Marlon Brando. But the combination of gender-bending and cathartic, almost shamanic power would become a major force in the spread of rock 'n' roll, particularly in the post-hippie era when the glam movement took hold in the UK and Europe. We saw that same incongruous blend of effeminate musical aggression with the Galloi during the Roman era.

LITTLE RICHARD

The prototype for the glam rockers was Richard Penniman, aka Little Richard. Cutting his musical teeth in the Holiness churches, Richard found his religion and sexuality constantly at loggerheads. He made his bones as a front man touring the rollicking gay speakeasies of the Deep South, and brought the androgynous violence of that subculture—along with the lacquer, lipstick, and guyliner of howlers like Esquerita—into the living rooms of staid Fifties America. Richard also brought some of the hardest, heaviest rock 'n' roll yet heard to the airwaves, informed by the howling passion of Pentecostalism. The violent intensity of his playing and performing seemed wildly at odds with his effeminate image, and Richard was a controversial figure in the early rock era.

In 1957, Little Richard quit rock for preaching at the height of his success, but he backslid to and fro throughout the years, enjoying a major revival in England during the Sixties. Ironically, he was usually more candid about his sexuality while preaching against it than when playing to a secular crowd. He enjoyed another comeback in the Eighties as a media personality, making appearances in films and on TV, famously haranguing the music industry at the Grammy Awards in 1987 for not acknowledging his work (which it would in 1993). As of this writing he continues to perform, most often as a gospel singer.

GLAM AND GLITTER ROCK

With the rise of the gay rights movement in the late Sixties, gender-bending became a new mode of rebellion against the status quo. In the early Seventies, the glam rock movement, alternately known as glitter rock, took hold in the UK. For the most part, the glam rockers were exceptionally enthusiastic heterosexuals who'd probably never heard of Attis or the Galloi, but recognized an elemental kind of power in the blurring of sexual identities.

The self-conscious hyperandrogyny of glam rock—ultrabasic, ultra-loud, sing-along proto-punk dolled up in satin and taffeta—seemed to inspire the wildest, most untamed impulses of these performers. Most of the glam bands failed to break big in the States, even those that were more freak than femme. Sweet had the odd hit, but Slade—whose insidiously catchy anthems made them superstars in the UK and Europe—inexplicably had none. Marc Bolan and T. Rex hit big with "Bang a Gong" in 1972, but not much after that. Gary Glitter scored with the instrumental "Rock and Roll Part 2," and the fe-macho Suzi Quatro landed an acting gig on TV's megapopular *Happy Days* (portraying "Leather Tuscadero"), but she wouldn't have a US career until going soft rock later in the decade.

Which in itself explains glam's failure to crack America—not only were the glam bands visually outrageous, they were musically aggressive, something increasingly out of fashion on US Top 40 playlists. Very few rock bands were able to squeeze in hits between all the disco and soft rock clogging up the airwaves, never mind the pounding, screaming blare of glam. But one gender bender upped the ante in ways mainstream culture wasn't used to, and established a long-running career marked by cultural, artistic, and, strangely enough, *financial* innovations.

DAVID BOWIE

Born David Robert Jones in 1947, David Bowie was raised in Bromley, England. Bowie bonded deeply with his troubled older half-brother, Terry, and Terry mentored David in music and the arts. Like his schoolmates, Bowie was smitten by rock from an early age, and Little Richard became his god. Taking up saxophone as well as singing, Bowie began performing with a series of local bands. When fellow Briton Davy Jones hit the big time on *The Monkees,* Bowie adopted a new surname, taken from the Alamo martyr Jim Bowie. In 1966, Bowie met Manfred Mann's manager Ken Pitt, who had lots of showbiz connections but not much experience with rock 'n' roll. Pitt saw Bowie as a cabaret or nightclub singer like Anthony Newley (one of Bowie's many heroes), and the pair's divergent visions would delay Bowie's rise to stardom for several years. Pitt did get Bowie signed to Decca Records, where Bowie recorded a self-titled debut that went nowhere. That pattern would continue until Bowie finally scored a novelty hit with "Space Oddity," released to capitalize on the Apollo 11 moon landing in 1969.

Bowie began sporting an overtly effeminate look which Pitt, though himself gay, disliked. Some would speculate that Bowie's gender-bending was a career move (T. Rex's Marc Bolan cited Bowie's *thousands* of female conquests when asked about Bowie's sexuality), since gay men were particularly influential within the British music industry. The story goes that Bowie met his future wife Angela because the two were both sleeping with "the same bloke." Significantly, that "bloke" was a talent scout for Mercury Records. Biographer Christopher Sandford summed it up best in *Loving the Alien*: "Bowie was an active heterosexual who also slept with men."

Angela played a major role in Bowie's ascent, and her driving ambition helped motivate her sometimes passive husband. Bowie went through styles as quickly as he did groupies—after trading in folk rock on *Space Oddity* (1969), *The Man Who Sold the World* (1970) offered up a theatrical strain of heavy metal. Switching gears, *Hunky Dory* (1971) served up bright, cabaret-tinged pop and earned Bowie a US hit with the anthemic single, "Changes." The album also paid tribute to Andy Warhol, whose flamboyant Factory entourage was a major influence on Bowie's glam pose. The same year, Bowie dumped Pitt in favor of Tony DeFries, a walking caricature of a showbiz manager whose firm was immodestly named "MainMan." It would turn out to be a smart move: Bowie's next album, *The Rise and Fall of Ziggy Stardust and the Spiders from Mars* (1972), made him a superstar in the UK and Europe. Bowie and the Spiders band repeated the formula on *Aladdin Sane* and a subsequent covers LP, *Pin Ups*. But with money always a problem, Bowie broke up the Spiders, who had threatened to strike over wages.

Bowie's next LP, *Diamond Dogs* (1974), continued in the glam vein, and cracked the US Top 10. A wildly theatrical stage show made the LP's tour a major success in the gloomy post-Watergate era. But halfway through it Bowie reinvented himself as a blue-eyed soul man and bewildered his fans with a Vegas-styled soul revue on the second leg of the tour. His next album, *Young Americans* (1975), worked the "plastic soul" conceit and gave Bowie his first No. 1 US hit with "Fame." But at the same time Bowie was nursing a monstrous cocaine addiction and had holed himself up in LA, hardly ever seeing the light of day.

Bowie's occult dabbling had become an obsession, resulting

in paranoid delusions. He kept his urine and other bodily fluids in jars (don't ask) and was convinced a coven of witches were planning to kidnap him and force him to impregnate them. Everywhere he traveled he dragged around a massive library of occult texts which he read and reread constantly. And yet his stamina and creative powers remained nearly superhuman. Glasses of milk and orange juice were the sum total of his diet, along with the occasional raw egg. He starred as an alien (appropriately) in *The Man Who Fell To Earth* (1976), directed by avant-garde filmmaker Nicolas Roeg. Immediately afterward, he recorded a new disco/rock fusion album, *Station to Station*, which many fans regard as his best.

While on tour in Germany, he met Romy Haag, a transgender cabaret star. Smitten, Bowie moved to Berlin and the two androgynes embarked on an intense affair. Wandering the city by day, Bowie recorded his vaunted "Berlin Trilogy" of albums with Brian Eno by night. The first LP was *Low* (1977), which his record company hated but is now widely acknowledged as a masterpiece. Hot on its heels was *Heroes*, whose emotional title track was a worldwide hit. The final LP of the trilogy was *Lodger*, which inspired three groundbreaking videos. One of these was "Boys Keep Swinging," in which Bowie showed off the drag queen moves he learned from Haag.

Bowie kicked off the Eighties with *Scary Monsters (And Super Creeps)*, which topped the charts in the UK and just missed the US Top 10. But he spent the next three years working in film and theater (including an acclaimed run in *The Elephant Man*) while waiting for his contracts with RCA and DeFries to expire. In 1983, Bowie signed a multimillion-dollar contract with EMI and released *Let's Dance*, produced by Chic maestro

Nile Rodgers. The album was a blockbuster, and sent Bowie on a stadium tour across the world. But mainstream superstardom seemed to bore Bowie, and his next two albums were moderate commercial successes but major critical flops.

With his credibility ebbing, Bowie assembled Tin Machine with Hunt and Tony Sales, who had previously played with Iggy Pop. Tin Machine's angry rock enjoyed a brief vogue until Bowie's boredom once again overshadowed the project. After a commercially unsuccessful reunion with Rodgers in 1993, Bowie looked to rekindle his muse with an avant-garde film soundtrack for *The Buddha of Suburbia*. That caught the ear of Eno, who reteamed with Bowie for *1. Outside* (1995), the first of a planned new trilogy. The critics howled, but Bowie repaired the damage done to his core audience with the album's sprawling, avant-garde madness. He quickly followed that up with the fan favorite *Earthling* (1997), which fused techno elements with heavy metal guitars.

Bowie reunited with Seventies producer Tony Visconti and the two served up some classic, old-school Bowie on *Heathen* (2002), which fully restored the artist's reputation. The pair quickly followed up with the following year's *Reality*, but Bowie's revival would be cut short. A lifelong chain smoker, Bowie had a coronary event onstage during the Reality tour. He's been largely inactive ever since. But his influence on rock 'n' roll is incalculable and it continues to this day.

THE NEW YORK DOLLS

If rock bands were paid royalties on ideas, then the New York Dolls would be billionaires. Widely despised during their brief existence, the Dolls' trashy mix of tranny chic and gutbusting hard rock would inspire armies of Eighties imitators who sold records by the truckload. The Dolls themselves were big Stones fans; lead singer David Johansen and lead guitarist Johnny Thunders consciously modeled themselves after the Glimmer Twins. The makeup and spandex came into the act when the shambling band couldn't cut it in the big clubs and they found that downtown gay clubs would book them when they prettied themselves up enough.

The Dolls' outrageous look and vibe compensated for their serious shortcomings as musicians, and they got themselves signed to Mercury. Their 1973 debut album flopped, though it earned them a dedicated glam fan base. The title of their second LP best summed up the Dolls' story—*Too Much Too Soon*. When that too bombed, the Dolls were dropped.

It all devolved into chaos when future Sex Pistols manager Malcolm McClaren inanely reinvented them as a bizarre Soviet-chic band for their notorious "Red Patent Leather" period and the Dolls quickly fell apart. Thunders formed the Heartbreakers and took them to England just in time for the punk explosion. Johansen later reinvented himself as a pompadoured lounge lizard named Buster Poindexter. Johansen and rhythm guitarist Sylvain Sylvain formed a new version of the Dolls for a festival appearance in 2004 and decided to continue with it; they have since recorded two new albums.

In between the two Dolls incarnations was the Eighties hair metal scene, which aped the Dolls' thuggish androgyny all the way to the bank. Bands like Poison and Cinderella offered up a Californian, Heather Locklear/Farrah Fawcett–type spin on the Dolls' drugged-out Brooklyn housewife look, and cooked up derivative bubblegum-metal stompers ready made for MTV airplay. So epidemic was all the rock 'n' roll cross-dressing that

Aerosmith—hardly the manliest band themselves—scored a massive 1987 hit with the anthemic "Dude Looks Like a Lady."

QUEEN

One band that combined glam, prog, and metal was Queen, a pack of college boy rockers led by a polysexual genius with a penchant for opera. Born Farrokh Bulsara to a Parsi Indian family, Queen leader Freddie Mercury was as outrageous and flamboyant as any Soho drag queen, but he and his band of virtuosos could rock harder, faster, and louder in their glory days than nearly all their more macho competitors.

Freddie Mercury moved to London and enrolled in art school. Smitten by hard rock, he fell in with Brian May and Roger Taylor, a guitarist and a drummer whose band had just split up. Bassist John Deacon signed on, and the band Mercury dubbed "Queen" was ready to take on the world. The band gigged the London circuit and developed a sound highly influenced by the hard rock of Hendrix and Led Zeppelin and the vocal harmonies of the Beach Boys. They signed to EMI and released their self-titled debut album in 1973, which made little impact. A second LP, cleverly titled *Queen II*, followed close on its heels and the band scored a UK hit with "Seven Seas of Rhye."

May took ill in 1974, so Mercury, Taylor, and Deacon worked up the basic tracks for the fan-favorite LP *Sheer Heart Attack* without him. Mixing in poppier tracks with the usual metallic thunder, the album's first single, "Killer Queen" (an ode to a transsexual prostitute), was a hit in the US and UK. The album also featured "In the Lap of the Gods," a two-part song suite whose operatic yowling and dramatic piano passages acted as a dry run for their signature song, "Bohemian Rhapsody," released the following year. "Rhapsody" was unlike anything yet heard on Top 40 radio, starting off as an Elton John–like lament, bursting into a gonzo operatic pastiche, then into a furious heavy metal refrain before ending with Mercury's mournful twinkling and a dramatic stroke of the gong. "Rhapsody" was featured on 1975's *A Night at the Opera*, which found Queen veering further away from Zeppelinesque stomps and deeper into Beatlesesque eclectica. Their next LP, *A Day at the Races* (1976), continued this trend, with Mercury taking on gospel in the hit "Somebody to Love."

Having taken the baroque rock concept to its limit, Queen then went back to basics with 1977's *News of the World*, which featured the double A-side "We Will Rock You"/"We Are the Champions." The latter was typical Queen piano/guitar rock (and was inspired by Queen's fanatical love of soccer, contrary to rumors it was a secret gay anthem), but the former was a stark chant that had the band stomping out the song's beat atop a grand piano. Queen topped *News'* triumph in 1980 with *The Game,* which featured their rock-disco smash, "Another One Bites the Dust." *The Game* produced several other major hits and spent 43 weeks on the *Billboard* charts, selling 4.5 million copies in the US alone. Queen also became notorious for their own elaborate after-show Bacchanalias, complete with satyrs, dwarfs, and naked dancers.

Queen delved deeper into dance music on *Hot Space* (1982). The one hit was "Under Pressure," an old-school rocker featuring David Bowie, but the album's synth-driven attempts at Eurofunk deeply alienated the band's American audience. Regardless, they became the biggest band in the rest of the world, winning the day at London Live Aid in 1985. Queen set a world record for concert attendance in Brazil in 1986, playing to well over 300,000 fans. Unfortunately, that record-breaking 1986 tour would also be their last.

The unabashedly promiscuous Mercury contracted AIDS, putting Queen off the road and slowing their progress in the studio. Mercury looked visibly gaunt in the videos they produced for the singles on 1991's *Innuendo*. A brief press released confirmed that Mercury was stricken with AIDS the day before he succumbed to pneumonia.

The story didn't end there—*Innuendo* was a hit everywhere, and a skit featuring "Bohemian Rhapsody" in the hit film comedy *Wayne's World* sparked a major Queen revival in the US. In 1992, an all-star tribute concert for Mercury featuring rock's biggest stars was held at Wembley Stadium—just as the great mythology of rock 'n' roll was about to implode. May and Taylor later teamed with Bad Company vocalist Paul Rodgers (Mercury's polar opposite, stylistically) and undertook several successful tours, but the project's album went nowhere and the band parted ways.

WALK ON THE WILD SIDE
BISEXUAL CHIC IN ROCK 'N' ROLL

Rockers who've crossed gender lines—or have been rumored to.

Elvis Presley—Others vehemently deny it, but some (including *Mod Squad* star Peggy Lipton) have claimed that the King liked a little jailhouse rock now and then.

Dave Davies—His brother Ray tried to trade the openly bisexual guitar hero to David Watts in exchange for a mansion.

Jim Morrison—Biographer Steven Davis claims the Lizard King had both male and female subjects.

Jimi Hendrix—Former bandmate Noel Redding and biographer Charles Cross say the guitar god sometimes excused himself to kiss the guys.

John Lennon—Several biographers have claimed the Beatle liked to hold more than hands.

Mick Jagger—Reportedly could find satisfaction with Angie *and* Jack Flash.

David Bowie—*David Bowie*.

Laura Nyro—The archetypal Seventies singer-song-writer could have married Bill *or* Jill.

Lou Reed—Walked on the wild side with a brother/sister team, among many others.

Debbie Harry—Has let both men and women know that the carpet doesn't match the drapes.

Michael Stipe—The REM star's ambiguous lyrics are a perfect match for his sexuality.

Darby Crash—Punk casualty told his boyfriends, "What we do is secret."

Sinéad O'Connor—Nothing compares 2 U. Or U.

Ani DiFranco—Wrote the unofficial bi anthem with 1992's "In or Out."

Kurt Cobain—What else could he say?

Billie Joe Armstrong—Came clean in the song "Coming Clean."

JOAN JETT

Strangely enough, the rise of MTV in the Reaganite Eighties would do away with most of the macho Seventies rockers, and replace them with a whole new wave of androgynous pop stars like Boy George of Culture Club, Annie Lennox of the Eurythmics, A Flock of Seagulls, The Human League, and Joan Jett, who were bending genders in both directions.

Joan Jett was born Joan Marie Larkin in Philadelphia. As a kid she worshiped Suzi Quatro, and aped the glam goddess's moves, sound, and even her hairstyle. Jett eventually made her way to Los Angeles, where she co-founded the Runaways, the notorious Seventies all-girl punk band. Manager Kim Fowley presented the teenage Runaways as aggressive jailbait, which didn't go over well in Middle America. But the small but fervent punk crowd loved it, and the Runaways landed plum support spots with stars like Cheap Trick and Van Halen. They were also big in Japan, as the saying goes, and were treated like royalty when they toured the country.

But things went sour quickly, and in short order the Runaways lost their manager, their recording contract, and their lead singer, Cherie Currie. Joan Jett took center stage, but she projected a much different image than the tall, blonde, and glamorous Currie. Jett modeled herself on male rockers as well as on Quatro, and her androgynous look betrayed a distinct Ramones influence. So did her music.

The Runaways split up and Jett went solo. When no record company would bite, Jett's manager formed a vanity label for her. She recruited an all-male backup band and recorded a covers-heavy debut LP. Her defiant punk-rock theme song, "Bad Reputation," earned her some airplay. Her next album was named for her cover of an obscure glam stomper, "I Love Rock 'n Roll," that stayed atop the Hot 100 for five weeks.

Although 1982 saw Jett at the peak of her popularity, she has continued to soldier on regardless of fame or fortune. She has scored hits here and there, and continues to release albums filled with punky originals and classic covers. In the early Nineties, Jett became a mother figure for the Riot Grrl movement, and recorded a comeback LP in 1994 with members of Babes in Toyland, L7, and Bikini Kill—bands all directly influenced by Jett's music and tough-as-nails attitude. A 2010 Runaways biopic had *Twilight* star Kristen Stewart playing Jett.

PRINCE

Prince was born Prince Rogers Nelson into a musical family in Minneapolis. He suffered from epilepsy as a child, which subsided over time. He was a genuine prodigy, able to play a dazzling array of instruments almost at will. He projected a distinct effeminacy while bedding women only slightly less glamorous than himself, and wrote lusty paeans to unapologetic carnality while espousing an eccentric but decidedly apocalyptic Christian spirituality. Full of contradictions, that one.

Prince made his debut at the height of disco with the *For You* LP, playing all 27 instruments on the album. A self-titled LP followed, garnering a couple of hits on the R & B chart. But with disco in the dumpster in 1980, Prince rolled the dice and radically revamped his sound for the *Dirty Mind* LP. His new sound was sparse, punchy new-wave funk, with lyrics celebrating incest and oral sex, as well as less controversial topics. Prince polished the formula on 1981's *Controversy*, but continued his obsession with sexuality and button pushing. The lyrics of *Controversy*'s title track are notable for combining the Lord's Prayer with the immortal couplet "People call me rude / I wish we all were nude."

On his next release, the double LP *1999*, Prince pulled out all the stops. This time the music was less sparse and more expansive, with rich synths and flashy guitars adding new levels of depth. The rock ballad "Little Red Corvette" was a major hit, and the album cracked the Top 10. It also earned Prince a movie deal, which would send him into the first rank of stardom the following year. *Purple Rain* was a fictionalized autobiographical film, presenting Prince as a heroic taboo smasher. The soundtrack LP was a monster, selling well over 10 million copies. It was also Prince's first LP to feature extensive musical contributions from his backup band, The Revolution.

In 1985, Prince rushed out *Around the World in a Day*, before *Purple Rain* had even fallen from the charts. The LP was an excursion into breezy Sixties pop that left a lot of fans scratching their heads. The bewilderment would continue with the movie *Under the Cherry Moon*, which bombed at the box office and won "Worst Picture" at the Golden Raspberry Awards. Prince recovered in 1987 with the double LP *Sign o' the Times*, a multi-platinum return to his surefire rock-and-funk formula. The set also had Prince largely returning to the one-man-band routine, with only occasional contributions from other artists. True to form, he rushed out 1988's *Lovesexy*, whose cover featured a nude Prince at his most effeminate ever, surrounded by giant orchids.

Though only two years past the multi-platinum *Sign o' the Times*, Warners felt Prince was in need of a career boost and had him cut a soundtrack for the studio's 1989 blockbuster *Batman*. Little of it was actually heard in the film but the album was enough of a hit, even if most critics were unimpressed. But yet again, Prince followed *Batman* with another film flop, *Graffiti Bridge*. After that, he worked in a more generically funky vein, and he spent a good chunk of the Nineties fighting his record company, which was trying to tame his relentless release schedule. Prince notoriously changed his name to a symbol until the dispute was resolved. He later escaped his contract, formed his own label, and sold records off his website. Prince remains popular as a live artist, but his adherence to the Jehovah's Witnesses sect and some controversial political statements have shaded his reputation with the hipsters. He still looks fabulous, however.

JANE'S ADDICTION

Jane's Addiction emerged from the LA goth scene (a goth scene in LA was even more unlikely than a punk one) of the mid-Eighties. Lead singer Perry Farrell had previously fronted a goth band, PsiCom, whose members all quit to join the Hare Krishna movement. Farrell met bassist Eric Avery, whose playing was influenced by moody post-punk. The pair completed the lineup with two unlikely comrades: drummer Stephen Perkins and guitarist David Navarro, whose their tastes were more in line with the Hollywood glam metal scene.

Jane's took the city by storm, defining and ruling the alt rock scene. The band offered up punk energy, post-punk atmospherics, and metal flash, and Farrell was a tireless entertainer whose vocal shortcomings were more than made up for by his shamanic energy and visual imagination. The band's first album was a live set recorded for an independent label, but its major-label debut, *Nothing's Shocking* (1988), hit the alternative scene like a freight train. *Shocking* tore through a dizzying array of moods and rhythms, incorporating metallic rockers, Chili Peppers–type funk, and even a bit of cocktail jazz. Soon, college rock jangle was out and power chords were in. Jane's had taught the scenesters that you could *rock* and still be hip. The band toured hard, but was menaced by the usual drug and ego problems, delaying the release of its 1990 album, *Ritual de la Habitual*.

A more sprawling affair than *Shocking*, *Ritual* displayed a range of musical influences, drawing comparisons to Led Zeppelin and the Grateful Dead. It also produced a major hit with the funky "Been Caught Stealing." Jane's then embarked on a grueling, yearlong tour that included Farrell's "Lollapalooza" brainchild, a touring festival of grunge and alt rock bands like Butthole Surfers and Nine Inch Nails, with rapper Ice-T and Siouxsie & the Banshees thrown in for seasoning.

THE FUTURE OF FEMME

Taking a more direct approach to the archetype was the queer-core movement, which wed gay-themed lyrics to pop-punk and often added generous servings of self-deprecating humor. The genre was predated by early-Eighties gay hardcore bands like the Dicks and the Big Boys, both from Austin, Texas. Queer-core pioneers Pansy Division went on to tour with Green Day in 1994 and serenaded teenyboppers with cuts like "Bill & Ted's Homosexual Adventure" and "Dick of Death."

With the rise of macho, frat-boy genres like grunge and nu metal in the early Nineties, androgyny would mostly fade from the rock scene, leaving only a few scattered acts like AFI, Tokio Hotel, and *American Idol* runner-up Adam Lambert to keep the neo-Galloi flame burning. But rock is ruled by cycles and trends, and a new glam explosion could be right around the corner. After all, teenage girls love nothing better than a hot guy in mascara and nail polish.

WITCHY WOMEN:
THE MODERN MYSTERIES OF ISIS

As a universal mother figure, Isis represented the home and family. But at the same time she was also the goddess of magic and sex. This made sense to the Romans—they *loved* sex, and omens and soothsaying were an important function of State. Magic was taken for granted and was an integral part of all religion.

But the Isis archetype had no presence in early American culture—no positive one at least. Theosophy changed that in the 19th century (see *Isis Unveiled*) and the image of the confident, spiritually minded yet sexy woman would reemerge in more freethinking circles. Isis also became popular with the emergence of Wicca and neopaganism in the Thirties and

Forties. And the Isis archetype also became a powerful one with the rock world in the Sixties.

GRACE SLICK

Probably the first modern Isis in rock 'n' roll is Grace Slick, the acid queen of San Francisco rock. Born Grace Barnett Wing in 1939, Slick moved to San Francisco in the waning days of the Beat movement. There she met an aspiring filmmaker and part-time musician named Jerry Slick, and the two were wed. Grace paid the bills working as a model by day while the Great Society—the band she and Jerry formed in 1965—wowed the hipsters at night. This band traded in a darker, more surreal kind of psychedelic rock than their Bay Area comrades, drawing on Indian ragas and other exotic musical influences. Slick's arch manner, keening yowl, and commanding stage presence were something new in rock 'n' roll. Her friend and rival Janis Joplin was drawing on traditional rock idioms, but Slick was more influenced by European and bohemian antecedents.

SF superstars Jefferson Airplane lured Slick from the Society when their own female singer went on maternity leave, and Slick brought the future Airplane hits "Somebody to Love" and "White Rabbit" along with her. Her lyrics tended to be sarcastic commentaries on the social mores Slick chafed under in her debutante days, and her compositions were often based in minor keys and featured slow, strange syncopations, giving her songs a witchy, droning feel. That effect was heightened by Slick's imposing stage presence, the mind-bending light shows, and of course, the drugs.

Though unmistakably feminine and voraciously sexual (her own conquests included Jim Morrison), Slick had a mischievous streak, which was often fueled by her weakness for booze. She performed topless at an outdoor festival, and in blackface on prime-time TV. Slick even planned to spike Tricky Dick Nixon's tea with LSD when her old deb connections landed her an invitation to the White House in 1970.

Slick's problems with alcohol resulted in a serious car crash in 1971, but her marriage to Airplane leader Paul Kantner offered a stabilizing influence. Together the two entered the Jefferson Starship project in the Seventies soft-rock gold rush, where a new Slick-inspired diva would ultimately take the witchy woman crown. Following a 1987 Jefferson Airplane reunion, Slick herself quit performing in 1989, saying she was repulsed by "old people playing rock 'n' roll."

STEVIE NICKS

Raised in Southern California, Stevie Nicks began her career duetting with her boyfriend Lindsay Buckingham. Their 1973 LP caught the attention of Mick Fleetwood, whose singer/ guitarist Bob Welch had quit Fleetwood Mac to pursue a solo career. With Buckingham and Nicks aboard, the new-model Mac recorded their now classic 1975 self-titled album, which hit the top of the US charts on its way to selling 5 million copies. Nicks's hypnotic ballad "Rhiannon" became the band's new signature song. "Rhiannon" was inspired by a novel about a woman possessed by the spirit of an ancient Welsh witch, and from that point on the witchy vibe hung over Nicks like a veil.

The pressures of stardom and the band's generous drug intake nearly broke it apart, but they opted to stick it out for 1977's *Rumours*, which has sold over 40 million copies worldwide. The album produced several hit singles, but once again a spooky Nicks number, "Dreams," took top honors. That pattern continued with band's thorny 1979 double LP *Tusk*. The only obvious hit was "Sara," Nicks's lush ode to her not-quite-secret affair with Fleetwood. Nicks also stoked her mystical aura with the witchy "Sisters of the Moon" and the ghostly "Angel."

Nicks had scored hits duetting with other artists, and she finally struck out on her own with her 1981 solo debut, *Belladonna* (shades of Hecate). Powered by the hit single "Edge of Seventeen," the album topped the US charts, outselling *Tusk*. Nicks worked tirelessly throughout the Eighties, juggling her solo career as well as her role in Fleetwood Mac. She even stayed on when Buckingham left in 1988, but took time out to overcome a long-standing struggle with tranquilizers, which in turn replaced a cocaine addiction that had nearly burned a hole through her nose. The classic Fleetwood Mac lineup reunited in 1997 for an MTV special and world tour, and the group remains active (sans the retired Christine McVie). Nicks has also continued to tour and record as a solo act.

PATTI SMITH

Since the Isis archetype in rock is all about strong women on the edges of the mainstream, it's no surprise that the punk movement would produce several of them. One of these is Patti Smith, a crucial figure in the development of punk and alt rock, and one of the foremost poets in rock. Raised in New Jersey, Smith dropped out of college in 1967 when she became pregnant. Giving the baby up for adoption, Smith moved to Greenwich Village, where she met the photographer Robert

Mapplethorpe. The two began an affair and circulated in the active poetry and art scenes in downtown Manhattan. Dabbling in music journalism, Smith also befriended (and collaborated with) Blue Öyster Cult, and would have a long relationship with BÖC's Allen Lanier.

In '74, Smith began performing in a duo with guitarist Lenny Kaye. The two enlisted other players for "the Patti Smith Group," whose first single was bankrolled by Mapplethorpe. That earned Smith a contract with Arista and the band recorded the 1975 LP *Horses*, which featured Smith's mythopoetic meditation on Van Morrison's Sixties classic "Gloria." Although Smith's "Gloria" begins with a defiant dismissal of Christian theology, she was raised a Jehovah's Witness and remains deeply spiritual. After an onstage accident that resulted in a broken neck, Smith returned to recording in '78 with *Easter*, which featured her hit version of "Because the Night." *Easter's* stirring, mystical title track has Smith proclaiming she is "the holy ground," "the endless seed of mystery," and "the evening star," and so on. Intentionally or not, Smith's litany is nearly identical to a typical ancient invocation to Isis.

In 1978, Smith met former MC5 guitarist Fred "Sonic" Smith, who inspired Patti's next two singles, "Frederic" and "Dancing Barefoot," both featured on *Wave* (1979). The two Smiths then retired from music to raise a family. They returned in 1988 with Patti's *Dream of Life* LP, but Sonic took ill and would die in 1994. Following his death, Patti returned to performing full-time with the Group in 1996, releasing the powerful *Gone Again* LP, an elegy for Sonic, Mapplethorpe, and others by then departed. It's worth noting that Isis was often called "the Widow." Smith has remained active in music and commands an almost universal respect in the rock community. Her most recent LP revealingly features a cover of Grace Slick's "White Rabbit."

KATE BUSH

While Nicks and Smith were rocking the States, a precocious young singer-songwriter working along similar lines emerged in the UK. Born to an English father and Irish mother, Bush enjoyed an idyllic upbringing in the British countryside. Her parents were both musical and Bush began writing demos that caught the ear of David Gilmour, who helped broker a contract for Bush with EMI when she was only 16. Combining a fascination with sex and mysticism with a shockingly powerful vocal range, Kate Bush bridged the gap between prog rock and the new art pop movement of the Eighties.

Her debut album, 1978's *The Kick Inside*, was a UK hit, as was the single "Wuthering Heights," which Bush sings from the point of view of Brontë's ghostly heroine, Catherine. Throughout her career, Bush explored such ethereal themes in her lyrics, much to the annoyance of some highbrow critics. The dazzlingly beautiful Bush also shocked audiences when she performed on *Saturday Night Live* writhing atop a grand piano in a gold-lamé catsuit. That kind of raw sexuality was out of fashion for rock in the dowdy late Seventies, though Michelle Pfeiffer later stole the routine in *The Fabulous Baker Boys*.

After a rushed sophomore effort, Bush went to the top of the UK charts with her third LP, *Never for Ever* (1980). The album displayed her growing prowess in the studio, as well as a burgeoning political awareness, resulting in UK hits like the anti-nuke "Breathing" and "Army Dreamers." A relentless perfectionist, Bush quit touring to focus on recording and video production. She made use of then new sampling technology on *The Dreaming* (1982), a dark, moody album whose abrasive atmospherics and multitracked vocals displayed the influence of post-punk bands like PiL and Killing Joke.

Trapped in the netherworld between prog rock and post-punk, Bush occupied an uncertain place in pop music until 1985's *Hounds of Love*, whose warm dance-pop was inspired by her relocation to rural Ireland. "Running Up That Hill," "The Big Sky" and "Cloudbursting" were the hits, but the centerpiece of the album was "The Ninth Wave," a stirring song suite that tells the story of a woman lost at sea who relives past lives (including an incarnation as an accused witch) and astrally projects into the cosmos. All very Seventies and cosmic, but Bush made it work in the cold-hearted Eighties.

The following year, Bush hit the UK Top 10 with "Don't Give Up," a duet with Peter Gabriel, and in 1989 she reteamed with David Gilmour for the album *The Sensual World,* which drew inspiration from James Joyce's *Ulysses.* In 1991, she scored a UK hit with a reggae cover of Elton John's "Rocket Man." And then, following 1993's *The Red Shoes,* Kate Bush disappeared. Rumors and legends grew, and Bush finally broke the silence in 2005 with *Aerial,* a double-disk set that many fans consider her magnum opus. Making no concessions to modernity, Bush unleashed a postmodern pagan liturgy to the sky and sea, with her familiar blend of lush, sensuous music, spoken-word passages, and Pink Floyd-esque found-sound flourishes.

Bush's mix of musical virtuosity and assertive individualism altered the DNA of the postmodern chanteuse. Along with Grace Slick and Stevie Nicks, Bush helped break the vixen/earth mother duopoly on women's roles in rock. In the wake of *Hounds of Love*, the Canadian singer Sarah MacLachlan, the American Tori Amos, and the controversial Irish artist Sinéad O'Connor drank deep from Bush's blending of music and mysticism, but they would enjoy greater commercial success in North America than the more idiosyncratic Bush enjoyed. A new genre of women singers following in Bush's footsteps inspired MacLachlan to create the Lilith Fair, a traveling festival of women artists that included adult-alternative hitmakers like Fiona Apple, Paula Cole, Natalie Merchant, and Lisa Loeb, all of whom owed at least a spiritual debt to Kate Bush.

SIOUXSIE & THE BANSHEES

If Kate Bush was the bright light of the new British rock revival of the late Seventies, she had a mad mirror image in London who was its black hole. In 1976, Susan Ballion, raised in Bowie's hometown of Bromley, renamed herself "Siouxsie Sioux" and redefined the witchy woman archetype with a fury and vengeance unseen this side of Britain's Hammer horror classics of the late Sixties. Like her punk compatriots, Siouxsie came of age in the glam era. As that movement faded, Siouxsie and her "Bromley Contingent" friends latched on to the Sex Pistols, acting as their instant entourage. Siouxsie became a master of provocation, parading around topless, or in bondage gear, or in Nazi regalia, or some combination of the three. Her first appearance with any Banshees lineup was an excruciating 20-minute improvisation where Siouxsie howled the Lord's Prayer and other random shards of lyrics while her band (which included future Sex Pistol Sid Vicious on drums) thrashed away behind her.

Siouxsie eventually settled on a lineup consisting of then-boyfriend Steve Severin on bass, drummer Kenny Morris, and guitarist John McKay. Defying rock convention, the Banshees fashioned a dark, angular take on punk inspired by the Velvet Underground and horror movie soundtracks. Though Siouxsie's lyrics were usually based in macabre and occult themes, the band lightened up with "Hong Kong Garden," which won them a Top 10 UK hit in 1978.

Unhappy with Siouxsie's imperious manner, McKay and Morris quit the band on the eve of a UK tour. Enraged but determined, Sioux and Severin enlisted Slits drummer Peter Clarke (aka Budgie) and Cure guitarist Robert Smith to fill concert and TV obligations. Budgie stayed on for their next album, *Kaleidoscope* (1980), which hit the UK Top 5. John McGeoch was hired on as full-time guitarist, and in 1981 the Banshees unleashed *Juju*, a goth rock landmark that brought an unprecedented witchy power to popular music. Egged on by the Banshees' eldritch throbbing, Siouxsie howled gruesome lyrics inspired by necrophilia, tabloid Satanism, and black magic.

One might suppose that a proper English girl like Siouxsie shouldn't have been harboring such dark thoughts, but her upbringing was anything but idyllic. Her alcoholic father died when she was 14, and soon afterward she contracted ulcerative colitis, an excruciating intestinal affliction that nearly killed her. That kind of physical agony can color one's outlook.

The Banshees lightened their approach a bit for 1982's *A Kiss in the Dreamhouse,* a collection of psychedelic paeans to polymorphous sex. But in 1983, McGeoch's drinking got him sacked and Smith was brought back. This lineup recorded 1984s *Hyena* LP, featuring morbid tracks like "Bring Me the Head of the Preacher Man" and "Pointing Bone," a song inspired by Aboriginal witchcraft.

The Banshees went through guitarists the way Spinal Tap did drummers, and Smith left to reform The Cure. John Carruthers signed on for *Tinderbox*, which saw the Banshees return to the arcane guitar rock of *Juju*. But Carruthers was no McGeoch, and despite the usual lyrical carnage, the album failed to recapture *Juju's* twisted intensity. The Banshees changed gears, expanding to a five-piece and trading in a more commercial alt rock sound. They found success in the US, but split up in 1996. Not missing a beat, Siouxsie and Budgie reformed The Creatures side project and picked up where the Banshees left off. After the duo divorced, Siouxsie carried on with a solo career.

COCTEAU TWINS

One of the many British bands to follow in Siouxsie's footsteps was Scotland's Cocteau Twins, composed of singer Elizabeth Fraser, guitarist Robin Guthrie, and bassist/pianist Simon Raymonde. Signed on the strength of a homemade demo submitted to the iconic 4AD label, the Twins became an underground sensation in the UK. The Twins' dark, droning noise was highly derivative of the Banshees but was distinguished by Fraser's hypnotic vocals, which would later be described as those of an "alien," a "witch," or in the words of one journalist, "the Voice of God."

The Twins were astonishingly prolific in their heyday, and Fraser's otherworldly strangeness had an immeasurable influence on female artists looking to circumvent the limited roles of vixen or earth mother. Ironically, their British breakthrough in 1984 came when Fraser and Guthrie recorded a mesmerizing cover of Tim Buckley's "Song to the Siren" for 4AD group project This Mortal Coil. "Siren" became a sleeper hit, spending over a hundred weeks on the UK independent chart. That year, the Twins also released landmark LP *Treasure*, which included another song to a Siren, "Lorelei."

The Twins reached their commercial peak with 1990's synth-heavy *Heaven or Las Vegas*. Things then got a bit rough; Guthrie and Raymonde developed drug problems. For Fraser, the pressures of motherhood and problems with her vocal cords kicked loose memories of childhood abuse, resulting in a breakdown that required hospitalization. After two underwhelming albums, the Twins rallied for a triumphant concert tour and returned to the studio the following year, only to have Fraser walk out forever in late '97, which may or may not have been triggered by her onetime lover Jeff Buckley's death earlier in the year. Eerily, Jeff was the son of the composer of "Song of the Siren." Even more eerily, he drowned in the Mississippi River.

The Cocteau Twins had a major influence in the UK and European underground pop scene, especially the "Shoegaze" scene, which featured such Fraser admirers as My Bloody Valentine and Lush. Kooky Icelandic poptart Bjork's early work with the Sugarcubes shows an unmistakable Cocteau influence, as does Delores Riordan's with the Cranberries. Irish New Age songstress Enya took the softer passages of the Cocteau sound directly to the bank, especially on her breakthrough single "Orinoco Flow," a Cocteau-like title if ever there was one.

ART DAMAGE:
HERMETIC ROCK

The word *Hermetic* calls up images of medieval alchemists, locked away in basement laboratories, breathing in deadly chemical vapors while desperately seeking to crack the code of Creation. The term itself comes from the legendary demigod Hermes Trismegistus, a synthesis of the Greek Hermes and the Egyptian Thoth, whose fabled *Corpus Hermeticum* was said to contain the secrets of the Universe. This tradition was revived with gusto in the Sixties when a host of new electronic gadgets lured musicians and producers into round-the-clock recording sessions.

The Hermetic strain in rock is almost as phallocentric as heavy metal and hardcore punk. Hermetic artists focus on technique and equipment, using the studio itself as a musical instrument. Hermetic bands are usually driven by artistic concerns more than commercial ones, and they often compete with one another to expand the formal constraints of form, technique, and technology.

The great Hermetic hero of the pre-rock era is undoubtedly the original American guitar hero, Les Paul (1915–2009). Paul not only created the solid-body electric guitar, but also pioneered multitrack recording, tape echo, and a whole host of other technological innovations aside from being a popular performer himself. Paul's work formed the foundation not only of Hermetic rock, but of rock 'n' roll itself.

PINK FLOYD

The first true Hermetic band was the Beatles, who retired from touring in 1966 and holed themselves up at Abbey Road for marathon sessions with George Martin. But the first prominent band to establish a distinct Hermetic identity from its inception was Pink Floyd. The band formed out of a group of friends in 1963: Syd Barrett on guitars and vocals, Roger Waters on bass, Richard Wright on organ, and drummer Nick Mason. Moving away from their choc-a-bloc R & B roots, Barrett began writing a body of arch, off-kilter pop songs, characterized by clever wordplay and unexpected chord breaks. The band plugged into the nascent psychedelic rock scene and began incorporating lengthy instrumental jams into its live sets, which were augmented by mind-blowing light shows at venues like the legendary UFO Club.

Following the success of the singles "Arnold Layne" and "See Emily Play," the Floyd recorded their first LP, *Piper at the*

Gates of Dawn. Though it's now considered a classic, recordings of their live sets prove that *Piper* didn't quite capture the power that the band could generate onstage. Floyd's future grew cloudy soon after *Piper's* release, when Barrett became increasingly erratic and unpredictable. Floyd enlisted David Gilmour to take up the slack on guitar, but Barrett was canned not long afterward. He contributed one track to the second Floyd LP, *Saucerful of Secrets,* but the band found it could do just fine without him, and delved more deeply into cosmic soundscapes on cuts like "Set the Controls for the Heart of the Sun."

Floyd continued in this vein for several more LPs, supplementing their income with soundtrack works for films like *More* and *The Valley.* With 1971's *Meddle,* the band's musical chaos began to cohere, and this set the stage for *Dark Side of the Moon* in 1973, at once their most successful and most atypical LP. *Dark Side* found Floyd at its most accessible, boasting 10 conventionally structured tracks. It also outsold all their previous records combined and stayed on the charts forever.

Perhaps feeling they'd compromised too much, their next LP, *Wish You Were Here* (1975), featured a mere four songs, one of them split over two sides. The title track was a pleasant ballad, but the 7-minute-plus "Welcome to the Machine" traded in harsh electronic noodling, and the bitter "Have a Cigar" mocked their own record company. Floyd followed that up with the Orwell-inspired *Animals* in '77. Again, the LP featured only four songs, again with one split in two. *Animals* was angrier and more abrasive than *Wish,* and acted as a showcase for Gilmour's innovative approach to electronic guitar effects.

But the band was falling apart, and they enlisted an outside producer after several years of self-production. Waters had devised an overarching concept he titled "The Wall," a nightmare story of a mad rock star who becomes a fascist demagogue, and the new songs were a mix of short musical vignettes and terse, heavy stompers laden with Wagnerian portent. Though much of the music and concept was Waters's, it was Gilmour's startlingly innovative guitar heroics and seductive vocal harmonies that were *The Wall's* selling point. This mirrored a strange dynamic within the band; Waters saw himself as the driving creative force of Pink Floyd, but it was Gilmour's lush, natural musicality that made them superstars.

The tension broke and Waters took full control on the poorly received 1983 LP *The Final Cut*. Waters declared that Floyd was over, but Gilmour and Mason disagreed and reconvened for 1987's *A Momentary Lapse of Reason*, a huge hit that introduced Pink Floyd to a new generation. Waters heckled the band from the sidelines, but this new Floyd continued on for several massive tours, eventually releasing two live LPs and one last studio album. The classic lineup re-formed one last time for a set at the 2008 Live8 benefit concert in London, shortly before Wright's death.

JIMI HENDRIX

At the same time Pink Floyd was making its name, a musician imported from America would strike terror in the hearts of every guitar player in England and would go on to influence, directly or otherwise, every single player who followed. James Marshall Hendrix was born in 1944 and grew up in a broken home in the Seattle area. Given his first guitar at age 15, the lonely, sensitive young Hendrix practiced constantly and developed a radically individual style in his endless hours of solitude. After a stint in the army, Hendrix honed his chops with a series of local bands, and then became a guitar-for-hire for the top soul and R & B artists of the time. One of these was Little Richard, whose flamboyant performances would have an enormous effect on the young whiz kid.

In New York, Hendrix caught the eye of Chas Chandler, a musician looking to move into artist management. Blown away by Hendrix's superhuman skill set, Chandler took Jimi over to England. Two top local players, drummer Mitch Mitchell and bassist Noel Redding, were enlisted for the Jimi Hendrix Experience. The trio began gigging in London and Paris, creating instant converts everywhere they played.

In 1967, the band unleashed its classic debut, *Are You Experienced?*, and nothing would ever be the same again. Jimi's breakthrough in the US came in June of '67 with an incendiary set at the Monterey Pop Festival, where the band played alongside such Sixties legends as the Who and the Jefferson Airplane. Everyone agreed that Hendrix blew them all off the stage.

Hendrix not only played the guitar, he used the equipment as an instrument, accentuating the harmonic overtones of the amplifiers' feedback and sustain. Jimi also made full use of the growing array of electronic effects being put on the market. He was astonishingly prolific, following up with *Axis: Bold as Love* before the end of '67. Hendrix essentially created the modern power ballad with the epic "Little Wing," since covered by artists such as Rod Stewart and Sting. Inspired by epic psych-outs like *Sgt. Pepper*, Hendrix recorded the *Electric Ladyland* double LP in '68, which boasted an all-star cast of players including Steve Winwood and Al Kooper and topped the charts in the US.

When Noel Redding and Hendrix had a falling out, Jimi played a legendary set at Woodstock with a pickup band he named Gypsy, Sun and Rainbows. That in turn evolved into the short-lived Band of Gypsys, a more soul-oriented outfit featuring Billy Cox and Buddy Miles. Hendrix began laying down tracks in New York during the week and touring on weekends with a new Experience composed of himself, Mitchell, and Cox. Tracks for what would be the posthumous 1971 LP *The Cry of Love* were recorded in Electric Lady studios in Greenwich Village, which Hendrix co-founded.

Tragically, Hendrix would die of an adverse reaction to a mix of red wine and sleeping pills in London in 1970, cutting short a remarkable career that could have gone in any number of directions. Dark rumors circulated about his manager and the ambulance crew, as the musician's death occurred at a time when other pivotal rock gods were dying.

Hendrix's prodigious drug use and sexual indulgences might paint him as a Dionysian, but his tireless work ethic and continual technical innovations—as well as his tendency to lock himself away in the studio—tell a different story. The shy kid obsessed with sci-fi and fantasy was always a major part of his persona, no matter how outrageous or extroverted he seemed onstage. And his dedication and virtuosity would have a tremendous impact, particularly on a new generation of British rock bands in the late Sixties and early Seventies.

KING CRIMSON

Comprising a gaggle of jazzbos and classically trained virtuosos fronted by singer Greg Lake and guitarist Robert Fripp, King Crimson pioneered a scorching and complex spin on psychedelia that came to be known alternately as art rock, progressive rock, or simply "prog."

Following Crimson's example, a whole host of prog bands emerged, some of them late-period psych bands that composed sprawling symphonies with self-indulgent soloing and neo-Tolkienesque fantasy lyrics. But after the band's 1969 landmark debut, *In the Court of the Crimson King*, Fripp found himself at sea when most of the band quit. (Lake left after Crimson's second LP to form Emerson, Lake, and Palmer.) Bands like Genesis and Yes offered up a more digestible version of prog and went on to earn hits while the Crims floundered, hobbled by personnel problems and musical confusion.

Fripp's fortunes brightened in 1972. Pile-driving bassist John Wetton signed on, bringing his uncannily Lake-like vocals aboard. Drummer Bill Bruford defected from Yes at the height of their popularity, bored with their increasingly poppy sound. Beginning with 1972's *Larks' Tongues in Aspic*, the new-model King Crimson offered up a new hybrid of prog and metal, alternating between cerebral jamming and power-mad freak-outs. By 1974's *Red*, the cerebral stuff faded and Crimson reached a new plateau of abstract musical violence, equaling or surpassing anything Black Sabbath ever put to vinyl. Though it didn't burn up the charts, *Red* would be a major influence on the grunge and alt metal scenes, influencing acts like Nirvana and Tool.

Drained by *Red's* intensity and increasingly obsessed with the mathematical mysticism of J.G. Bennett, Fripp dissolved Crimson after a tour and live album. He became an itinerant guitar wizard, playing with Brian Eno on the groundbreaking ambient LPs *No Pussyfooting* and *Evening Star*, doing session work for Blondie, David Bowie, and Talking Heads, as well as producing LPs by Peter Gabriel, Daryl Hall, and the Roches.

In 1980, Fripp formed a new-model King Crimson, inviting singer-guitarist Adrian Belew and bassist Tony Levin to join him and Bruford in developing a whole new kind of Hermetic rock 'n' roll. Beginning with 1981's *Discipline,* the new Crimson built their songs around dense, noodly rhythms, over which Belew crooned and sprayed his trademark guitar wizardry. As with the *Red*-era Crims, this lineup produced three studio LPs and a live set before splitting up. In the early Nineties, Fripp relaunched King Crimson and they've carried on in one form or another since then, unleashing all sorts of mind-bending sound experiments along the way.

BRIAN ENO

Fripp's partner in crime over the years has been Brian Eno, probably the definitive example of the Hermetic archetype in rock history. Eno began his career as a militantly androgynous "nonmusician" bleating out atonal shards of untutored synth noise for art/glam legends Roxy Music. But Eno soon found himself growing bored with the repetitive demands of a successful rock band, and set off for a solo career in 1973.

Eno's first solo LP, *Here Come the Warm Jets,* enlisted the cream of early-Seventies art rock players and set them to work on a weird mélange of styles that essentially created the templates for post-punk and new wave. Eno repeated the process on *Taking Tiger Mountain by Strategy,* and then vastly expanded his sonic palette on 1975's *Another Green World,* which featured career-peak performances by Fripp, Phil Collins on drums, and bass virtuoso Percy Jones.

In a mad blaze, Eno defined the modern ambient style on *Discreet Music*, rejoined Fripp for *Evening Star*, and recorded with Krautrockers Cluster before reenlisting Fripp, Collins, Jones, and other stars for *Before and After Science*, which refined the formula established on *Green World*. After that achievement, Eno took a break from solo work to join David Bowie in Berlin for the latter's famed "Berlin Trilogy," contributing to *Low* and *Heroes*, both released in 1977, and *Lodger*, in 1979.

During all this, Eno found time for a series of groundbreaking ambient explorations, releasing *Music for Airports*, *Music for Films*, and a set with the German duo Cluster, all in 1978. "Rock music isn't capable of producing that spiritual quality anymore," Eno said. "Despite all the criticism that's been made of psychedelic music, it certainly was committed to the production of an expanded awareness."

THE TALKING HEADS

Eno's beliefs notwithstanding, he still signed on to produce Devo's first LP and the Talking Heads' second. The Heads were formed at the prestigious Rhode Island School of Design by singer/guitarist David Byrne, bassist Tina Weymouth, and drummer Chris Frantz. The band relocated to New York, playing on the nascent punk circuit and at art-school parties. Multi-instrumentalist Jerry Harrison signed on and the band recorded its debut, *Talking Heads '77*, for Sire. The Heads' sound was tense and wiry, and their image was button-down nerdy. The band serenaded shaken New Yorkers with their single "Psycho Killer" in the midst of the Son of Sam murders, and the song was a huge, timely hit. Eno expanded the Heads' dry, scratchy palette of sounds considerably for *More Songs About Buildings and Food,* and the band reached the Top 40 in early '79 with a druggy cover of Al Green's "Take Me to the River."

After producing the Heads' 1979 classic *Fear of Music* (which produced another paranoia-rock classic in "Life During Wartime"), Eno and David Byrne began a landmark body of experiments on African musical themes, resulting in the classic 1980 Talking Heads LP *Remain in Light* and the 1981 Byrne-Eno opus *My Life in the Bush of Ghosts,* widely cited as a primary influence on late-Eighties hip-hop. After Eno departed, the Heads broke through to pop stardom in 1983, when they filmed the seminal concert documentary *Stop Making Sense,* directed by Jonathan Demme. That marked an artistic high point for the Heads, whose sound subsequently devolved into a light new-wave pop. By the time David Byrne landed on the cover of *Time,* the Heads' creative glory days were long behind them.

PETER GABRIEL

Another prog vet who moved into the futurist rock sphere is Peter Gabriel, former lead singer for Genesis. In the early Seventies, Gabriel became known for his outrageous costumes and performances, confounding audiences with his flamboyant behavior and rambling onstage monologues. But Genesis was largely a cult act during Gabriel's tenure, and his final album with the band was 1975's two-LP epic *The Lamb Lies Down on Broadway,* a concept album based on Gabriel's nightmare vision of New York City.

Tension with the band peaked when Gabriel lapsed into a

depression after his first child was born with serious health problems, and he left following the tour in support of *Lamb*. Happily, Gabriel earned a hit on his first solo LP in 1977 with "Solisbury Hill." The rest of the album was polished mainstream rock (crafted by Pink Floyd/Alice Cooper producer Bob Ezrin), not quite what Gabriel wanted to be playing. He enlisted Robert Fripp for a stripped-down second LP, setting the stage for his landmark 1980 set (also self-titled). Gabriel enlisted an all-star cast, including Fripp, Kate Bush, and Phil Collins, around whom producer Steve Lillywhite sculpted a dark, dense electronic rock sound. Bush duetted on the antiwar "Games Without Frontiers," whose surreal video features a typically manic performance by Gabriel.

Gabriel took full advantage of an exploding variety of new electronics on his next album, 1982's *Security*. The key track on that set was "Shock the Monkey," for which Gabriel produced a terrifying video depicting a businessman's dissociative breakdown. Gabriel then made his mainstream move with *So* (1986), a radio-friendly batch of soft rock which rocketed to the top of the charts with the award-winning animated video for "Sledgehammer." Next, drawing in a host of musicians from around the world, Gabriel composed an epic 1989 soundtrack for Martin Scorcese's *The Last Temptation of Christ*, for which he won a Grammy and a Golden Globe Award. Gabriel takes ages to create his meticulously crafted albums, but he has become an elder statesman of British art rock. He's been active in political and environmental causes over the years as well.

SONIC YOUTH

In the midst of Eno's Seventies hyperactivity, he found time to produce 1978's *No New York* compilation, documenting the so-called No Wave scene that coalesced around extremist noisemakers like Mars and DNA. No Wave didn't last long at all and even most diehard punks couldn't stomach it, but one band inspired by the self-conscious artiness of No Wave would develop a radically dissonant style that would have an enormous influence on independent rock in the Eighties and Nineties.

Sonic Youth—guitarist/singer Thurston Moore, his wife, bassist/singer Kim Gordon, drummer Steve Shelley, and guitarist Lee Renaldo—fused the accidental innovations of No Wave to garage punk and various avant-garde influences and created a perennially hip style that alternates between elegy and assault. Sonic Youth used odd tunings and treatments (playing their guitars with drumsticks, etc.), adding ear-bleeding volume to hipness and irony before they had become marketing tools. Though their profile is considerably lower these days, the band has endured by staying committed to an esoteric musical vision. Even a best-of CD created for the Starbucks coffee chain couldn't tarnish their evergreen indie cred.

RADIOHEAD

Radiohead began life straddling the grunge and Britpop movements and scored a major hit in 1993 with "Creep." But it was with its second album, *The Bends* (1995), that the band began to show off, drawing upon influences as varied as Pink Floyd, Queen, Echo and the Bunnymen, and Nirvana. Radiohead expanded its sonic horizons even further with 1997s *OK*

Computer, generally recognized as one of the most important albums of the Nineties. The album's first single, "Paranoid Android," earned comparisons to "Bohemian Rhapsody," and the album was a commercial success as well, going double platinum in the US.

Then, Radiohead dived headfirst into post-punk and post-rock idioms on 2000's *Kid A*, a polarizing set of electronic noise, ambient experiments, and abrasive bebop skronking. Despite the controversy, the album went to No. 1 in the US and UK. A companion set from the same sessions, *Amnesiac*, was released the following year. The band stumbled on 2003's *Hail to the Thief*, a halfhearted compromise between conventional rock and their recent experimentalism.

After an extensive bout of touring, Radiohead escaped its contract with Capitol and released its 2007 album *In Rainbows* on its website. Synthesizing all the various contradictory impulses the band had juggled in the past, *In Rainbows* was hailed as a return to form. Radiohead has survived nearly all its early Nineties contemporaries, and perhaps the group's refusal to repeat themselves is a major part of that. It's not a guarantee, but adherence to Hermetic principles often lends artists a longevity others can't manage.

Fans of prog, post-punk, and art rock are usually thoughtful types who are in it for the long haul, as are the artists themselves. Hermetic principles have even migrated into the metal realm, and several cult metal acts like Opeth, Tool, and Mastodon are heavily influenced by prog and its various offshoots.

METAL MILITIAS:
THE NEW KORYBANTES

The use of guitar amplifier distortion was at one time more an accident than an innovation. Amplifiers were modest in size in comparison with today's behemoths, and as bands cranked it to fill larger halls, that typical distorted rock sound was actually the sound of equipment failure. But in the late Sixties, a movement emerged that would make distortion the object of near-religious devotion and inspire an elaborate, dedicated, and widespread culture of machismo and musical violence not seen since the days of the Korybantes. Rockabilly rebel Link Wray is generally credited with the first intentional use of distortion on his 1958 hit "Rumble," perhaps the first instrumental to be banned from radio (albeit for its violent title).

Wray poked holes in the paper cone of his amplifier's speaker to achieve the effect.

THE KINKS

"Rumble" lit a generation of young guitarists on fire, but the first to make the distorted guitar sound part of his style was Dave Davies of the legendary British band the Kinks. Davies experimented with a number of different techniques to develop a reliably raunchy sound, nearly electrocuting himself in the process. But he and his brother Ray developed a vocabulary of simple repetitive riffs inspired by R & B horn charts, and earned a string of hits like "You Really Got Me," "All Day and All of the Night" and "Tired of Waiting."

Davies kept his secrets close to his vest and it took a couple of years for the sound to catch on while other players wrestled with the notoriously temperamental equipment of the time. Gibson solved these problems in 1965 with the Maestro Fuzz-Tone, made famous by Keith Richards on "(I Cant Get No) Satisfaction." The Kinks themselves would branch into lighter styles, including folk rock and music hall, and their popularity suffered for it. But punk rock and Van Halen's incendiary cover of "You Really Got Me" inspired them to bring the old sound back, and they enjoyed a string of successful albums in the late Seventies and early Eighties.

THE WHO

One band that copped to knocking off the Kinks' formula was the Who, a London-based foursome who got their start playing amphetamine-fueled "maximum R & B" at the height of England's dapper Mod scene. The Who first adapted the Kinks' loud, simple riffs as their own with "I Can't Explain" and then with the anthemic "My Generation," both of which were hits. The fractious players were constantly trying to outdo each other, so guitarist Pete Townshend used heavy riffs as a foundation over which John Entwistle and drummer Keith Moon could unleash a dizzying blizzard of notes while their pugnacious singer, Roger Daltrey, howled and barked. The band also became infamous for the players' expensive habit of destroying their instruments at the end of their sets. The cumulative effect was loud, aggressive, and hypermasculine.

The Who's power-mad approach to hard rock had its roots in complex social interactions in England. Pete Townshend would later explain that his loud, aggressive guitar playing and onstage mayhem was a response to the bullying of the WWII generation, who, having lived through combat and Hitler's bombing campaign, looked on the Sixties kids as "pussies." The increasing stridency in British rock was the new generation's response.

Townshend stretched the Who's riff-rock formula in new directions to create the "rock opera" *Tommy.* But it would be the Who's blistering live shows that would set a new standard for heavy metal and hard rock. Surrounded by walls of speakers, the Who unleashed a tidal wave of noise unlike anything heard before. *Live at Leeds* (1970) captured the elemental mayhem of the Who onstage, a sprawling, improvisational sound built not only on distorted guitar but distorted bass as well. In 1971, the Who streamlined their sound on *Who's Next,* adding extended synthesizer passages to the thunder. Townshend's songwriting became increasingly sophisticated (another rock opera, *Quadrophenia,* followed in 1973), and the band would become one of the top rock bands of the Seventies, alongside the Stones and Led Zeppelin.

CREAM

Cream was rock's first "supergroup," made up of the hottest players on the London scene. They were also the first successful band to perfect the new hard rock sound. Influenced by raunchy Chicago blues, Eric Clapton developed a fat, fuzzy tone that would become the prototype for later rock and metal soloists. Jack Bruce and Ginger Baker were a nimble rhythm section that soared and swung where less capable players plodded. Their 1966 debut, *Fresh Cream*, synthesized blues, rock, and pop, giving lie to Clapton's claim that he left the Yardbirds to pursue a purist blues approach. Their first US tour had a powerful impact in San Francisco, and soon the psych bands were exploring the same heavy blues direction as Cream. Virtuoso outfits following Cream's lead popped up, such as Electric Flag, Fleetwood Mac, and the Jeff Beck Group, the latter featuring a young Rod Stewart, future Stone Ron Wood, and former Yardbird Beck.

But Cream's long, noisy, drawn-out jams were not blissed-out surrenders meant to keep young asses shaking; Clapton later admitted their epic live improvisations were just an excuse to show off their chops. These bad habits would seduce a legion of other bands, provoking an eventual backlash with punk rock. Cream split up in 1968, and Clapton went on to become a Seventies soft rock star. The band reunited in 2005 for gigs at Royal Albert Hall and Madison Square Garden.

HEAVY METAL THUNDER

The exact origin of the term *heavy metal* is still controversial. Steppenwolf sang of "heavy metal thunder" on "Born to Be Wild," which may well have inspired journalists to begin using the tag to describe over-the-top hard rock bands. In the Sixties, the heavy, blues-based hard rock of bands like Cream, the Jimi Hendrix Experience, and Deep Purple came to be known as "acid rock," originally a catchall term for the more eclectic Haight-Ashbury bands. Acid rockers like Blue Cheer, Vanilla Fudge, and Iron Butterfly are often cited as the first proto-metal bands, serving up a stripped-down, cranked-up version of hard rock defined by its worship of volume and excess. Of these, Blue Cheer is the most important, establishing the vaguely blues-based fuzz-tone overkill that defined early metal.

Blue Cheer released two albums in 1968, and together they established the Cream-on-Quaaludes, bottom-heavy pounding that Led Zeppelin and Black Sabbath would make their own the next year and the year after that. The first, *Vincebus Eruptum,* would earn them a hit with their cover of Eddie Cochran's "Summertime Blues," which gave mainstream radio its first full blast of the heavy metal sound. But the band was erratic, and went through a number of rapid-fire personnel and stylistic changes. Iron Butterfly's 17-minute opus "In-A-Gadda-Da-Vida" also hit in the summer of '68, though it lacked Blue Cheer's go-for-broke intensity.

There was a period when heavy blues and heavy metal were contiguous, but this would quickly change when Black Sabbath's debut LP unmistakably defined the new genre. Led Zeppelin's two albums embodied the shift, with ponderous blues dirges giving way to more expansive and diverse epics.

This approach inspired dozens of successful bands to serve up their own variations on the basic sound. Deep Purple brought classical elements into the sound, Jon Lord's organ trading complex riffs with Ritchie Blackmore's guitar.

Detroit's Grand Funk Railroad sold out Shea Stadium peddling its working-class R & B spin on the formula. Boston's Aerosmith fused Stonesy blues-rock with Zepesque guitar thunder and enjoyed a string of hit albums in the Seventies, before the group's drug habits hobbled them by decade's end. The classic lineup cleaned themselves up and picked up where they left off in the mid-Eighties, going on to greater success than ever before. Bands like ZZ Top and Lynyrd Skynyrd served up a Dixie-fried spin on heavy blues, inspiring the Southern Rock movement. Ireland's Thin Lizzy brought a Celtic poesy to the mix, becoming major stars in the UK and earning the odd US hit. Bloodthirsty guitarist Ted Nugent came up in the Amboy Dukes, a freewheeling psych outfit which devolved into a metallic boogie band. Nugent hit the big time when he went solo in the mid-Seventies and brought a slicked-up version of the MC5's onstage mania to a wider audience.

But throughout the Seventies distinguishing hard rock and heavy metal was a tricky business. Led Zeppelin despised the term *heavy metal*, and took pains to point out the broad range of musical styles it traded in. Kiss certainly looked like a metal band but its music was standard-issue hard rock. Blue Öyster Cult traded in the dark mysticism and macho theatrics of metal, but its eclectic sound was deeply rooted in Sixties acid rock. Rush had the glorious excess and the piercing vocals, but was too self-consciously intellectual and prog-obsessed to fit in with the metal mutants.

The move to a distinctly separate heavy metal sound would

start in the mid-Seventies and quickly evolve by the start of the next decade. Right on schedule, a bunch of boozy misfits from Down Under would start building the wall of separation.

AC/DC

AC/DC was made up Scottish emigrants to Australia, including brothers Angus and Malcolm Young on guitars and the roguish Bon Scott on vocals. AC/DC gigged tirelessly, sometimes putting three sets a day in three separate venues. In 1975, they released *High Voltage* and *TNT*, both filled with scuzzy, stripped-down hard rock that put special emphasis on the guitar thunder, often overwhelming Bon Scott's vocals. The band toured relentlessly, finding common cause with the punks when touring the UK.

AC/DC had its US breakthrough with *Highway to Hell* (1979), which found the band's sometimes sloppy sound cleaned up by notorious taskmaster Robert "Mutt" Lange. But *Highway to Hell*'s success would come back to haunt the band during the rock witch-hunts of the Eighties. The album's title track was that hoariest of rock clichés—a road song, celebrating and lamenting the rigors of touring. Even so, ridiculous rumors circulated that the band's name was an acronym for "Antichrist/Devil's Children." But the last track on *Highway to Hell,* "Night Prowler," was something else entirely. A bluesy dirge about a stalker, the song took on a hideous notoriety when a real-life serial killer named Richard Ramirez took it as his personal anthem. An avowed Satanist *and* AC/DC fanatic, Ramirez claimed that the song inspired his brutal home-invasion murders in 1985.

While preparing for the follow-up to *Highway*, Bon Scott

died of alcohol poisoning and was replaced by British singer Brian Johnston. In 1980, the new lineup unleashed *Back in Black*, which served up a polished and refined version of the band's trademark attack. The album, with Lange having polished away any remaining vestiges of punk or any other such sloppiness, went platinum many times over. The new AC/DC sound followed the template set down by British blues rockers Free on their 1970 hit "All Right Now"—lean, blues-based riffing, topped with clipped lead guitar and bluesy bellowing. Young even appropriated Kossoff's trademark vibrato. Johnson was more of a shrieker than the gruff-voiced Scott, and he fit right in with the new generation of opera-trained metal screamers. The band has continued in that *Back in Black* format ever since, and they are considered the gray eminences of metal today.

JUDAS PRIEST

AC/DC gave the headbangers hope when heroes like Black Sabbath, Led Zeppelin, and Deep Purple were in decline or splitting up. And back in grimy Birmingham, Judas Priest resolved to be the definitive heavy metal band and worked relentlessly toward that goal. Taking its macho Conan-the-Barbarian-meets-Mad-Max look from the gay S/M underground, Priest served up a reverse spin on glam gender-bending.

Rocka Rolla, from 1974, had Priest still mired in the idioms of the day but showing signs that a faster, leaner metal makeover was straining at the leash. *Sad Wings of Destiny* (1976) was more certain, boasting a more streamlined and recognizably metallic sound, as well as dark comic book/horror movie ambiance and grim violent lyrics that veered into S/M territory on tracks like "Island of Domination" and "Tyrant." *Stained Class* (1978) featured baroque arrangements and dramatic sword-and-sorcery lyrical indulgences like "Saints in Hell" and "Beyond the Realms of Death." Priest's thunderous sound still struggled with murky production, but this was unmistakably *heavy metal*, owing nothing to the blues or to the druggie grooves of acid rock.

In 1979, Priest released *Hell Bent for Leather* (titled *Killing Machine* in the UK) and the live set *Unleashed in the East*, both boasting dramatically improved production, which finally allowed the band's metallic innovations to shine through. These albums would have a profound effect on the development of the genre: what fellow Brummies Sabbath established in 1970 Priest had redefined by decade's end.

Following a string of Priest maelstroms, 1980's *British Steel*, 1982's fan-favorite *Screaming for Vengeance*, and 1984's *Defenders of the Faith*, the band stumbled. *Turbo (1996)* was a halfhearted attempt to capitalize on the pop-metal fad dominating MTV's playlist. Priest was facing an army of young, faster competitors and was struggling to stay relevant. The band regained its footing with 1990's *Painkiller*, but after a triumphant world tour, Halford quit. Priest then recruited Ripper Owens from a tribute band, later inspiring the Mark Wahlberg film *Rockstar*. The Owen-led Priest fared poorly, and Halford returned in 2005. The band is now considered the honored torch-bearers of British metal.

IRON MAIDEN

Following in Judas Priest's footsteps was London's Iron Maiden, whose early sound was closer to third-wave punk bands like the UK Subs and Stiff Little Fingers than Black Sabbath or AC/DC—albeit with Ritchie Blackmore–influenced lead guitar thrown atop the charging rhythms. After replacing growly vocalist Paul Di'Anno with a more traditional heavy metal screamer named Bruce Dickinson, Maiden's 1982 breakthrough LP *Number of the Beast* brought both a dentist-drill guitar sound and cinematic vision to metal.

Like Priest, Maiden offers a dark fantasy world of violence, fire, and machismo designed to appeal to the shaky egos of working-class adolescent males. The metal movement would become a virtual religion to the working class, particularly at a time when its economic prospects were uncertain. Reagan and Thatcher were ripping away the old industrial economy and blue-collar jobs were being sent overseas at a blinding rate. The unmistakably masculine world of heavy metal allowed a kind of virtual reality of music, fantasy, and community within which fans could bond. Indeed, rock history teaches us that the louder the music, the more likely it is to inspire religious devotion. Dionysus would understand.

In the Eighties, the rock press was largely dominated by baby boomers who thought metal was a piss-poor substitute for the hard rock heroes of their teenage years such as Cream and Jimi Hendrix. But the writers were passing judgment on metal's working-class fans as well as the music. In response, those fans started their own fanzines and tape trading networks, obsessing on bands no one had yet heard. "We were like secret societies," fanzine writer Ron Quintana later revealed. Out of this underground would emerge bands that would establish platinum as the new standard in heavy metal.

MOTÖRHEAD

Many Eighties metal fans consciously drew inspiration from the hardcore scene and its do-it-yourself ethic. At the same time, Motörhead, a power trio fronted by former Hawkwind bassist Lemmy Kilmister, would bridge the gap between the metal and punk audience. To a casual observer at the time, there was little to distinguish early Motörhead from hardcore punk, other than better production and playing (and somewhat longer songs).

But noise was noise, and Lemmy sung his odes to drugs, violence, and jailbait over the band's relentless hammering in a ravaged voice strongly resembling that of an Orc. Even though Motörhead had a huge following in the UK and Europe, they were too raw and weird for American audiences. Though they influenced legions of popular bands, they've remained commercially marginal. Regardless, they stick to their guns, and their longevity, as much as their refusal (or inability) to compromise, continues to inspire admiration.

METALLICA

Improbably, two American metal fans would take the building blocks of the Motörhead sound and combine them with bits and pieces from other obscure British metal bands to become the genre's new standard bearers. James Hetfield and Lars Ulrich were true-believin' hard-core metal fanboys, but hadn't yet gotten their act together for a band. Opportunity knocked in the form of an underground metal compilation LP, and Hetfield and Ulrich put together a provisional version of Metallica for "Hit the Lights." Encouraged by the response, the boys recruited bassist Cliff Burton and guitarist Dave

Mustaine (later replaced by Kirk Hammett) and practiced morning, noon, and night.

Metallica didn't fit in with the older, more experienced alpha males of the LA scene, but neither did a lot of their fans. So an alternative scene developed with Metallica is its breakout stars. A New Jersey retailer started up Megaforce Records for underground metal and signed Metallica. The label's first release was Metallica's *Kill 'Em All,* which combined Motörhead's reckless abandon with slicker touches borrowed from Iron Maiden. The album climaxed with "Metal Militia," a self-referential ode that unconsciously pays tribute to the Korybantes as well.

A second LP, 1984's *Ride the Lightning,* showed the growing influence of H. P. Lovecraft, and mixed the speed rock with slower material. The group's next LP, *Master of Puppets* (1986), ripped Metallica away from the underground and put them atop the metal mountain. The album's driving virtuosity and angry political bent earned the band praise from critics outside the metal ghetto and changed the rules for metal from then on.

By the late Eighties, Metallica, Megadeth, Slayer, and New York's Anthrax were the provisional leaders of the metal movement, though hundreds of bands were forming every day, determined to usurp their thrones. Metallica was shaken when bassist Cliff Burton was killed in a highway accident on an icy road in Sweden. Jason Newsted took his place, but was never accepted as a full member by Metallica and left in 2001. Having taken the thrash concept to its logical conclusion with 1988's *And Justice For All,* Metallica concentrated on songwriting— rather than mere riff assembly—in their self-titled 1991 album, better known as *The Black Album.* The album was a monster hit, earning the band play on mainstream rock stations with anthemic cuts that veered back toward traditional metal like "Sad But True," "Enter Sandman," and "The Unforgiven."

Some metal diehards grumbled at the makeover, but the band was perfectly positioned to weather the grunge typhoon that would sweep nearly all the big metal acts of the Eighties off the charts in the early Nineties. Bands that had taken wealth and stardom for granted for years barely knew what hit them when acts like Nirvana and Pearl Jam took over the charts in 1992, offering up old-school hard rock under the new tag *grunge.*

Which begs the question: what *is* the difference between hard rock and heavy metal? Ultimately, metal is all about the noise, the fetishization of volume, speed, and distortion. Bands like Van Halen and Def Leppard were often stuffed into the metal pigeonhole, but they offered catchy, tuneful sing-alongs that most metal bands were either incapable of or not interested in writing.

Metal is also a visual aesthetic, with bands embracing dark, violent imagery derived from fantasy literature and the S/M underground. Hard rock can be as loud and extreme as metal, but the emphasis is usually on traditional song structures and melodies, not just the guitar thunder. All the speed and volume of metal can often blur into static, mitigating the impact. This may ultimately account for the successful revival of old-school hard-rock aesthetics in the grunge and post-grunge era, as bands like Soundgarden, Smashing Pumpkins, Stone Temple Pilots, and Pearl Jam brought back the catharsis and rage of classic hard rock as well as some old-fashioned songcraft. But aggressive, hypermasculine noise comes in a variety of flavors, as we'll see in the next archetype.

GOING UNDERGROUND:
MITHRAIC ROCK

The ancient Mithraic cults were an all-male fraternity whose members met underground and bathed themselves in blood. Their rituals were dark, weird, and unsettling, and their iconography was violent, confrontational, and disturbing. They were deeply moralistic and prone to asceticism. They saw the world as a cosmic theater of war in which an eternal struggle was being waged between irreconcilable forces of light and dark.

That's also about as perfect a description of hardcore punk as I can muster.

The origins of hardcore are diffuse, but one city stands out as its primary incubator. The Seventies punk scene in Los

Angeles was fairly quiet until the newly minted police chief Daryl Gates decided he needed a scapegoat to crush. A punk scene that was the usual mix of bohemians and misfits soon found itself facing batons, tear gas, and helicopters after every gig. The publicity Gates finagled from these raids helped attract thrill-seeking surfers and skateboarders, who'd previously looked at punk rock as sissy stuff. They brought a new level of violence into the clubs with slam dancing, stage diving and frequent fistfights.

But long before the mayhem erupted in California, politically charged hard rock with an emphasis on rowdy live performance was being perfected by a succession of bands who saw noise as a political tool. The first of these was The Motor City Five, aka the MC5, which roared out of Detroit in the racial chaos and upheaval of the late Sixties.

THE MC5

The MC5 drew upon R & B and soul idioms for its pummeling proto-metal sound. Affiliated with radical celebrity/political prisoner John Sinclair and his White Panther Party, the MC5 were the only major rock band with the balls to play Chicago during the blood-spattered Democratic Convention in 1968, which they did for eight hours straight.

The band became legendary for its electro-shockifying onstage assaults. Their debut live album, *Kick Out the Jams* (1969), projected a raw, elemental fury that may have been equaled but has never been surpassed. Shamanic to the core, the MC5 were completely consumed by the power of their music, which could lift them up and fling them across the concert stage like rag dolls. Their first studio album, *Back in the USA* (1970), took a lot of the firepower out of the MC5 sound, disappointing some hard-core fans. Their second LP, *High Time* (1971), worked hard to repair the damage done by *USA*, but with the Yippie/radical movement in tatters, the band faded. In the end, the same radical/political ferment that gave their music its earthshaking power ultimately prevented the MC5 from reaching their potential, commercially at least. Guitarist Wayne Kramer reassembled the MC5 in 2003, without singer Rob Tyner, who died in 1991.

THE STOOGES

Led by madman singer James Osterberg, aka Iggy Pop, the Stooges were the MC5's "kid brother band," who made up for their lack of chops with druggy, unhinged proto-punk and over-the-top theatrics. The Stooges recorded their self-titled debut album for Elektra, home to Iggy's hero, Jim Morrison. Getting a lot of press but few buyers, the Stooges' second album added dissonant free jazz to the mix, sending their commercial prospects into the toilet.

The band's members all developed the usual drug problems, and Iggy was institutionalized at one point. But Bowie was a huge fan and took the controls for their third album, 1973's seminal *Raw Power*, which saw the debut of new guitarist James Williamson, whose sound recalled the glass-grinding overdrive of the MC5. But even Bowie's fame couldn't make the LP a hit and the band returned to its old habits. Iggy eventually cleaned up and Bowie produced two solo LPs for him, which earned a following in the UK. Like nearly everyone else, the Stooges reunited in the early 21st century. Williamson— long retired from rock—returned to the band in late 2009 to replace original guitarist Ron Asheton, who had passed away earlier in the year.

THE RAMONES

The punk underground of the Seventies was immersed in pre-hippie nostalgia. It was also studiously anti-intellectual and often politically reactionary. The short, sharp, spiky garage rock of bands like the Count Five, the Seeds, and the 13th Floor Elevators was a favorite on boho jukeboxes. New York's Ramones took all these elements and threw in some incongruous servings of power chords and girl-group melodicism to construct a brilliantly moronic sound. The fuzzed-out skrong of Black Sabbath was a prime reference point for guitarist Johnny Ramone (John Cummings), while bassist Dee Dee (Douglas Colvin) and Tommy (Thomas Erdelyi) bashed out a reliably steady beat, allowing Joey (Jeffrey Hyman) to show off his strange repertoire of Ronnie Spector and Elvis Presley vocal tics.

The Ramones got signed and quickly whipped out a series of classic LPs, touring the punk circuit relentlessly. With punk becoming a big story in the UK, manager Danny Fields flew them over to England. The Ramones would change the sound of English punk literally overnight. Indeed, punk bands all over the world owe a major debt to the boys from Queens for having perfected the fast/loud punk template.

The band peaked in the late Seventies but carried on until the mid-Nineties, operating mostly as a punk nostalgia act. Tragically, all three of the principal Ramones—Joey, Johnny, and Dee Dee—have passed away.

THE SEX PISTOLS

At the same time the Ramones were perfecting what Linda Ronstadt labeled their "moron music," a pack of young New York Dolls fans were tenaciously learning to play on stolen equipment in London. The unnamed band featured Steve Jones on guitar, Paul Cook on drums, and Glen Matlock on bass. They had started hanging around in 1975 at a King's Road boutique named SEX, whose proprietor, Malcolm McLaren, was trying to figure out a way to combine his great loves— rock 'n' roll and media provocation. McLaren's sidekick Bernie Rhodes spotted an ugly, hunched-over teenager from East London and figured he was just the ticket for McLaren's band. The young John Lydon joined the band that McLaren dubbed the Sex Pistols and was renamed Johnny Rotten by Jones in reference to his rotten teeth.

The band tore through the usual handful of old garage rock covers, but Rotten and Matlock also cooked up some originals with subversive lyrics such as "Anarchy in the UK" and "No Feelings." They started off their performing career playing to hostile crowds, but at each performance a few outcasts tuned in to what was lurking beneath the racket.

Soon every city or town they played had its own punk band—that's how potent the Pistols were as a cultural force. They also had a relentless schemer to push the media's buttons and keep the band outfitted in the latest decadent fashions. But the outrage was a double-edged sword. Nearly every date on their Anarchy tour met with protests and cancellations. The Pistols were reduced to touring under a pseudonym ("SPOTS" or "Sex Pistols on tour secretly") and Johnny Rotten and Paul Cook both suffered beatings at the hands of outraged patriots when they announced that their next single would take potshots at the Queen—during her Silver Jubilee, no less.

Things quickly descended into parody when the nimble Matlock was replaced with Rotten's old chum John Ritchie, aka Sid Vicious, who couldn't play worth a damn and was usually too doped up to try. An album was made, but by the time it was released the Pistols were on their last legs. A harrowing American tour in early '78 finished the band forever. Sid and girlfriend Nancy Spungeon holed themselves up in New York's Chelsea Hotel, where someone—either Sid or a notorious dealer he owed money to—stabbed Nancy to death. Sid was arrested for the crime and then OD'd.

But beneath all the outrage, the Pistols were moralists, shouting down the predations of the elite and the aimless hedonism of the hippie counterculture. Their scorching sound was a wake-up call that jolted Seventies England out of its narcoleptic stupor. There *was* no future in England's dreaming, as Johnny Rotten screamed—a parasitical aristocracy was sucking away the country's life force.

THE CLASH

The Pistols' top rivals were assembled by Bernie Rhodes after leaving McLaren's employ. The Clash coalesced when guitarists Mick Jones and Keith Levene brought in a lanky art student named Paul Simonon on bass simply because he looked cool. Casting around for a singer, they settled on John Graham Mellor, aka Joe Strummer, who'd been shaking up the sleepy London scene with a ragged proto-punk band named the 101ers. Strummer had attended a private boarding school—and his father was a genuine spy with the Foreign Office—but he idolized Bo Diddley and Elvis Presley and wanted to rock. The foursome tried out a number of drummers before settling on a red-haired powerhouse named Terry Chimes. Rhodes told the band to dump all the love songs and write tunes with a political edge. Fueled by cheap speed, Clash gigs became spontaneous displays of untrammeled rage.

The Clash's first album took England by storm in early 1977. Claiming that the band was run like a cult, Chimes quit and was replaced by new drummer, Nicky "Topper" Headon. The Clash then unleashed a string of singles that expanded the punk palette with touches of reggae and R & B. Blue Öyster Cult impressario Sandy Pearlman took the reins for the Clash's second LP, *Give 'Em Enough Rope* (1978), the band's first US release. But the band's thunderous hammering ran afoul of an entrenched generation of aging baby boomers, who had no taste for punk rock excess. To "break" America, the Clash resolved to radically tone down their studio sound. By the time they packed it in, the Clash's records bore little resemblance to their early salvos—or their live shows.

After an intense period of writing and rehearsing in a London garage, the Clash worked up a batch of radio-ready rock ditties and took to the studio. But their producer, Guy Stevens, turned out to be an erratic drunk who ruined an expensive new piano and nearly killed Mick Jones while swinging a ladder around the studio. The band sent Stevens home and worked up the tracks with engineer Bill Price, who co-produced the Pistols' debut. The result was *London Calling* (1979), a double LP of retro rock 'n' roll styles that caught the ear of the music press and rock radio stations in America and cracked the US Top 30.

But the band was already falling apart. Headon had nearly

died of an OD on a previous tour, but he continued using. Strummer and Jones were constantly at odds over musical direction, Strummer's retro-rock impulses clashing with Jones's pop enthusiasms. In late 1980, the group released *Sandinista!*, a *triple* LP filled with every style imaginable but punk rock, which drove their company to cancel a US tour. Unbowed, Rhodes flew the Clash to Europe, where they were first-division arena rock stars. Returning to the US, the Clash stumbled into a PR coup when a planned series of NYC club dates was shut down by the fire department, sparking a near riot. The story made the national news and the Clash became the hottest ticket in town.

But it wasn't enough. The Clash disintegrated—spiritually, at least—during the recording of their lifeless 1982 commercial breakthrough, *Combat Rock*. On the eve of a UK tour, Strummer vanished for a month, and when he returned, Headon was canned. Chimes was rehired, and his arena-shaking backbeat inspired the band to return to hard rock basics for a lengthy US/UK tour (which included a slot of stadium dates opening for the Who). But soon afterward, the Clash fell apart for good, and Jones was fired in September of '83.

A new, punk-centric Clash lineup was formed and set off on a backbreaking marathon tour in 1984, but Strummer couldn't handle the pressure and ceded control to Rhodes. The result was 1985's *Cut the Crap*, a widely ridiculed attempt to fuse Eighties hip-hop with punk, released a few weeks after Strummer had dissolved the band. By then, the Clash's reputation was in tatters, and would remain so until a 1988 best-of, *The Story of the Clash, Vol. 1*, reminded the world what a potent force the band had once been, despite the myriad compromises and botched opportunities.

The Clash may never have realized their immense potential, but they nonetheless played a crucial part in helping to establish punk rock as a viable—and lasting—force. Even if records like *Combat Rock* lacked the catharsis of their early work, the Clash's mainstream success allowed them to reach people in places that more traditional punk bands never could. Certainly, the curious young Americans who caught the Clash on their marathon tours in 1982 or 1984 got a blast of honest-to-God punk rock for their money. That spirit would take root and gestate over the next 10 years, setting the stage for a new wave of Clash-inspired bands who'd storm the charts with power-chord punk when grunge collapsed following the death of Kurt Cobain.

BLACK FLAG

An outsider visiting LA in the late Seventies probably would never figure it was ripe for a punk rock revolution. But the glitz and glamour of Beverly Hills hid the real LA: a dirty, crowded, working-class city with bad air and worse traffic. For millions of working-class Angelenos, the big money in Hollywood only made their lives harder, driving up the cost of living and driving out blue collar jobs to make room for more mansions and malls.

Based in Hermosa Beach, Black Flag arose out of this malaise in 1977 and began gigging in late '79. In 1981, Black Flag expanded to a five-piece with the addition of a bald bruiser named Henry Rollins, whose muscles and puritanical machismo would be more influential than his music. This lineup recorded the first Black Flag long-player, 1981's *Damaged*. But the band quickly tired of the scene they inspired. Hardcore became ever more reductionist in the early Eighties, and in response Black Flag grew their hair out and rediscovered their cock-rock roots.

Unable to record because of legal issues, Black Flag spent much of '82 and '83 writing and rehearsing. Band leader Greg Ginn looked to bands like Black Sabbath for inspiration, but the Flag's new sound—with its free jazz tinges and murky tone—resembled nothing so much as an Eighties take on the Stooges, which Rollins would play to the hilt with his Iggy-like long hair and bare, muscular chest. Black Flag reemerged in 1984 with *My War*, a record filled with slower, sludgier material. *My War* kicked off an impressively prolific period in the band's career, with a total of six LPs and an EP before they ended. The hardcore faithful hated the new sound, but it would have a powerful influence on the nascent grunge community. But the band was constantly chafing under Ginn's iron fist, and split up in 1986.

THE BAD BRAINS

As with the Pistols, every city that Flag played usually produced its own hardcore scene. Rollins hailed from the only other US city that already had one: Washington, DC's, hardcore scene was launched by the Bad Brains, an astonishing band of African American musicians who began their career as a jazz-fusion outfit. Attracted to the anarchic energy and radical politics of punk, the Bad Brains dived in and ramped up the speed and technique, even adding touches of metal. They discovered reggae (and Rastafarianism) and expertly incorporated dubbed-out jams into their attack.

After their fans' exuberance led to the group being banned

from the DC club circuit, the Bad Brains moved up to NYC and set the hardcore nation afire with their landmark 1982 cassette-only debut. But the Brains' relationship with the punk community would always be strained due to their singer H.R.'s militant homophobia. The Bad Brains would split up shortly after releasing *Rock for Light*, a 1983 LP produced by new wave maestro Ric Ocasek, but they reformed in 1987 as a pioneering groove-metal outfit. They underwent a series of lineup formations and stylistic shifts, never fully reaching their early potential. More recently, Beastie Boy Adam Yauch encouraged the Brains to return to their early sound, producing the 2007 CD *Build a Nation*.

MINOR THREAT

A younger band took the local hardcore crown when the Bad Brains split from DC. Formed from the remnants of hardcore pioneers the Teen Idles, Minor Threat would far outshine Black Flag's influence in many ways. Their sound was less chaotic than that of their LA counterparts, and the band also injected a lifestyle philosophy into hardcore. Dubbed "straight edge" by lead singer Ian MacKaye, this lifestyle would form the basis of a new puritanism: shunning smoking, drinking, drugs, and even sex. Needless to say, straight edge ran counter to the Dionysian impulse that was the lifeblood of rock 'n' roll. But it would fit right in with an ancient Mithraic cult.

The straight edge philosophy took root in Boston (which of course had its own legacy of puritanism), adopted by thrashers like SS Decontrol and DYS. New York hardcore seemed indifferent to straight edge, though it became a logical choice for bands like the Cro-Mags, who were affiliated with the Krishna

Consciousness movement. Despite the puritanical discipline implied by straight edge, the original hardcore movement fell apart in the mid-Eighties, plagued by increasing violence and unfortunate lapses into cheeseball heavy metal. Following Minor Threat's breakup in 1983, MacKaye formed Fugazi, an experimental post-punk band which remained true to the straight edge philosophy.

Despite incorporating musical influences from metal, grunge, and even hip-hop, hardcore has remained a militantly Mithraic subculture. Hardcore shows are usually played in sparse, unconventional venues and attended almost exclusively by athletic teenage males. Many bands still preach the straight edge, often throwing veganism and radical environmentalism into the mix. But the scene has been plagued—rather, *defined*—by violence and gang activity, particularly in Boston. An underground series of videos titled *Boston Beatdown* has compiled street fights inside and outside of shows, attracting serious police scrutiny. But as long as there are angry young men in need of a musical rite of passage, hardcore punk will live on.

PRINCES OF DARKNESS:
THE NEW PLUTONIANS

A (very) brief history of Satan: Dionysus was often identified with Pluton, the Underworld god of bounty and riches. Pluton was later identified with Hades, or Pluto in the Roman pantheon, and Dionysus himself had a dark, savage aspect, as we saw in the Bacchanalia. But with the rise of Christianity, a dualist cosmology emerged that would conflate Satan—who was an "adversary" (a kind of celestial prosecuting attorney) in the Old Testament—with the Zoroastrian Ahriman as well as the nastier aspects of Pluto and the Egyptian Set to create a new god of evil and darkness. And almost from the start, disgruntled Christians sought to caucus with the loyal opposition, and thus the "black mass" was born.

Some rock 'n' roll bands would latch on to the Plutonian archetype as a way to shock and provoke the mainstream. This trend first became explicit in the late Sixties as influences from Satanism and black magic became fashionable in some quarters. There was a highbrow kind of Plutonian energy that traded in art and sexual transgression, as a well as a more sensationalistic, lowbrow stream that wallowed in horror and gore. The two streams would run parallel in the Seventies and Eighties and converge in the Nineties, sending shock waves through the mainstream media not felt since the earliest days of rock 'n' roll.

THE VELVET UNDERGROUND

The Velvet Underground channeled a darkness from Decadent poetry and literature that may have scared listeners off in the hippie days but would have a far-reaching impact on later bands, both musically and lyrically. Indeed, it was through the Velvets that themes of death and decadence would become fair game in rock 'n' roll.

Velvets leader Lou Reed had a relatively conventional suburban upbringing on Long Island. This being the Fifties, however, part of that conventional upbringing was undergoing shock treatment to zap away his homosexual tendencies. Surviving that, Reed attended Syracuse and majored in creative writing. He developed a yen for free jazz, whose aimless skronking would influence the Velvets' noise jams. After getting his degree, Reed moved to New York and scored a songwriting gig for a knockoff label. There he met John Cale, an avant-garde musician from Wales, and the two clicked creatively. Reed enlisted two college buddies, guitarist Sterling

Morrison and drummer Maureen "Mo" Tucker, and so the Velvet Underground was born.

At the same time, superstar artist Andy Warhol was fishing around for a rock 'n' roll band to add to his media empire, and the Velvets fit the bill. Warhol took the band under his wing, landing them a plum gig at Max's Kansas City, one of New York's most fashionable new clubs. Warhol thought the Velvets lacked sex appeal and strong-armed the band into letting statuesque German fashion model/actress Christine "Nico" Paffgen join in on vocals.

The Velvets' dark, droning music was everything that the pop scene of the time was *not*. Reed wrote songs about addiction ("Heroin," "Waiting for the Man"), kinky sex ("Venus in Furs"), and violence ("There She Goes Again"), and the band also performed moody ragas like "All Tomorrow's Parties" and "The Black Angel's Death Song." The effect was druggy and weird, but in an ungroovy way that scared off the Flower Children. Warhol dreamed up a multimedia extravaganza for the Velvets' first tour that he titled "The Exploding Plastic Inevitable." It didn't win many fans. Cher walked out of a show at LA hot spot The Trip, declaring that the Velvets would "replace nothing but suicide." A review in the *Chicago Daily News* concluded that "the flowers of evil are in full bloom."

Their first album went nowhere, and after the Velvets lost both Nico and Warhol they set to work on their second album, *White Light, White Heat*. The lyrical concerns stayed much the same, particularly on the 17-minute epic "Sister Ray," which offered up transsexual prostitutes, drugs, and murder. The LP barely scraped the Top 200, but would have a huge influence on glam, punk, and similar styles. With money and attention low, the Velvets replaced Cale with Doug Yule and set to work on a self-titled LP featuring a more traditional rock sound. *Loaded* (1970) continued the move toward basic rock and produced two of the Velvets' best-known songs, "Sweet Jane" and "Rock and Roll." But success continued to elude them and Reed quit the band a month before *Loaded* was released.

Reed went on to a solo career, and his 1972 *Transformer* LP was produced by David Bowie and Mick Ronson. The LP featured "Walk on the Wild Side," Reed's homage to Warhol's transgender "superstars," the first Top 20 single to make reference to "giving head."

BLACK SABBATH

If the Velvet Underground traded in an elitist, decadent brand of Plutonian energy, then England's legendary Black Sabbath was its populist counterpart. Arising out of the grim industrial environs of Birmingham, Sabbath were heavy metal's first superstars, and their early records remain the foundational works of the genre.

Sabbath arose from the ashes of a band appropriately named "Mythology." Looking to explore the new heavy blues sound, guitarist Tony Iommi and drummer Bill Ward enlisted Bill "Geezer" Butler on bass and singer John "Ozzy" Osbourne, who recently had been released from a harrowing prison stint only to find himself dealing with Iommi, his former schoolyard tormentor. The band began life as "Earth" but changed its name to Black Sabbath after the 1963 Italian film (though the name may also have been a nod to their spiritual forebears, Blue Cheer). Horror films were enjoying a resurgence, and the band decided to create a musical equivalent of the genre.

Sabbath's sound featured overdriven, distorted guitar and

bass, playing endlessly repeating blues riffs in the deepest registers possible. Butler worked up lyrics based on the occult horror stories of authors such as Dennis Wheatley and H.P. Lovecraft. The critics (predictably) hated Sabbath's 1970 self-titled debut, but the kids ate it up. Sabbath intended their second album to be titled *War Pigs*, after a blistering cut that pictured generals as "witches at black masses," but their label changed the title to *Paranoid*, after the LP's driving, proto-punk single. The lyrics were bleak and the sound heavy, but the *Sturm und Drang* was relieved with the hypnotic sci-fi ballad "Planet Caravan." As with the first LP, *Paranoid* sold well, but the band was largely ignored by radio.

Sabbath went from strength to strength, though the usual touring pressures and expensive drug habits were already starting to take their toll. Their third LP, *Master of Reality* (1971), continued in the same vein as its predecessors but boasted better production. The key tracks were featured on the first LP side, starting with "Sweet Leaf" (a paean to ganja) and ending with "Children of the Grave," a *Midwich Cuckoos*-gone-antiwar stomper. In between was "After Forever," whose Calvinist lyrics were laid over a metal blitzkrieg, as was "Lord of this World" on side two. Sabbath achieved something unique in history: gospel songs that sounded like they written in the deepest pits of Hell.

But the drugs were catching up (as they always do), and intraband squabbling marred the recording of *Vol. 4* (1972). The band loosened up the metal attack on the following year's *Sabbath Bloody Sabbath*, but by this time the booze 'n' drugs had got worse, leading to Butler's hospitalization. Still, a 1974 tour was a triumph and seemed to lift the band's spirits. Sabbath rallied for *Sabotage* (1975), in which their trademark

bone-rattling metal was laced with jazz, pop, and even operatic passages. *Sabotage* was praised as a surprisingly mature
and inventive work upon its release, but the band's luck began
to sour on the resulting tour, and Ozzy was sidelined after
a motorcycle accident. Sabbath's next LP, 1976's *Technical
Ecstasy*, was a departure from metal that left fans scratching
their heads in confusion. After a grueling six-month tour, Ozzy
quit Sabbath to form his own band.

When his new band fell apart, Ozzy sweet-talked his way
back into Sabbath. The band had to dump songs written in his
replacement's vocal range and start from scratch, attempting
to write while they recording and often finding they were too
stoned to do either. The album *Never Say Die* was released in
'78 and Sabbath toured with Ozzy back on a salaried basis.
But the tired, aging metal masters were reportedly humiliated
every night by their fiery young opening band, Van Halen.

When they staggered home from the tour, the band was in
a drink 'n' dope shambles, and Ozzy was sacked in 1979. He
was replaced by the late Ronnie James Dio, an elfin screamer
formerly of Ritchie Blackmore's Rainbow. Refreshed, Sabbath
burst back onto the scene with 1980's *Heaven and Hell* and
then hit the road for a phenomenally successful tour, marred
only when Ward's drinking got him fired. He was quickly
replaced with Vinnie Appice, brother of Carmine, drummer
for metal pioneers Vanilla Fudge. Ward would end up home-
less before kicking the sauce.

Ozzy hit rock bottom too, but was pulled out of a self-
pitying stupor by Sharon Arden, the daughter of Sabbath's
manager, Don. Looking to make a name for herself, Sharon
got Ozzy cleaned up and paired up with a new band, featuring
a hotshot young American guitarist named Randy Rhoads.

Ozzy released *Blizzard of Ozz* in late '80, and the LP was a hit. But his comeback wasn't without incident—he horrified his new record company by drunkenly biting off the head of a dove during a business meeting. Two years later, Ozzy had to be treated for rabies when he did the same to a bat that a fan threw onto the stage—he had assumed it was a rubber fake.

Ozzy and Sabbath both enjoyed similar success until Dio left in 1983 to form his own band. Ozzy had got it much worse a few months earlier when Rhoads was senselessly killed during a joyride he took in a small plane while the band's bus was stopped near an airstrip.

Through the next two decades, Iommi soldiered on with a number of different "Black Sabbath" lineups. Ozzy too worked his way through a number of different guitar heroes but enjoyed far greater success than his old schoolyard tormentor. Inspired by the success of Lollapalooza, Sharon created a metal package tour named Ozzfest in 1996. The festival went nationwide in 1997 with a partial Black Sabbath reunion as headlining act. Ward rejoined that December for a successful tour and live album. A reunion LP was begun but later shelved due to Ozzy's solo commitments. Ultimately, Sabbath's reunion only served to remind fans how potent the metal godfathers were—and how superfluous their countless imitators are in comparison.

Sharon then scored another coup—an MTV reality series titled *The Osbournes*. The show was successful but many fans believed it painted Ozzy in an unflattering light. More recently, the Dio version of Sabbath toured and recorded under the banner "Heaven and Hell." Dio's death in 2010 has led to talk of yet another Black Sabbath reunion.

ALICE COOPER

Sabbath's horror-movie rock would have a lot of competition in the early Seventies, with two major American acts adding ghoulish theatrics to the mix. The first of these was a band that outraged even jaded Los Angeles with its cross-dressing and onstage theatrics, as well as a manic, maniacal singer who claimed to be the reincarnation of a 17th-century witch. The Alice Cooper Group was so outrageous that freak-father Frank Zappa signed the band to his label, Straight Records, in 1969.

Led by a minister's son born Vincent Damon Furnier, the Alice Cooper Group's first two albums for Straight, *Pretties for You* and *Easy Action,* earned them nothing but scorn. Their luck began to turn when they met producer Bob Ezrin, who glossed the band's sound up on their third album, *Love it to Death (1971)*, which featured the hit "I'm Eighteen." *Killers* was released hot on its heels, earning the band another hit with "Under My Wheels."

The band attracted a dedicated, working-class audience who expected outrageous entertainment for their money—and got it in spades. Live snakes, guillotines, angry dwarfs, electric chairs, stage magicians—anything that aroused a cheap thrill was fair game. But despite all the ghoulish imagery, Alice Cooper's music was no-frills party rock, with only the odd morbid track like "Dead Babies" or "I Love the Dead" added for seasoning. But the pressures of success set tensions and egos flaring, which led Cooper and Ezrin to relaunch the brand with Cooper as a solo artist.

After *Muscle of Love* (1974), the last record to feature the original Alice Cooper Group, Ezrin enlisted topflight session players for a new Alice Cooper band. The first fruit of this new regime was 1975's *Welcome to My Nightmare* LP and

TV special. Along with the slick hard rock, Ezrin ensured that *Nightmare* and subsequent Cooper albums had at least one radio-ready love ballad. *Nightmare* had "Only Woman Bleed," which reached No. 12 and put the LP in the Top 5.

The story goes like all the rest: Cooper's drinking got out of control, and his limited vocal range got lost in the ornate, orchestral productions being assembled for him. One last outing with Ezrin, 1978's *From the Inside*, produced the obligatory hit ballad, but the album fizzled. Cooper's chart prospects were dim for most of the Eighties, but brightened with his 1989 comeback, *Trash*, which featured members of Aerosmith and Bon Jovi. Since then he's played the metal elder statesmen role and continued to tour and record.

KISS

As Cooper's notoriety began to wane, New York's Kiss was there to pick up the slack. Comprising singer/guitarist Paul Stanley, singer/bassist Gene Simmons, guitarist Ace Frehley, and drummer Peter Criss, Kiss mined the same vein Alice did: meat-and-potatoes hard rock with comic-book visuals and an elaborate, theatrical stage show. New York Dolls guitarist Syl Sylvain put it best when he described Kiss as "truck drivers who decided to do something for Halloween."

After earning a dedicated regional following, Kiss was signed to Neil Bogart's Casablanca Records, a label better known for its disco acts. But Kiss's live shows were their main boast, and a slightly premature live album, *Alive* (1975), made them superstars. A live take of the Dionysian anthem "Rock and Roll All Nite" earned Kiss their first hit. Kiss then hired Bob Ezrin to sweeten their sound for 1976's *Destroyer.* "Shout

It Out Loud" was a hit, but the Cooper-like ballad "Beth" (sung by Peter Criss) was a *smash*, winning over the teenage girls who'd been previously resistant to Kiss's charms. Hedging their bets, Kiss had Criss sing their next single, "Hard Luck Woman," an uncanny Rod Stewart soundalike.

Kiss's outrageous makeup and horror movie costumes provided perfect fodder for a merchandizing blitzkrieg, and their logo and likenesses were slapped on everything from comic books to T-shirts to toys. But the creative juices seemed to be running dry—a second live album (*Alive II*) was followed by *Double Platinum* (1978), a greatest hits set, signaling premature creative exhaustion within the group.

Then, in 1978, Kiss took an unprecedented gamble: each member released solo albums simultaneously. Preorders were high, but only Frehley's produced a big hit (a cover of a 1975 glam hit, "New York Groove") and Casablanca was inundated with unsold copies. Kiss next signed on for a TV movie, *Kiss Meets the Phantom of the Park,* aired just before Halloween of 1978. The low-budget film featured lousy special effects and voice actors dubbing Kiss's speaking parts, none of which shored up the band's cred. They scored a major hit with the disco-tinged "I Was Made for Loving You" in '79, but album sales and concert attendance began to slip and both Criss and Frehley soon left the band.

Kiss dropped the makeup for its Eighties incarnation, but returns were continuing to diminish. After a long period of commercial decline for the band, Criss and Frehley rejoined in 1996 for a smash-hit world tour, but it turned out that they were just hired hands, and both eventually quit again. Simmons and Stanley bought the rights to their characters and continue to tour with other players filling their roles.

PUBLIC IMAGE LTD.

Cooper's and Kiss's shock value was overshadowed by Seventies punk bands like the Sex Pistols, who made their elders' comic-book fantasies seem trite. But the Plutonian archetype would be taken to another level by many of the bands that rose from the punk movement. One of these was Public Image Ltd. (aka PiL), John Lydon's return to his arty, pre-punk roots. Lydon enlisted Clash castoff Keith Levene and Cockney madman/bassist Jah Wobble for one of the most iconic singles of the era, 1978's "Public Image." PiL's early formula deconstructed the Pistols' sound, and Lydon brought a dark, death-fixated vision to the lyrics.

Their debut, *First Issue*, also featured "Annalisa," based on the murder of Annaliese Michel, a mentally disturbed German girl who was starved to death by a pair of "exorcists." Inevitably, it turned out that Michel suffered from severe epilepsy, not demonic possession. From there, PiL's music and lyrics only got darker and weirder. Their next single was "Death Disco (Swan Lake)," which was included on their landmark 1979 album *Metal Box*. Another pivotal track, "Poptones," was sung from the viewpoint of a murder victim whose naked body is left out in the rain. But Wobble was sacked after a US tour in 1980, and PiL's new songs were built entirely around brutal drum riffs, with smatterings of guitar, synth, and found sounds thrown over the pounding din.

The resulting 1981 album was titled *Flowers of Romance*, an ironic tribute to Sid Vicious. Lydon kicked off the festivities by yowling, "Doom sits in gloom in his room" in a pseudo-Arabic lilt. The distinctly Lovecraftian "Under the House" had Lydon moaning in terror about a rotting corpse coming out of the wall. "Go Back" was an Orwellian nightmare of a resurgent fascism. And so on. An exec at Virgin Records later called *Flowers* one of the most uncommercial albums ever made. PiL got the hint and decided to pursue a more commercial alt rock direction.

KILLING JOKE

PiL's pounding noise and grim worldview inspired another London band that would become even more influential. Fusing disco, punk, metal, and reggae into a seamlessly aggressive whole, Killing Joke's 1980 debut LP was so impressive that legendary DJ John Peel thought they were an established band recording incognito.

By stripping heavy rock to its most primal elements, Killing Joke would influence numerous alt rock and metal bands, including Jane's Addiction, Ministry, Tool, Faith No More, and Metallica. The Joke's mix of dance rhythms, detuned synths, distorted vocals, and down-tuned guitars also had an enormous influence on industrial metal acts like Nine Inch Nails and Marilyn Manson. Nirvana lifted the riff for "Come as You Are" from the Killing Joke stomper "Eighties" and Mötley Crüe borrowed the distinctive rhythm for "Dr. Feelgood" from "Love Like Blood." Neither lift was much appreciated by the Jokers.

Central to the Joke's mystique was their deep involvement with the occult, particularly the teachings of Aleister Crowley. (Rumor has it that Killing Joke leader Jaz Coleman is one of only a handful of luminaries allowed into Jimmy Page's fabled Crowleyana library.) In 1982, the band famously decamped to Iceland, where they claimed they would sit out the imminent apocalypse. The band was undaunted when the world didn't end and continued on with their unholy racket ever since. More recently, the late Heath Ledger borrowed Coleman's psychotic jester makeup and disheveled hairdo for his Oscar-winning turn in *The Dark Knight* (2008). Ledger also revealed that he modeled his Joker on the version featured in an Alan Moore graphic novel, titled—of course—*The Killing Joke*.

DENIZENS OF DARKNESS: CULTS AND THE OCCULT

To a certain kind of Christian, rock 'n' roll will be forever known as "the Devil's music." This demonic reputation goes all the way back to the days of the blues, when legendary singer Robert Johnson was said to have sold his soul to Satan in exchange for worldly success. Later rockers toyed with devilish imagery, such as Screaming Jay Hawkins and Arthur Brown. But along with all the acid and patchouli and good vibrations in the Sixties came a more serious kind of mysticism with a much darker tone. The Rolling Stones' semi-ironic ode to Lucifer, "Sympathy for the Devil," touched a nerve in the rock realm and unleashed a torrent of occult energy from that point forward.

As we've seen, **Aleister Crowley** has his followers in the rock realm, the most prominent being Jimmy Page. But the Great Beast has other, lesser-known admirers in the outré-rock world: Ministry sampled some rare spoken-word passages of Crowley in 1988 with "Golden Dawn," and goth bands such as Coil, Current 93, Fields of the Nephilim, and Kommunity FK also drew inspiration from the Thelema founder.

The Process Church of the Final Judgment was a London-based cult created by two former Scientologists, Robert and Mary De Grimston. They worshipped a unique godhead—Jehovah, Jesus, Lucifer, and Satan—and were rather keen on Hitler as well. Their black-caped followers were a well-known sight in Britain in the Sixties and their house magazine, *The Process*, featured interviews with rock stars like Mick Jagger and Paul McCartney. They attracted a new generation of admirers long after their demise, including members of Throbbing Gristle and Skinny Puppy.

The Church of Satan was formed in San Francisco in 1966 by former carny Anton LaVey. The Church attracted a strange mix of thrill seekers, including Fifties bombshell Jayne Mansfield and Rat Packer Sammy Davis Jr. Occultists like Kenneth Anger and Bobby Beausoleil were tight with LaVey even if they weren't down with the Church's program per se. Other local rockers may have partied with the Dark Lord, but few copped to it at the time.

Explicitly satanic rock began to surface in the

late Sixties. Led by the glamorous Jinx Dawson, acid rockers **Coven** are credited with introducing the "devil's horns" hand sign familiar to metal fans. Their first album, ironically named *Witchcraft Destroys Minds and Reaps Souls*, featured a 13-minute toe-tapper titled "Black Mass." Coven scored an unlikely hit in 1971 with "One Tin Soldier," a decidedly *un*-satanic anthem included on the *Billy Jack* movie soundtrack.

The proto-prog outfit **Black Widow** was Coven's UK counterparts. Their 1970 single "Come to the Sabbat" was banned in the UK for satanic content. More recent satanic superstars include Marilyn Manson, Eurometal icon King Diamond, Glenn Danzig, and underground provocateur Boyd Rice.

Charles Manson was not only the leader of his very own cult, he also jammed with some of the era's top rockers, thanks to his association with Beach Boy Dennis Wilson. Stars like Neil Young and Jimi Hendrix were impressed with Manson's manic creativity, but that wasn't enough to put Charlie on the charts. Manson would later become a kind of star in his own right, though not so much for his music. Preaching an apocalyptic vision of race war, Manson tried to kick off the proceedings with a series of gruesome murders that stunned LA and poisoned the garden for the entire Love Generation.

David Bowie was rock's most studious

occultist, dragging around an enormous library of magickal texts everywhere he roamed in the Seventies, including those of his favorite authors Arthur Edward Waite (Crowley's Golden Dawn nemesis) and Dion Fortune. His landmark 1976 LP *Station to Station* took its title from the Kabbalah, which Bowie referenced in the title song. Bowie's occult dabblings, combined with a crushing work schedule and a coke intake that could have killed a platoon, led to fits of delusion, paranoia, and political extremism in the late Seventies, but also to a remarkable string of classic records. More recently, Bowie confesses to an interest in the ancient Gnostics.

THROBBING GRISTLE

Another influential band to emerge from the post-punk underground was Throbbing Gristle (TG), pioneers in—if not the *creators* of—the industrial genre. TG was formed by former members of a sexually explicit performance-art troupe named COUM Transmissions, Genesis P. Orridge (Neil Megson) and Cosey Fanni Tutti (Christine Newby). The pair was joined by electronics whiz Chris Carter and multi-instrumentalist Peter Christopherson, and together the foursome declared war on music, decency, and sanity.

TG resolved to shock England out of its malaise using

lyrics and imagery drawing heavily on crime, fascism, and the occult. Inspired by American survivalists, they took to wearing military fatigues and used their array of homemade electronics not to entertain but to literally assault their audiences with sound. Lyrically anticipating the death metal movement, TG unleashed blasts of hate with titles like "Blood on the Floor," "Dead on Arrival," and "Maggot Death." They sang odes to serial killers Ian Brady and Myra Hindley as well as a burn victim the tabloids dubbed the "Hamburger Lady." Their hilariously misnamed 1979 album *20 Jazz Funk Greats* had the band standing atop an English cliff that was a popular spot for suicides.

Outraging even jaded punk rockers, TG's flirtations with fascism became increasingly *un*-ironic. Sensing that the game had gone too far, TG split up in '81. But the extremism of Throbbing Gristle made its mark, giving rise to electronic noise terrorists who traded in the industrial category, such as Skinny Puppy, Front 242, and Cabaret Voltaire. For a brief time in the late Eighties, industrial dance music owned the clubs, spreading its wicked tentacles out into more commercial spheres.

MINISTRY

One of the best-known industrial bands, Ministry, began as a commercial dance-pop band. But Ministry's second album, *Twitch* (1986), saw singer/leader Alain Jourgensen dropping the synth pop and hijacking the songbook of industrial dance pioneers Cabaret Voltaire, complete with pounding drum machines, sampled noises, and half-whispered, English-accented vocals. For their next album, *The Land of Rape and Honey*

(1988), Ministry turned its sights on Skinny Puppy, lifting that band's recipe of violent beats, blasts of synth, and bits of dialogue from horror movies and the like. Ministry then paid tribute to Killing Joke on *The Mind is a Terrible Thing to Taste* (1989), a virtual remake of the Joke's 1981 LP *What's This For?* Their next album, *Psalm 69*, added Slayer-style riffing, earning them MTV airplay. From then on, Ministry traded in a more generic thrash metal sound before splitting up in 2008.

NINE INCH NAILS

Cleveland's Trent Reznor drew from the same esoteric sources as Ministry but added a mournful melodicism to leaven the mix. Working under the trade name Nine Inch Nails, Reznor released the classic *Pretty Hate Machine* in 1989, which blended industrial angst with solid songcraft. The album was a major underground hit, rocking the clubs with hit track after hit track.

Reznor hired a stage band and toured tirelessly (including a star-making spot on the first Lollapalooza tour), honing a more aggressive guitar-driven sound. After the bleak, disjointed *Broken* EP in '92, Reznor broke big with *The Downward Spiral* (1994), whose success was powered by two gloomy hits, "Closer" and "Hurt." Significantly, *The Downward Spiral* was recorded at 10050 Cielo Drive—the house where Sharon Tate and her friends were killed by the Manson gang. Friends like Tori Amos reported that this was a very dark time for Reznor.

Reznor's struggles with depression delayed *Spiral's* follow-up, *The Fragile*, for five years. By then, introspection and self-pity had gone out of fashion and frat boy rockers like Limp

Bizkit and Korn were selling a more aggressive spin on the sounds Reznor had perfected with NIN. His next album, *With Teeth*, would be another six years in the making as Reznor's depression gave rise to chronic drug and alcohol abuse. He cleaned up and released his 2008 album *The Slip* for free on the Internet, and toured with Jane's Addiction (the NIN/JA tour, as it was called) in 2009.

DEVIL MUSIC—FOR REAL THIS TIME

The religious right declared war on heavy metal in the late Seventies, and spent the next several years trying to destroy the genre with lawsuits, record burnings, and anti-metal propaganda books and films. The ludicrous "backward masking" witch-hunt was the basis of many of the suits. The pitch was that even though the bands were singing the usual spiel about fast cars and snow dogs, they were secretly embedding commands to worship the Abominable One under the clamor—messages that your brain could somehow pick out and magically play backward like a tape recorder. Most of the suits were thrown out of court, but the attack kept coming, drawing on the immense wealth and power of the religious right and its shadowy corporate overlords.

In the end, all the fundamentalist bed-wetting had the exact *opposite* effect, inspiring legions of metalheads to drop the old party anthems and pledge allegiance to the Dark Lord *openly* in the lyrics. By the end of the Eighties an international movement had taken all the wildest, most hysterical exaggerations and distortions of anti-rock preachers, thrown in gore and horror movie aesthetics and gruesome urban legends built around Seventies heroes like Alice Cooper and Black Sabbath, and built an entire musical genre (and industry) around it.

The granddaddy of all Eighties satanic metal bands was Venom, a trio of British bodybuilders with questionable musical chops. But what they lacked in skill Venom more than made up for with excess, unleashing devilish anthems like "In League with Satan," "Burn This Place to the Ground," and "One Thousand Days in Sodom," as well as albums like *Welcome to Hell* and *Possessed*. Serious metal fans saw Venom as a joke, but the band's work ethic and perseverance was enough to earn them a dedicated fan following. Venom's unapologetic dedication to satanic shock tactics would inspire hordes of imitators, many of whom would overshadow the originators.

Foremost among these was Slayer, a Southern California thrash band that rose out of the underground metal scene in the early Eighties. Slayer took Venom's basic template but pulled it off with more skill. Rap label Def Jam scooped up Slayer for their major-label debut, *Reign in Blood* (1986), but got more than they bargained for with "Angel of Death," a gruesome musical tribute to Nazi war criminal Josef Mengele. The rest of the album was only slightly less offensive, and Columbia refused to distribute it. Geffen stepped in and the album went gold.

Blood marked the peak of Slayer's media notoriety. From then on the band settled into a routine of bone-breaking extreme metal, servicing a dedicated core of followers. But as the outrage died down, the band was eventually overshadowed not only by the mainstream success of rivals like Metallica, but by a horde of even more extreme bands.

THRASH AND GRINDCORE

The thrash metal genre was primarily inspired by hardcore punk. One of the major influences on satanic metal was the Misfits, a New Jersey–based punk band formed in 1977 that combined ghoulish costumery and theatrics with drive-in horror movie lyrics and iconography. Many of the black metal bands would draw inspiration from the Misfits' muscles-and-makeup punk rock update on the Kiss template.

Following the dissolution of the original Misfits, leader Glenn Danzig formed Samhain, a similar outfit that explored more serious occult themes. Samhain evolved into Danzig, which traded in a stripped-down hard rock that steadily progressed toward metal, and boasted satanic-themed lyrics sung in Danzig's Elvis Presley-meets-Jim Morrison-in-Hell croon.

A more serious influence came from England. The band Discharge, also formed in 1977, developed a brutal, extremist approach to punk that would give rise to thrash. Lead singer Calvin "Cal" Morris was a brawny, deep-throated bruiser whose lyrics evolved from standard punk rants to short bursts of brutal sloganeering that made no concessions to melody or meter. This style reached its apex in the landmark 1982 album *Hear Nothing See Nothing Say Nothing*. Discharge presented itself as antiwar, but its violent lyrics, gruesome cover art, and extreme thrash noise exuded pure violence. And Morris's *basso profundo* growl anticipated the infamous "Cookie Monster" vocals that death metal and grindcore later traded in. Discharge's influence on heavy metal is incalculable, and metal superstars such as Metallica, Anthrax, and Sepultura have covered Discharge songs in tribute.

Another band directly inspired by Discharge was Napalm Death, leaders of the grindcore movement. Storming out of the UK, grindcore shunned even the nods to musicality Mega-deth and Metallica offered. Napalm's songs were usually short blasts of face-punching noise, with deep, growly vocals and an extreme, anarchist political outlook. Other bands like Doom and Extreme Noise Terror followed in their wake, upping the metallic ante and throwing the ball back into America's court.

DEATH METAL

The various memes from hardcore and thrash collected into the death metal scene, which took Slayer's excess to even greater extremes and threw in the "Cookie Monster" vocals for added effect. Sunny, suburban Florida was the unlikely epicenter for the genre, boasting such bands as Morbid Angel, Possessed, and Deicide. But an even more malignant brand of metal came from Buffalo, New York. Drawing on the mindless mayhem of Eighties slasher flicks and horror comics, Cannibal Corpse brought outrage to new depths, their albums like *Tomb of the Mutilated* and *Butchered at Birth* boasting mind-numbingly offensive album covers and song titles. ("Hammer-Smashed Face" is by far the most innocuous.) The Florida bands worked similar musical themes, but eschewed mutilation fantasy in favor of satanic radicalism. Similar outrages would emerge in the black metal scene that grew from the same roots as death metal but branched off in a different direction.

Emerging from Scandinavia in the mid-Eighties, black metal upped the ante when it came to religious and political extremism, spilling over into murder and arson. Black metal bands like Emperor, Satyricon, and Immortal (among many others) even sported satanic variations on Kiss's armored costumery and Kabuki makeup. The black metal scene took inspiration from goth, incorporating keyboards, choirs, and other symphonic trappings, alienating some meat-and-pota-toes metal diehards, particularly in the US.

Immersed in *Lord of the Rings* and *Dungeons & Dragons*, some Scandinavian black metal enthusiasts even opened up their history books and discovered that their Nordic fore-fathers didn't abandon their old gods through reasonable persuasion but at the end of a bloodstained Christian sword. Seeking to avenge their martyred Viking ancestors, some Norwegian black metal acolytes declared war on Christianity and set over 50 churches ablaze (many of them national land-marks) between 1992 and 1996.

MARILYN MANSON

The dark memes that grew out of the Velvet Underground and Black Sabbath wound their malign way through a multitude of bands during the classic rock era and beyond. But in the Nine-ties, the opposing poles of Plutonian rock converged and took possession of an unlikely host. Born and raised in the Ohio heartland, young Brian Warner had a conservative religious upbringing. But when he found himself in the death metal homeland of Florida, his spiritual life took a very strange turn, eventually leading him to Anton LaVey's Church of Satan.

Warner was out to shock everyone: conservatives with his satanic philosophy and antiauthoritarian politics, homophobic headbangers with sporadic outbreaks of onstage gay sex, and everyone in between with his fascination with sexual predators and child molesters. Warner took the Alice Cooper concept to its illogical extreme, giving his band members pseudonyms that combined female celebrities with male serial killers. Hence the world was introduced to "Twiggy Ramirez," "Madonna Wayne Gacy," "Daisy Berkowitz," "Zsa Zsa Speck," and so on. Similarly, his music combined macho metal with dance rhythms and old synth pop covers by androgynous forebears like Depeche Mode and Patti Smith.

Sensing a kindred spirit, Trent Reznor signed Marilyn Manson to his label, Nothing Records. Conservatives got wind of Warner's irresponsible button pushing when Marilyn Manson's cover of the Eurythmics' "Sweet Dreams (Are Made of This)" became a hit on MTV, putting professional harpies like William Bennett and Joe Lieberman on his trail. In response, Manson unleashed the *Antichrist Superstar* album in 1996, declaring that the religious right was simply an American adaptation of fascism, suppressing individuality and creativity in the service of corporate profit and endless war. *Antichrist* featured Manson's best-known anthem, "The Beautiful People," whose video had Warner parading around on stilts in androgynous mock-Nazi gear.

The media attacks got worse when the band was made scapegoats for the Columbine High School massacre in 1999, despite the fact that the two killers weren't even fans of their music. Marilyn Manson fought back in 2000 with the album *Holy Wood (in the Shadow of the Valley of Death)*, which inspired Warner to read some of the more gruesome passages in the Bible onstage while on tour. More recently, Warner has alienated previous supporters like Reznor with his drug use, and pretty much everyone else with a gruesome music video in which he acts out an imaginary beating death of his on-again, off-again girlfriend, actress Evan Rachel Wood.

Despite that controversy, Marilyn Manson and the death metal and black metal brigades aren't scaring anyone anymore.

Without outraged church groups dogging your heels, doing the devil's bidding isn't nearly as fun. A strange codependency between fundamentalism and fringe metal developed in the early Eighties, and the two opposing (but temperamentally similar) factions used each other as a villainous pretext to justify their own need to act out and revel in extremism. After a while, it became something of a charade—and more than a little tedious—and the rest of the world moved on. Besides, we all have much more worrisome problems to deal with these days.

WOE IS ME:
THE MODERN MYSTERIES OF ORPHEUS

Orpheus was known for his mournful songs and his tragic life, and so it is with the Orpheus archetype. This rock cult rose to dominance in the grunge era, and mutated and spread into the nu metal and emo variants, threatening for a time to turn rock 'n' roll into one big pity party. The problem is that self-pity often (if not usually) masks self-obsession, and the miseries and moperies of neo-Orphic artists turned the rage of rock inward, leading to a kind of atomization in the overall community. The irony of this is that many of these styles were—and are—consumed by the most completely socialized generation in American history. Maybe all the static from Facebook and MySpace and cell phones simply leads to a new kind of isolation.

The Orpheus archetype expressed itself first in folk, which already had a long and storied history of sad songs tracing back to the medieval troubadours, and to the original followers of Orpheus long before them. The archetype popped up again in the 20th century with crooners like Johnny Ray and Roy Orbison, and would filter back into rock during the early Sixties, when rock and folk began to merge. From there a whole host of artists would bring the Orpheus archetype out of the coffeehouses and into the arenas. By the early Seventies, sad songs would be very big business indeed.

NEIL YOUNG

With his bleak worldview, plaintive, whiny voice, and angry guitar hacking, Neil Young is the very embodiment of the modern Orphic rock star. Born in Canada, Young traveled to LA in 1965 to seek a career in music, and eventually joined longtime collaborator Steven Stills in the legendary Buffalo Springfield, best known for their protest anthem "For What It's Worth."

The Springfield never caught the big breaks, and they split up in 1968. Young recruited a backing band he named Crazy Horse, and in 1969 released the seminal *Everybody Knows This Is Nowhere*, which featured the groupie anthem "Cinnamon Girl," the murder ballad "Down by the River," and an overall minor-key, downer vibe. Relentlessly prolific, Young also joined Crosby, Stills and Nash, with whom he recorded the anti-Nixon protest anthem "Ohio," written in horror over the killings of four war protesters at Kent State University in 1970.

The year 1970 also saw the release of Young's seminal

After the Gold Rush LP, which featured another fiery protest anthem, "Southern Man," written after the singer was beaten up at a bar in Alabama for having long hair. Young followed up *Gold Rush* with *Harvest*, one of his most popular LPs, which contained one of his biggest singles, "Heart of Gold." The mood of the album was rustic and homey, but also distinctly downbeat. His next studio album was *On the Beach* (1974), which *Rolling Stone* labeled "one of the most despairing albums of the decade."

Young's spirits were darkened further when his band's guitarist and a friend both OD'd. He used his next album, *Tonight's the Night,* as their eulogy. Young remained productive and in 1979 released a live album and concert film both named *Rust Never Sleeps*. The title track was Young's tribute to punk rock and new wave, which inspired him to experiment with his folky, country rock formula. *Re-ac-tor*, from 1981, had Young toying with faster, new wave–influenced rhythms, and on *Trans* (1982), he treated his vocals with the robotic-sounding Vocoder. The year 1983 saw his rockabilly pastiche *Everybody's Rockin',* which was followed by a country album. Exasperated, Young's label sued him for delivering deliberately uncommercial records. Undaunted, he continued to experiment until 1989, when he released *Freedom*, a landmark comeback album featuring the scathing protest anthem "Rockin' in the Free World." A new generation discovered his music, and he discovered them; he eulogized Kurt Cobain in his 1994 album *Sleeps with Angels,* and recorded with Pearl Jam the following year.

Young, along with Crosby, Stills and Nash, was a pioneer in the mellowing of rock in the late Sixties—a symptom of exhaustion and deep disillusionment, as well as the overall malaise that gripped the nation. CSN&Y didn't shy away from politics, but many artists who followed in their footsteps used the new soft rock synthesis to warble inoffensive pop to a nation tired of controversy. Young has enjoyed a prolific and cantankerous career, returning to political activism in 2006 with the *Living with War* album, which was followed by a CSN&Y reunion that confronted their aging yuppie audiences with antiwar and anti-neocon politics.

JAMES TAYLOR

In the context of the political upheavals of the Sixties, the singer-songwriter and soft rock movements were a retreat. The so-called Greatest Generation was still firmly entrenched in power and was in full reaction mode against the counterculture. In their eyes, rock 'n' roll was public enemy number one. But the soft rock that began appearing in the early Seventies was far less of a threat, and was able to bypass some of the filters put up in the anti-rock reaction (hard rock was nearly invisible on prime-time TV), helping to heal the generational rift caused by the excesses of the Sixties. Subsequently, many artists rode the soft rock formula all the way to the bank—or at least their labels did.

One of these was James Taylor, who set the template for the sensitive singer-songwriter movement of the early Seventies. Born into a wealthy New England family, Taylor excelled at music but also suffered from depression. His struggle became so overwhelming that he was institutionalized. After his release, he was determined to pursue a music career and landed in the New York folk circuit before relocating to London. There he caught the ear of Paul McCartney and was one of the first acts signed to Apple, the Beatles' in-house label.

Taylor's debut went nowhere, and his luck went from bad to worse when he suffered a debilitating motorcycle crash in late '69. While recuperating, Taylor wrote a batch of new songs that would make up the bulk of his commercial breakthrough, 1970's *Sweet Baby James*. Taylor drew upon his hospital experiences and the suicide of a close friend for the soft rock standard "Fire and Rain."

Taylor's lilting, introspective music struck a chord in a generation trying to adjust to life after the revolution. The album was a smash hit, establishing Taylor and the soft rock movement as forces to be reckoned with. Taylor married singer Carly Simon, and the two would become the "It couple" of the early Seventies soft rock scene. But Taylor would struggle with addiction issues, shattering his marriage. He would eventually recover, and he continues to tour and record as an elder statesman of the singer-songwriter revolution.

NICK DRAKE

Across the ocean, Taylor's claim as the new Orpheus would be challenged (spiritually, at least) by a British singer who would only find success decades after his tragic death. In many ways, Nick Drake was the star-crossed mirror image of James Taylor. The parallels are compelling—Drake was also born into a wealthy family and showed an aptitude for music, playing a number of instruments in school. Like his American counterpart, Drake suffered from depression. Unlike Taylor's, the talented English singer's career—and ultimately his life— would be destroyed by the disease. As with Taylor, Drake's 1969 debut was a commercial disappointment, selling less than

5,000 copies in the UK. Unlike Taylor, Drake's other records would follow suit.

Drake's depression was further aggravated by his failure, as well as by his prodigious drug use. Painfully shy, Drake hated performing live and refused to promote his records. His melancholy reduced his singing to a nearly indecipherable mutter, redeemed by the hauntingly beautiful melodies that it carried. Frustrated by the intrusive production and orchestration of his first two albums, Drake recorded *Pink Moon* entirely alone, with barely any overdubs. When he handed in the masters for *Pink Moon*, they were so raw they were mistaken for demos. The album was a commercial disaster and sent the already troubled artist into a tailspin, which ended with a fatal overdose of his prescription antidepressants. But *Pink Moon's* title track would earn Drake new attention when it was featured in a popular Volkswagen commercial in the Nineties. Artists like Belle & Sebastian and Elliot Smith (himself later a suicide) would find inspiration in Drake's wispy, intimate music throughout the decade.

IAN CURTIS

A few years after Drake's passing, the grinding dreariness gripping the British heartland inspired a new kind of Orpheus who would turn all the rage and fury of punk inward. The most prominent—and by far the most influential—of these bands was Joy Division from miserable, rainy Manchester. Inspired by the punk wildfire started by the Sex Pistols, suburban Mancunians Ian Curtis, Peter Hook, Bernard Sumner, and Stephen Morris formed the dark, angry post-punk band Joy Division, taking their name from a brothel at Auschwitz. Like many punks of the time, the band was openly flirting with Nazi imagery, something they would later come to regret. Joy Division's first EP, *An Ideal for Living* (1978), caught the ear of a local TV personality named Tony Wilson, who formed the legendary Factory Records especially for them. Wilson put Joy Division in the studio with madman producer Martin Hannett, who took their raw punk noise and polished it to an atmospheric sheen influenced by dub reggae and David Bowie's Berlin albums.

The resulting album, *Unknown Pleasure* (1979), took the indie charts by storm and inspired a wave of Joy Division imitators overnight. Hannett's dark, chilly sound acted as a perfect counterpoint to Curtis's mournful baritone and pitch-black lyrics, which made every song sound like a suicide note. Like his ancient Orphic predecessors, Curtis saw the world as miserable, fallen, hopeless.

Curtis had a very compelling inspiration for his dark vision. He had been diagnosed with epilepsy just as the band was hitting its stride and his seizures had become increasingly violent, sometimes striking while he was performing onstage. He also began showing symptoms of bipolar disorder, and was prone to violent mood swings. In "She's Lost Control," Curtis projected his harrowing epileptic fits onto an unnamed girl "clinging to the nearest passerby" who "screamed out, kicking on her side."

Curtis then began an affair with a glamorous Belgian journalist, and the havoc it wreaked on his marriage formed the basis of Joy Division's most iconic single, "Love Will Tear Us Apart." As Curtis's health worsened under his marital and career pressures, his already-bleak vision became terminal. Incorporating keyboards, the band took on a more elegiac,

Doors-like sound for its second album, *Closer* (1980).

Aside from more mundane miseries, Curtis drew on historical horrors for tracks like "Atrocity Exhibition," in which a carnival barker invites the listener to witness "mass murder on a scale you've never seen." The simple, repetitive lyrics to "Dead Souls" are perhaps his most chilling. Looking back at historical cruelties and forward to a life of debilitating physical and mental illness, Curtis begs for someone to "take these dreams away," where the "mocking voices" of dead souls "keep calling" to him.

"Dead Souls" was released posthumously on *Still* (1981) and was made famous when Nine Inch Nails covered it for the 1994 hit soundtrack to *The Crow*, which was the last film of up-and-coming star Brandon Lee, who was accidentally killed on set.

Curtis's wife, Deborah, filed for divorce in early 1980, and the singer was hospitalized in April after overdosing on his medication. After sending his wife to her mother's house one spring evening on the eve of his band's first US tour, Curtis hung himself. His band would carry on as New Order, another name taken from fascist history.

In Joy Division's wake came a horde of gloom-mongers who took inspiration from Joy's later-period, synth-driven era. The most successful and influential of these was Depeche Mode, which began as a cheery pop-disco outfit but darkened considerably when songwriter Vince Clarke split to form Yaz with singer Allison Moyet. Depeche Mode slowly built up a cult audience in the US before breaking big with their 1990 album, *Violator*.

Other bands would draw inspiration from Joy Division's earlier work. By far the most successful of these would join

Depeche Mode at the top of the US charts in the heady period before grunge hit.

THE CURE

One of the first bands to follow in Ian Curtis's dark footsteps was the Cure, who could wallow in despair one minute and bounce around like pixies the next. The English band was formed by singer/guitarist Robert Smith, joined over the years by a revolving cast of sidemen. Their first LP, *Three Imaginary Boys* (1979), was terse, stripped-down pop-punk, whose lyrics were moody and detached without trading in miserabilism.

The band developed a lush, synth-driven post-punk sound on 1980's *Seventeen Seconds*, which featured ethereal pop tracks like "A Forest" and "Play for Today." Smith's writing became increasingly gloomy and downbeat on *Faith* (1981), featuring Curtis-like dirges such as "The Drowning Man" and "The Funeral Party." Combining grim, nihilistic lyrics and dark, pounding music, 1982's *Pornography* opened with the memorable lyric "It doesn't matter if we all die."

The Cure shocked fans by following that gloom-a-thon with the synth pop about-face "Let's Go to Bed." The contrast between *Pornography* and the singles that followed set a pattern for the rest of the band's career: lush gloom alternating with bouncy pop. (Smith mocked this schizophrenic approach when he titled the Cure's 1998 album *Wild Mood Swings*.) The Cure scored a string of alt rock hits throughout the Eighties, culminating in the 1989 chart smash *Disintegration*. Somehow they found themselves headlining Giants Stadium in New Jersey, securing their place as the most successful band to emerge from the original post-punk movement.

THE SMITHS

By 1983, Ian Curtis's heartfelt despair had been reduced to a woe-is-me cliché in UK indie pop, so much so that a fellow band of Mancunians became major stars in their homeland by parodying it. The Smiths were the brainchild of Steven Patrick Morrissey, a diehard Oscar Wilde disciple, and Johnny Marr, a guitar virtuoso whose chord dictionary started where everyone else's stopped. The pair recruited bassist Andy Rourke and drummer Mike Joyce and worked up a cheery, nostalgic amalgam of Sixties pop sounds while Morrissey archly crooned about how terrible his life was.

The Smiths' song titles said it all: "Heaven Knows I'm Miserable Now," "Bigmouth Strikes Again," "Please Please Please Let Me Get What I Want," "Last Night I Dreamed That Somebody Loved Me." Morrissey's tongue was always planted firmly in cheek, parodying the self-pitying teenagers who bought his records by the boatload. But the band was a bit too esoteric to ride the "New British Invasion" wave and remained a cult concern in the US. The Smiths split up for the usual drug/drink/ego problems in 1987, and Morrissey simply segued into a soundalike solo career as if nothing had happened.

RITES OF SPRING

Another obscure Eighties band whose influence has far outgrown its sales is Rites of Spring, a Washington, DC, post-hardcore band. Formed by Guy Picciotto in 1986, Rites of Spring evolved past the bonehead reductionism of hardcore, adding in shards of melody and lyrics more concerned with everyday frustrations than taking crucial stances against society. For their crimes, Rites of Spring earned the tag "emocore," short for emotional hardcore, a scarlet letter that continues to infuriate the band's former members. Gestating in the hyperactive post-grunge indie scene, emocore mutated into emo, a catchall tag thrown at indie rock bands given to mopey lyrics, arid musical sounds, and androgynous fashion statements.

It's important to note here that the Eleusinian Mysteries were the original "rites of spring," and that the composer of the famous ballet *The Rite of Spring*, Igor Stravinsky, also composed the score for a ballet based on the myth of Orpheus as well as a piece for chorus and orchestra titled *Persephone*. The power of the Collective Unconscious is mighty indeed.

GRUNGE

But before emo would take hold, grunge rose up from the underground and hit the mainstream like a neutron bomb. By the time the smoke cleared, the Classical Age of Rock would be over.

Grunge (old musician slang for the sound created by bad musicians using cheap equipment) had been gestating in the underground for several years before Nirvana stormed the charts. Bands such as Cleveland's MX-80 Sound established its basic parameters in the Seventies, and San Francisco's Flipper perfected the grunge template in the Eighties, building inexplicably catchy tunes out of dumb-ass bass riffs, dumber lyrics, and excruciating layers of feedback and fuzz tone. Flipper spawned a whole host of "noise rock" imitators like Pussy Galore and the Butthole Surfers, but Boston-based legends the Pixies would take the big bass-line-and-noise-guitar formula of the early grunge bands and craft irresistible melodies with it.

The style took hold in the Pacific Northwest, where the ripped-jeans-and-flannel look of the early grunge bands was already the height of fashion. Scenesters there latched on to the don't-give-a-shit attitude of grunge, adding heavy doses of old-timey cock rock and an incongruous mopey nihilism to the mix. Soon the worldly, prosperous city of Seattle found itself host to thousands of would-be rock stars who looked like they just stepped off the stage of *The Jerry Springer Show*. Foremost among these were Kurt Cobain and Krist Novacelic, the founders of Nirvana, whose first album, *Bleach*, was released in 1989.

NIRVANA

Nirvana's grunge-by-numbers might not have gone very far without a great singer like Cobain. Producer Butch Vig brought Cobain's rich, complex, emotionally charged (if often indecipherable) singing straight to the fore on the band's second album, *Nevermind* (1991). The album seemed a most unlikely hit, but a deep recession had soured the nation's mood, and grunge's Orphic mopery struck a deep chord. Labels went on a grunge-signing binge and soon rock radio was filled with it, all because terrified suits didn't want to miss out on the next Nirvana.

The band enlisted grunge guru Steve Albini for its new studio album, *In Utero*. The record company was unhappy with Albini's work and an outside producer was hired to remix the singles. The album was a hit on the strength of the instant-classic single "All Apologies," but sold less than half as well as *Nevermind*. The band toured, but Cobain's behavior became increasingly erratic, and there were two suicide attempts.

When the band finished its tour, Cobain holed himself up in his Seattle home in April 1994 and died from a self-inflicted shotgun wound.

As with Curtis, Cobain's real pain would become a cartoon in the hands of a horde of generic grunge bands peddling fake misery. But returns began to diminish, and as the economy recovered no one felt like being miserable anymore.

Even so, many bands signed in the grunge gold rush revealed themselves to be highly credible and competent rock bands. Acts like Pearl Jam, Smashing Pumpkins, Stone Temple Pilots, Alice in Chains, Soundgarden, and the Foo Fighters (featuring Nirvana's multitalented Dave Grohl) released some rich and challenging music, and helped to revive the hard rock genre in a big way after a long metallic sleep in the Eighties—even if the lyrics did get a bit maudlin now and then.

But younger kids had been turned off by the anger and darkness of the Seattle *über alles* days. Instead of offering a wonderland of fantasy, sex, and power for kids to escape into, grunge simply reflected the unhappiness, awkwardness, and insecurity of its audience back at them. Album cover art was once a popular art form among kids, and helped add to the mystique of the music inside. But grunge album covers— already hampered by the smaller CD format—were almost all ugly and inept, and arrogantly so. *Everything* in rock culture had become ugly, gray, lifeless, and contrived, for reasons no one could quite understand. By the time the rock world finally kicked the grunge habit, slut pop and boy bands reigned unchallenged. One radio station (New York's Z100) even ran on-air promos *apologizing* to its audience for its nonstop grunge overload during the movement's peak.

It's no wonder that prefab pop filled the void. Kids will

always need to escape the cruelty of adolescence. They will always need to project their wish-dreams onto slightly older kids who then act them out. Something had been shattered— a *trust*—and it would take several years to sift through the rubble and find the great mythology of rock 'n' roll lying dead beneath it. Whether or not it can rise from the ashes is very much an open question.

CODA

Why then does all of this matter? The ancient Mysteries are long gone and rock 'n' roll is now an established commercial art form, largely innocent of any deeper spiritual significance. The days of sociologists predicting a new religion arising out of rock culture are long since past, as is most of the ridiculous hysteria aimed at the form from religious (and political) extremists.

It is tempting to refer to rock 'n' roll as a cultural phenomenon in the past tense. The music is still everywhere you turn, but it's no longer at the center of young people's lives. Rock 'n' roll has become a soundtrack—a backdrop—to kiddie shows and computer games and Internet chat rooms and networking sites and everything else young (and not so young) people are focused on today. Rock 'n' roll is not dangerous or controversial anymore, and it really hasn't been for more than a generation. Tipper Gore and the PMRC (Parents Music Resource Center) in the mid-Eighties were the last gasp of resistance from the old Establishment, and that was more posturing and yuppie nostalgia than a real threat. Even 2008 vice-presidential candidate Sarah Palin—who claims to represent small-town, conservative Christian values—waltzed onstage at campaign events to Heart's lurid "Barracuda," looking every inch a rock 'n' roll MILF.

But perhaps the fact that so many people take rock for granted is not due to overexposure or familiarity, but just the opposite. Too many of us accept the very limited canon of "classic rock" songs, which usually comprises two or three overplayed hit songs each from a relatively small handful of big-name artists. But all of these artists also have large back catalogs of great songs that never get played on the radio. And for every one of the accepted classic rock bands (think the Beatles, Stones, Who, U2, etc.) there are a dozen other great bands that mined the same musical territory but never caught the breaks to put them over the top. There is an enormous amount of great, unheard music to explore within the 1965 to 1994 time frame covered in the preceding sections. You could spend the rest of your life doing so.

Most—nearly all—of the artists who channeled the ancient archetypes discussed here were completely oblivious to what they were bringing into the world. But that simply serves to demonstrate just how powerful these memes are, and how hardwired they are into our consciousness. Human experience is vast and complex, but it has a tendency to organize itself along certain patterns. In ancient times, people grouped themselves according to these patterns and formed cults that venerated certain ideals and symbols. The same process continues today, only in a secular, cultural context.

Even when I was a teenager, I sensed that rock 'n' roll was simply a new incarnation of something very, very old, and I was fortunate enough to be tuned in at a time when artists were kicking at the music's boundaries as well as digging at its roots. I'm also old enough to have suffered the total contempt and dismissal of older generations for the music I lived for, as if it were all some historical mistake that grew up overnight like, well, like mushrooms. I knew in my gut that they were wrong, but it took me a lifetime to prove it.

A FUTURE HISTORY OF ROCK 'N' ROLL

The best popular culture is anything but disposable. As we've seen, it's part of an often unconscious process in which we act out dramas and archetypes that are embedded in our cultural DNA—and quite possibly, our *actual* DNA.

So if bands today aren't resonating with the same cultural power that bands like the Beatles did, it may not be simply that there are too many other distractions; it may be that the new bands aren't *trying* to tap into those same archetypal streams—at least not trying in a way appropriate to these times. And maybe they aren't trying because they aren't even aware of them. There's no shortage of bands paying tribute to (read: imitating) the rock styles and heroes of the past. But that's just phony Beatlemania, as Joe Strummer once said. Shag cuts and flare bottoms don't *mean* anything anymore— neither do Mohawks or nipple rings. Of course it doesn't help that there's no shortage of fortysomethings still trying to keep the old flames burning, with their dyed black hair, greenish tattoos, and trousers desperately straining at the buttons.

But it's not all bad news. Not at all.

Video games like *Rock Band* and *Guitar Hero* have turned kids' attention not only back toward the old stars but to the classic rock form itself. Songs that sound played out to one generation are a revelation to their children, especially when digital technology allows them to step into the old gods' shoes. It could very well be that games (and other digital entertainments) are the next step in rock 'n' roll's evolution. These games allow the player to become co-creators with the gods of rock, and to step into the immersive environments you once needed drugs for.

With the possibility of multiplayer interactivity and embedded narratives there's no telling where it all could lead. If grunge took a lot of the mystery and grandeur and escapism out of rock 'n' roll, these games are doing a lot to put it back in. It will be fascinating to see how various memes will enter into rock from other games. And with ancient mythology making such a powerful comeback in the movies—and potent new myths like *Harry Potter* and *Twilight* manifesting themselves as well—a whole new world of cultural possibility could be just around the corner. And sure enough, the old Greek gods have been digitally reborn as well with the popular *Gods of War* video game series and the Percy Jackson series of novels.

There are signs of hope on the horizon. Even if the Internet has allowed fans to merrily download thousands of dollars' worth of music without paying a dime, it has created a whole subgenre of artists who've found success outside the increasingly limiting filter of the record industry, and YouTube and other Internet outlets make all music current and available, no matter how old it may be. Even the optimal native format of rock 'n' roll—the vinyl record—is staging a major comeback.

While we may be past the Classical Age of Rock, there may still be a Golden Age to come. But it will only come when a new generation of musicians can tap into the deep well of archetypal and spiritual energy that has animated this music for thousands of years and make it relevant to *these* times. Maybe that will "change the world."

ABOUT THE AUTHOR

Christopher Knowles is the author of the Eagle Award-winning *Our Gods Wear Spandex: The Secret History of Comic Book Heroes* and the critically acclaimed *Clash City Showdown: The Music, the Meaning, and the Legacy of The Clash.* He's also co-author of *The Complete X-Files: Behind the Series, the Myths, and the Movies,* the authorized companion to the long-running TV series.

Christopher was a longtime associate editor and contributing writer for the five-time Eisner Award-winning magazine *Comic Book Artist* and contributing writer for the UK-based monthly *Classic Rock.* He lives in New Jersey with his wife and family.

TO OUR READERS

Viva Editions publishes books that inform, enlighten, and entertain. We do our best to bring you, the reader, quality books that celebrate life, inspire the mind, revive the spirit, and enhance lives all around. Our authors are practical visionaries: people who offer deep wisdom in a hopeful and helpful manner. Viva was launched with an attitude of growth and we want to spread our joy and offer our support and advice where we can to help you live the Viva way: vivaciously!

We're grateful for all our readers and want to keep bringing you books for inspired living. We invite you to write to us with your comments and suggestions, and what you'd like to see more of. You can also sign up for our online newsletter to learn about new titles, author events, and special offers.

Viva Editions
2246 Sixth St.
Berkeley, CA 94710
www.vivaeditions.com
(800) 780-2279
Follow us on Twitter @vivaeditions
Friend/fan us on Facebook